2016 Gold Medal Winner for Social Issues / Public Affairs

Guardianship

Praise for
Guardianship

ARCHDIOCESE OF LOS ANGELES

"Thank you very much for sending me a copy of the book *Guardianship*, written and assembled by M Larsen. Asking the Lord's continued blessings upon you… " **His Eminence Cardinal Roger Mahony, Archbishop Emeritus of Los Angeles**

ARCHDIOCESE OF GALVESTON-HOUSTON

"This letter acknowledges receipt of your October 21, 2016 correspondence to Daniel Cardinal DiNardo, the Archbishop of Galveston-Houston, regarding Forced Professional Guardianship Fraud. Your letter and accompanying documentation characterizes forced guardianship fraud as akin to human trafficking, which is an issue that the Church takes very seriously. Prior to receiving this information, Cardinal DiNardo and I were not aware of this activity. We will become more educated on the subject and are grateful to you for bringing it to our attention." **Most Reverend George A. Sheltz, Auxiliary Bishop & Chancellor**

Guardianship

F R A U D

• • •

Written and assembled by M Larsen

Factual accounts regarding misconduct of guardians, judges, lawyers, nursing homes, legislators and others, and how well over $41 Trillion has been removed from victims and their families through court-appointed guardianship are from some of the following sources in this book:

AARP Magazine
American-Statesman
CNN Report
Las Vegas Review-Journal
Las Vegas Tribune
LateLine, Australia
MainStreet, On-Line Financial News
Money Magazine
National Association to Stop Guardianship Abuse
New York Daily News
South Jersey Times
The Indianapolis Star
The Wall Street Journal
The Washington Examiner
3rd District Court of Appeal Investigation
U.S. Attorney's Office, District of Nevada

ISBN: 0692586210
ISBN 13: 9780692586211

Dedication and Appreciation

• • •

Dedicated to all the victims of this international crime and their families and friends. Also dedicated to all of those working to end this crime. The author is grateful to those who sent professional guardianship fraud information to the Senate on Aging Committee, FBI, U.S. Attorney General, governors, national news media, professors in many of the top US law schools, law enforcement, and many others. This book is to help shine light on the serious crime of professional guardianship fraud to the general public.

Special appreciation to the journalists and others whose articles and photos have been used in this book: Barbara Hollingsworth; Juliette Fairley; *Money Magazine*; Gerald Boland; Janet Phelan; Angela V. Woodhull, PhD; Anthony Domanico; Tony Plohetski; Steve Miller; National Alliance for the Dissolution of Guardianship; M.P. Roberts; Colton Lochhead; Steve Marcus; T.S. Radio: Gerald's Story; US Attorney's Office; Conor Shine; Steve Cannane; Michael Volpe; Madeline Buckley; Doug Franks; Patty Reid; Kevin Pizzarello; Robert Sarhan, MD; Skender Hoti; Barbara Stone; Teresa Tozzo-Lyles; Susan Warren; Glynnis Walker; Shayna Jacobs; Corky Siemaszko; Gary; National Association to Stop Guardianship Abuse; Darcy Spears; Susan Hindman; *Sacramento Daily Journal*; Jessica Beym; Stuart Isett; Donna Ennis; Carrie Hill, PhD; Arian Campo-Flores; Ashby Jones; KTNV TV; Mike Christ; Marjie Lundstrom; Lou Ann Anderson; Teddy Moore; Kristi Hood; Dr. Terri Kennedy; Eric Hilt; as well as those whose quotes have been used to emphasize the enormity of this crime.

www.GuardianAbuseCases.com

Introduction

• • •

U.S. Senator Amy Klobuchar states in her website: "Most long term care workers adhere to ethical standards that ensure the safety and well-being of their clients. However, there are cases when long-term care workers do not have the interests of seniors in mind. **In these instances, too many vulnerable adults are abused and financially exploited by court-appointed guardians and conservators – the very individuals charged with protecting their well-being.**"

KILLERS OF THE FLOWER MOON, The Osage Murders and the Birth of the FBI, a book by David Grann, is a true story about how government appointed guardians over wealthy Indians murdered them for their money. This quote is from that book:

> A conspiracy is everything that ordinary life is not. It's the inside game, cold, sure, undistracted, forever closed off to us. We are the flawed ones, the innocents, trying to make some rough sense of the daily jostle. Conspirators have a logic and a daring beyond our reach. All conspiracies are the same taut story of men who find coherence in some criminal act.
>
> --Don DeLillo, *Libra*

Older, retired and/or defenseless citizens are being put to their death in illicit guardianship courts that operate under color of law. Their families are being falsely imprisoned and retaliated for speaking up to expose these crimes against humanity.

Those with financial assets are targeted by rogue attorneys and guardians who strategically use a conjured "incapacity" which they obtain from their colluding medical providers as a justification to force defenseless adults into a guardianship nightmare – they are living adults in a system of probate laws dealing with the dead. They lose all of their civil rights and liberties. They have less rights than death row prisoners. Health Care Agents or fiduciaries designated by an elderly person in documents they have prepared are often cast aside or simply ignored and cases exist where Living Trusts and similar instruments, once thought impenetrable, are broken making room for the fee-for-service professionals / attorneys in a system with no checks and balances. They are forcibly removed from their home. Their family members are barred from seeing them on the basis of perjured false accusations against them by the predator attorneys and guardians who are financially extorting them. Not only are these disabled and retired citizens being terrorized, but their family members and others who expose this syndicate are also victims… they are being threatened, retaliated and falsely arrested. (See "Who Guards the Guardians?" Five Part Series by Diane Dimond / Crime & Justice Reporter / *Albuquerque Journal*)

When the money runs out, the Taxpayers will pick up the tab for Medicaid, Social Security dollars and other applicable tax-payer funded programs. More often, when their funds are all gone, they are illegally chemically restrained with psychotropic drugs to cause their death.

These activities fall under the Hobbs Act in the United States. It is a form of homeland terrorism.

We have a litany of laws to protect our older Americans, including The Elder Abuse Victims Act, The Elder Justice Act, The Community Choice and the Senior Financial Protection Act and mirror laws of each state. However, all these laws go out the window when an American adult is forced into guardianship because law enforcement ignores enforcement when violations take place in a color of law court.

The guardian industry is a cottage crime syndicate, a well-oiled machine using legal sabotage to ensnare and exploit the public. They use secretive, rigged legal maneuvers to carry out their subterfuge. Rogue firms and judges are a special breed of predators like child abusers who molest the vulnerable. Anyone with assets is their prey. **Brooke Astor was preyed upon by her own son, an attorney, decorated Marine, and U.S. Ambassador with the help of other attorneys to steal millions she was leaving to charities.**

This crime undermines every one of our inalienable rights and our core values under the United States Declaration of Independence and the Constitution. This syndicate that has taken control of our court system is doubly offensive – it engages in crimes of the most heinous nature and its operation under color of law is unconstitutional.

This is not a State issue. The States themselves are the perpetrators of this crime. It has become a state-sponsored and run operation. The citizens of every state are affected and Federal Taxpayer Dollars are being used up. All of the Federal agencies are involved, Social Security Fraud, Health Care Fraud, Medicare Fraud, IRS Fraud for failure to report the income from this color of law operation, U.S. Codes are being violated, and Federal Taxpayer Dollars are being used up. This problem will not be changed unless there is a public outcry for legislation reform that has a nationwide reach and that has jurisdiction over Civil, Constitutional and Human Rights Issues.

Government officials took an oath of office under Title 5, Section 3331 of the United States Code to support and defend the Constitution of the United States and faithfully discharge the duties of their office. However, millions of American families are being shattered by this simulated guardian court proceeding.

This country was based on the concepts of individual liberty and property rights. Guardianships destroy not only these freedoms, but also the spirit in which they were established. **Nothing is more sacred and more protected by the Constitution than the protection of our families,**

our right to life, liberty and the pursuit of happiness, our right to due process, religious freedom and freedom of speech.

We have millions of older Americans who are barred from seeing their children and their families who are in reckless endangerment and being put to death by guardianship torture and terrorism. This problem is of international epidemic proportion. Attorney Margaret Dore of Seattle, Washington believes the only way to fix this problem is to take guardianship supervision and oversight of assets away from the judicial system. Separate organizations with state or federal controls such as the Real Estate Division or Banking Division that have built-in oversight and accounting systems must be used instead of the court system that has no oversight management training nor asset controls. At least $41 Trillion has disappeared in this racket. (Google: Margaret Dore Bar Bulletin)

This is a book about lies, chemical restraints, theft, torture and premeditated murder committed by judges, lawyers, guardians and other professionals throughout the United States on a daily basis. I have used quotes in this introduction to illustrate that the crime of professional guardianship fraud is deeply entrenched in our legal system and how easily judges and lawyers steal your money. Some quotes come from articles in the book and some articles may not have all of the authors and sources identified. I apologize for omissions. The purpose of the book is to make the reader aware that this international crime is rampant in the United States. I hope you share this information with your loved ones.

...usually after the victims are purportedly diagnosed with a disease such as Alzheimer's (often by a non expert without medical evidence), then, in spite of protests by family members, the family court has historically and consistently approved the bilking of the hard earned assets of elderly or disabled persons by crooked for-hire guardians under the color of often-ignored Nevada laws. —**Steve Miller, former Las Vegas City Councilman**

Once under guardianship, you have less rights than a criminal. — ***Money Magazine***

There is a large transfer of wealth occurring. This is happening to approximately five million seniors a year, and their wealth is disappearing from the general population into the hands of a few professional guardians, attorneys, and court personnel acting in conspiracy to obtain the victim's wealth with little public knowledge. —**American-Statesman reporter Tony Plohetski**

The victims of professional guardianship fraud are chemically restrained, families torn apart, and life savings, heirlooms, jewelry, art, cars and stocks are looted from family by these thieves. —**Barbara Stone, commenting on the Catherine Falk Bill**

The final state of elder cleansing, according to Ditkowsky, occurs when the elder, now isolated and placed into a facility, is drugged to death. —**Intellihub**

You are a target because you have assets. You don't necessarily have to be very old. You can even be quite lucid. That won't stop these predators. When it comes to removing your rights and your money, these folks are experts. —**Money Magazine**

"Jared Shafer's Clark County Family Court Lackeys Removed from All Guardianship Cases—Shafer and Wells Fargo Bank Sued for RICO"...*Up until that point, no one in Las Vegas media would ever believe such a horrible thing was happening right under our eyes to our most vulnerable citizens.* —**Steve Miller, former Las Vegas City Councilman**

...older Americans are being robbed of their freedom and life savings by a legal system created for their protection. Although relatives are the most common exploiters, the damage they cause generally stays within the confines of their own families. By contrast, greedy professional guardians can wreak havoc on a far larger scale. In many states, there are few

prerequisites for entering the guardianship business: no special training, no licensing process, no enforceable professional standards. —AARP: **The Magazine, January/February 2004**

Law enforcement pretends it is a "civil" matter. These are crimes being committed against our most vulnerable citizens—special victim crimes. They are being falsely imprisoned, kidnapped, and their assets are looted—it is a virtual free for all. **—Barbara Stone**

A simple slip-and-fall can put someone into the guardianship of unknown persons with no knowledge to family and friends until the deed is done. Forced incompetency; get control over everything and the ward [senior] *loses all rights.* — **Robert W Melton, Pinellas County internal auditor, "Dirty Tricks of Guardianships—The Need for Change," April 2004**

*The current system does not work. This reality is most apparent when a wealthy individual falls victim to these involuntary proceedings and his or her wealth becomes a ripe plum to be shared by the Judge's favorites. Judges and their favored professional conservators and guardians, expert witnesses, and court investigators have unspoken agendas; money, power and control. When an elderly individual is brought into court and forced to prove his or her competence, we soon see that the system does not work. We have a system rife with court-sanctioned abuse of the elderly. Why? Judges override protections that have been put in place in the codes. It happens every day. Judges disregard durable powers of attorney—the single most important document each of us can create to determine our care should we become incapacitated. Judges ignore our lists of pre-selected surrogate decision-makers. —***Diane G. Armstrong, PhD, excerpt of prepared statement before the US Senate's Special Committee on Aging, February, 2003**

*This [guardianship] is an area ripe for fraud and where most fraud abuse has in fact occurred. —***Karleen F. DeBlaker, clerk of the Circuit Court, Pinellas County, Florida 2004**

Lyon County and former Public Administrator Richard Glover must pay $2.1 million to the heirs of a man whose Wellington home was looted after his death in May 2006, a federal jury ruled Tuesday. The verdict stemmed from a civil rights lawsuit filed by Mathis and his two brothers who accused Glover, a public guardian who handles the affairs of people deemed mentally or physically incompetent, of illegally seizing and stealing nearly $1 million of heirlooms and other property from the home of their 85-year-old father shortly after his death. —**Carri Geer Thevenot,** *Las Vegas Review-Journal,* **November 11, 2015**

They have enough hand-picked lawyers on the Bar Associations, in the legislature, in judicial positions and on various commissions, boards, and other influential positions to control the corrupt courts we are forced to endure. Should a citizen 'file a complaint' that complaint is heard by the very 'lawyers' that are responsible for the nature of the complaint. In other words, lawyers set the rules, interpret the rules, administer the rules, and impose penalties if they feel the rules have been broken. —**National Association to Stop Guardian Abuse: The Trial Lawyers Association: Holding Our Courts Hostage, State of Washington**

...guardianship can divest an elderly person of all the rights and freedoms we consider important as citizens. —**Chairman of the Senate Special Committee, Larry Craig**

Instead of serving to protect the assets of incapacitated persons, the existing guardianship system presents the opportunity for unscrupulous guardians to loot the assets of their wards and enrich themselves with impunity. —**New York Grand Jury**

Outside of execution, guardianship is the most radical remedy we have. —**Elias Cohen, Philadelphia attorney and gerontologist**

Contents

CHAPTER 1

Guardianship Fraud and the Legal System

• • •

The judiciary is by law immune from prosecution, and thus unaccountable to anyone, for anything and everyone is subject to the jurisdiction of the judiciary. A broken system, by definition, will provide injustice, which is a serious threat for the property, life and liberty of every person in this country, far more, than the threat caused by terrorism.

JUDGES, LAWYERS USE GUARDIANSHIPS TO PREY ON ELDERLY

By: Barbara Hollingsworth September 9, 2012 *Reprinted with Permission*

Local Opinion Editor *The Washington Examiner*

THINK YOUR WELL-TENDED NEST EGG will protect you from the depredations of old age? Don't count on it.

Little has changed since the D.C. Court of Appeals ruled almost a decade ago that Probate Judge Kaye Christian abused her power by ordering retired economist Mollie Orshansky, creator of the federal poverty line, removed from her sister's care in New York and placed in a District guardianship against her will.

Even multimillionaires cannot prevent a judge from appointing a total stranger to take complete control of their affairs—and banish family members who object.

That's what happened to five-term D.C. Council member Hilda Mason and her husband, Charles, a Harvard graduate who traced his lineage back to the Plymouth landing. Despite Charles' $22.5 million fortune, this power couple ended their lives in squalor.

Blind, wheelchair-bound and suffering from diabetes and skin cancer, Charles spent his last days in dirty clothing and worn-out shoes, with fingernails so long they curled around his fingers.

"He looked like a hobo," one witness told *The Washington Examiner.* His frail wife suffered a broken collarbone when one of her "caregivers" ran her over with a four-wheel-drive vehicle.

At the time of Hilda Mason's death in 2007, debris and broken furniture littered every room of the couple's once-stately Shepherd Park home. The roof leaked and the house was infested with rodents and insects.

As attorneys helped themselves to the couple's assets, Episcopal Senior Ministries reported that "there appears to be no individual or group that is currently responsible for the cleaning/condition of the house."

According to a Jan. 9, 2001, court transcript, a clearly competent Charles Mason testified before the same Judge Christian that he no longer wanted the Virginia attorney he had previously hired to represent him.

Less than three months later, Charles was declared incompetent after an adverse reaction to a psychotropic cocktail landed him in Suburban Hospital's psychiatric ward.

The judge refused to dismiss the lawyer, but OK'd a settlement agreement allegedly signed by Charles Mason after he had been declared incompetent that prohibited his own wife from "interfering" with his care.

Guardianship abuse is not limited to people with money, as Laura Francois-Eugene, a supervisor at the Department of Homeland Security, learned the hard way.

Her mother's only financial resources are her modest D.C. home and a small monthly Social Security check. But after a fall left the elderly woman temporarily paralyzed, Probate Judge Franklin Burgess appointed a conservator to handle her affairs despite the fact that her daughter had previously been named her legal guardian.

Francois-Eugene told *The Washington Examiner* she is forced to pay for her mother's food, dentures, medicine and clothing out of her own salary because the court-appointed conservator has been hoarding her mother's Social Security benefits.

The same thing is happening to another 91-year-old woman, a former D.C. Public Schools employee forced into a guardianship after Maryland lawyers characterized her daily walk as "wandering."

"Some lawyers took all my money," she told us, adding that she can't access her own pension or Social Security benefits, even to buy herself an ice cream cone.

The National Association to Stop Guardianship Abuse has documented hundreds of cases in which family members are denied any say in their loved ones' care, even as court-appointed fiduciaries are given total control. After the estate is sucked dry, the wards are often dumped onto Medicaid rolls—if they're still alive.

Advocates call the pattern "Isolate, Medicate, Steal the Estate." They're meeting with Sen. Amy Klobuchar, D-Minn., on Capitol Hill today seeking an end to well-intentioned guardianship laws gone horribly awry.

Editor's Note: Ms Klobachur never appeared for this meeting.

Barbara F. Hollingsworth is *The Examiner's* local opinion editor

The articles and stories included in this book illustrate the betrayal of American families found in probate courts in America. It is also an international crime. Professional guardianship fraud has been called the No. 1 crime against elderly and disabled citizens in America

FINANCIAL ABUSE BY PROFITEERING GUARDIANS AWAITS AGING BOOMERS AND HEIRS

By: Juliette Fairley   September 23, 2014 9:02 a.m. EDT

MainStreet

In May 2008, Larry Mills filed in Texas to become legal guardian of his then 80-year-old mother, Willie Joe Mills, who'd had a stroke. But by July 2009, Judge William McCulloch in a Harris County probate court appointed a third-party guardian who was also an attorney.

"The guardian put Mama in memory care with dementia people, then he sold her house for $86,000, cashed out $1 million in CDs and put it all in a trust before she was declared incompetent," said Sherry Johnson, who is one of three of Mills's adult children. "She never had a trial or due process."

The nightmare Willie Joe Mills and her heirs experienced is part of a growing trend. Some 37 percent of judges, court managers and clerks who responded to a Center for Elders and the Courts survey revealed that guardianship filings have increased over the last three years and 43 percent noted an increase in caseloads.

In most states, it is not uncommon for the elderly to lose their individual rights around residence, medical care, assets and property once they are placed under guardianship. The consequences can be detrimental for families—financially and in terms of the older relative's health.

LASTING EFFECTS OF THE SWINDLE

Willie Joe Mills's trust was reportedly billed on a quarterly basis by the guardian to pay his monthly salary to manage the elderly woman's affairs, but Johnson claims her mother's health began failing once she was placed under care at Silverado Senior Living in Kenwood, Texas.

"She had pneumonia and urinary tract infections and the facility medical staff failed to treat her because the guardian told them not to," said Johnson. "The guardian used a Do Not Resuscitate document my mother signed to avoid treating minor health problems that could have been arrested."

There are federal regulations that protect seniors in government funded retirement homes. "But if it's a private retirement institution, it is more difficult to find a remedy under federal law," said Phil Ross, an elder care and civil rights attorney in Texas.

In 2012, there was $1.6 million in Willie Joe's trust, according to Johnson, and in 2013 there was $1.5 million. She has yet to receive an accounting for 2014.

"I'm not sure I'll receive my inheritance, because the judge and probate court have tied the hands of Wells Fargo bank," said Johnson. "I would have never thought Texas law would allow the judge, guardian and probate court to do what they are doing to my family and many others."

"We are seeing financial exploitation of the elderly by court appointed third-party guardians where there is little oversight," said Debby Valdez, president of Guardianship Reform Advocates for the Disabled and Elderly (GRADE) in San Antonio, Texas.

Elder abuse is commonly thought of as identity theft or telephone scams but chances are a significant number of the 77 million Baby Boomers approaching the threshold of retirement and old age will face physical abuse, sexual abuse, psychological abuse, neglect, abandonment, isolation and financial and fiduciary abuse at the hands of those they hoped would assist.

MONEY TALKS

"Baby Boomers are the last generation of great wealth, so it stands to reason that things are going to get a whole lot worse and quickly," said Elaine Renoire, president of the National Association to Stop Guardianship Abuse in Indiana.

Symptoms of elder abuse include sudden depression, withdrawal in social settings, bloodied under garments and abrupt changes in financial documents.

"A caregiver's refusal to allow visitors is another red flag," said Kerry Peck, attorney with Peck Bloom and author of *Alzheimer's and the Law* (ABA Book Publishing, 2013). "Dehydration, unusual weight loss, poor hygiene and unsafe living conditions are others."

HELP THAT HURTS

Typically, Adult Protective Services (APS) is the first point of contact responsible for investigating alleged abuse.

"When APS receives reports of elder abuse, case workers go into the home to investigate and ameliorate the situation with legal, medical, psychological and social services," said Karen Roberto, director with the Center for Gerontology at Virginia Tech.

And therein lies another potential for abuse in states where anyone can reportedly initiate a guardianship by simply placing a telephone call to the probate court.

"We receive two to three phone calls a week from families whose elderly parent or family member is being forced into guardianship under the guise of protection by an APS phone call or visit," Valdez told *MainStreet*.

Our broken judicial system affects the lives of everyday people. In the case of professional guardianship fraud, it has been said to be worse than executing someone because the ward, who becomes non-person, suffers exploitation, perhaps sexual assault, prolonged abuse and suffering, and the person's family and friends suffer as well.

THE GULAG OF GUARDIANSHIP: THE LEGAL SYSTEM MEANT TO PROTECT OUR ELDERLY IS A NATIONAL DISGRACE
By: *Money Magazine*

We'd like to alert you to a growing problem in America. It's adult guardianship. It strips seniors (and the disabled) of nearly all of their rights and, with little oversight, the abuse and fraud is out of control. Please read this important information below and tell all your friends.

If you have no assets and little income, you are safe from adult guardianship. Guardianship is all about money.

Guardianship "protects" your assets from misuse and you from exploitation. That is its stated purpose. There are statutes in every state which cover the conduction of guardianship. These laws are designed to control the behavior of the courts and the guardian. Guardianship is a legal proceeding which puts the person under guardianship at the mercy of the courts and the guardian. A guardian is charged with the legal right and duty to care for a person who is determined to be unable to care for themselves.

The potential for exploitation and neglect in guardianship is enormous. For that reason, every state in the nation has passed laws designed to control the conduction of a guardianship.

These laws are universally ignored.

Imagine the effect of giving someone unlimited and unsupervised access to your money with little or no oversight. Imagine having someone determine every aspect of your life. If you or a well meaning relative try to fight this system, the court allows the guardian to use your money to fight you! You are effectively imprisoned in a system designed for your "protection."

Money magazine refers to the "gulag of guardianship" and calls it "a national disgrace."

It is a system riddled with abuses now. It will, if possible, get even worse as baby boomers provide a stream of new victims.

Across America, and particularly here in Florida, with its large retirement community, is a system infested with abuse and fraud. If you've got a nest egg for your retirement, watch out! A professional guardian or an heir may get control of your money by alleging that you can no longer manage your affairs. You pay the court costs for this charade. Those examining you won't consider illness or the effects of drugs on your wits. Forget "due process."

Should your guardian be predisposed to fraud and abuse, there's very little you can do. You are at the mercy of your court-appointed guardian. There are a few rights that you keep. One is the right to privacy. Should a family member want to investigate suspicions of embezzlement, this right to your privacy is invoked. Convenient isn't it?

In 2003, after hearing guardianship horror story after horror story, the Chairman of the The Senate Committee on Aging called for a US government Accountability Office (GAO) report on guardianship. The report indicates that only four courts in our entire country have exemplary guardianship programs: Broward County, FL., Rockingham County, N.H., San Francisco County, CA., and Tarrant County, TX. Is your county among these?

Once under guardianship, you have less rights than a criminal.

1. The right to marry—STRIPPED
2. The right to vote—STRIPPED
3. The right to apply for government benefits—STRIPPED
4. The right to have a driver's license—STRIPPED
5. The right to travel—STRIPPED
6. The right to seek or retain employment—STRIPPED
7. The right to contract—STRIPPED
8. The right to sue and defend lawsuits—STRIPPED
9. The right to manage property or to make any gift or disposition of property—STRIPPED
10. The right to determine his or her residence—STRIPPED
11. The right to consent to medical and mental health treatment—STRIPPED
12. The right to make decisions about his or her social environment or other social aspects of his or her life—STRIPPED

You may believe your health care surrogate, your durable power of attorney, and a pre-need guardianship will protect you. They won't. A guardianship will nullify the best of plans.

What does it take to become a professional guardian in Florida?

1. 18 years old or older
2. No criminal record
3. 40 hour course

Want to fight it? Call Elder Abuse. Nothing. Call the Police: "It's a Civil Case." No one listens to your plight. The guardian will use your money to fight to keep you as their "ward." Your family wants a different guardian? The guardian is likely to accuse your family of abuse and prevent them access to you. Judges frequently rule in favor of the guardian, even if that guardian has a trail of civil cases and very suspicious activity.

You are a target because you have assets. You don't necessarily have to be very old. You can even be quite lucid. That won't stop these predators. When it comes to removing your rights and your money, these folks are experts. It is a very rare and lucky individual who is able to regain their rights. Unfortunately, the process still removes most of their assets by guardian charges and attorney fees fighting to keep you in the gulag.

The following are some quotes about guardianship abuse and fraud from highly respected sources:

"This [guardianship] is an area ripe for fraud and where most fraud abuse has in fact occurred." — Karleen F. DeBlaker, clerk of the Circuit Court, Pinellas County, Florida (4/2004)

Reports of guardians stealing from their wards' bank accounts and otherwise abusing guardianship powers are surfacing with disturbing regularity. "This problem is going to get bigger and bigger," says E. Bentley Lipscomb, AARP's Florida state director and a former state secretary of elder affairs.— "Guardians Drawing Increased Scrutiny," AARP Bulletin

It is a system that in practice often serves lawyers over clients. Even as the court's lax oversight allows guardians to neglect their responsibilities, it also permits some lawyers to take unnecessary control of people's lives. —*Washington Post*, 2003

The current system does not work. This reality is most apparent when a wealthy individual falls victim to these involuntary proceedings and his or her wealth becomes a ripe plum to be shared by the Judge's favorites.— Diane G. Armstrong, PhD, author of *The Retirement Nightmare: How to Save Yourself from Your Heirs and Protectors: Involuntary Conservatorships and Guardianships*, from an excerpt of her prepared statement before the US Senate's Special Committee on Aging, February, 2003.

The denial of these rights is the consequence of a court determination that an individual is legally "incompetent" or "incapacitated" and the appointment by the court of a guardian to act as surrogate decision maker on the person's behalf. The real tragedy is that mounting evidence suggests that many of these individuals—having been stripped of their right to self-determination—are being poorly served, and even victimized and exploited by the very persons or agencies appointed to protect them and to make decisions on their behalf. — *House of Representatives, Select Committee on Aging Report*

"...older Americans are being robbed of their freedom and life savings by a legal system created for their protection." and "Although relatives are the most common exploiters, the damage they cause generally stays within the confines of their own families. By contrast, greedy professional guardians can wreak havoc on a far larger scale. In many states, there are few prerequisites for entering the guardianship business: no special training, no licensing process, no enforceable professional standards." — *AARP: The Magazine, January/February 2004*

"These are not isolated, occasional blips. This constitutes a significant portion of the cases out there. They were flat-out rip-off situations." — Robert L. Aldridge, elder law attorney and a member of ElderLawAnswers.com

Re: forced incompetency: Visit assisted-living facilities [and retirement communities] and establish employee contacts; obtain voluntary limited financial guardianship; if there is money in the estate, do paperwork to force an evaluation of competency; get control over everything and the ward [senior] loses all rights. — Robert W. Melton, Pinellas County internal auditor, "Dirty Tricks of Guardianships—The Need for Change," April 2004

Once judged incompetent and placed under a conservatorship [or guardianship], a citizen becomes a nonperson, with fewer rights than a convicted felon in a penitentiary. — Robert Casey, editor, Bloomberg Wealth Manager

"This is something that ought not to be taken lightly. Seniors have become victims of the legal process. When you become old, you should not, by the action of a court, automatically lose your rights just because some family member or impersonal administrator calls you incompetent." — Senator Larry Craig, Chairman, US Senate's Special Committee on Aging, February, 2003

Case Study Illustrates the Gulag of Guardianship

Guardianship Gulag: Elder Abuse Falsely Confines Woman
By: Gerald Boland Guest Editorial: May 10, 2015

When Gerald Boland and Mary Jane Snell complain to hospital Memorial Medical Center (MMC), Las Cruces about accommodations and care, MMC's alleged retaliation is to maliciously petition (Third Judicial District Court) for guardianship! Guardians Sandy Meyer and Alaina Johnson (dba ADVOCATE SERVICES OF LAS CRUCES, LLC) immediately take dictatorial control to permanently separate-isolate Mary from Gerald.

Hospital MMC misuses Gerald's information about Mary's fear (phobia-panic) of medical scene as a risk-management ploy to divert attention away from negligence allegations by Mary and Gerald. MMC hires a cadre to falsely diagnose Mary incapacitated, appoint guardians, and commit victim to nursing home where they sadistically, knowingly, induce sustained mental-emotional-panic, trauma, and deep-deep-depression, crying, and forced separation!

Mary asked the (unnecessary) appointed guardian Sandy Meyer, "why are you doing this to me, what did I ever do to you?" A logical woman's question, being abruptly swept away to a nursing home!

Sagecrest Nursing & Rehab disregards Mary's reported fall on January 31, 2015, guardians disrespect Mary with indifference to her strongly spoken desire to be released to come home and resume life. Guardian's indifference, court's indifference, Guardian ad Litem's indifference, court visitor's indifference and psychologist's indifference weakens Mary by design.

Elder abuse, false diagnosis, hypnotic-psychotropic medications that double mortality and can induce a cardiac-arrest, and false confinement that deliberately traumatize Mary, continues since January 21, 2015! Mary is competent at home and elsewhere, only meds for hypertension and allergies, just scared-panicked around doctors, hospitals, and nursing homes.

This is the worst form of colorable legal/medical malpractice! Forced abduction, forced confinement, forced medications, forced separation from significant other; guardians hypothecate (steal) and liquidate all property! Mary's name securitized for more theft in Court Registry Investment System [(CRIS) Accounts and (CUSIP) accounts)] using Treasury-Direct accounts to exploit and transfer wealth from Mary. A forensic-criminal-audit must be performed!

Community (Baptist and SDA) Pastors please urgently help! Call to speak with Mary Jane Snell at Sagecrest 1-575-522-7000 and visit her (Room 115). She needs lots of reassuring hugs, love, and prayers! Yes America! Judicial-medical malpractice enabled "woman-stealing" in America! This evil must cease!

Community Call and Pastor Visits Requested

WHAT CAN THE COMMUNITY DO?

Phone Judges and State Guardianship Program Administrator! Let's free Mary Jane Snell from misdiagnosis and false-imprisonment! There're verifiable 'allegations' of Judicial misconduct, Guardianship abuse, mind destroying medical-Quackery, Nursing Home negligence, and State Administrator(s) neglect; hereafter (JGQNHSA) wrongdoers harming Mary!

I humbly ask all caring people, to please help free Mary! Respectfully call/leave messages pleading Mary's freedom and dismissal of cases D-307-PQ-2015-00003 and D-307-CV-2015-00133! Call Third Judicial District Judge(s) James T. Martin 1-575-523-8292 and Judge Manuel I. Arrieta 1-575-523-8225 assistants and Marina A. Cordova, Supervising Attorney & Guardianship Program Manager, Developmental Disabilities Planning Council (DDPC), Office of Guardianship (OOG) 1-505-841-4586 (http://www.nmddpc.com) to cease and desist all abuses, judicial indifference, willful error, impropriety and constructive fraud.

Mary's continued nursing home false-imprisonment defines the insidious explicit and implicit forms that JGQNHSA coordination takes on. People calling for Mary's freedom demonstrates the grounds in law and precedent, affirming that by JGQNHSA coordinated wrongdoing—judges are the most vulnerable to impropriety, cover-up, and conflict of interests.

Judges do cover-up for each other! In the last 226 years since the creation of the Federal Judiciary in 1789, only eight of its judges were removed from the bench! People phoning, investigating, and exposing wrongdoing—reveals judicial dishonesty, indicts judicial credibility to impartial application of law; and refutes proclaimed institutional responsibility for the integrity of the Judiciary and of legal process. Calling them will give publicity to review their decisions damaging Mary.

JGQNHSA's deliberate-knowing but not stopping wrongs damaging Mary are 'accessories after the fact!' Moreover, by giving implicit or explicit reassurance that JGQNHSA wrongdoers will not condemn and report their wrongdoing to we the people, other authorities, or the media eliminates deterrence of adverse consequences to the commission of more wrongdoing; JGQNHSA become 'accessories before the fact!'

"Wrongdoing" and "coordinated wrongdoing" as opposed to "corruption" encompass more conduct and impose a lower burden of proof to be borne by civil-criminal investigations. Mary's false confinement at Sagecrest Nursing and Rehabilitation, L.C., is Elder Abuse, against her will, over her objections and without consent. Please make that call! Everyone's freedom and property are at risk for such a misused method of diagnosis with legalese rubber-word "incapacitated."

Attorneys will usually betray their own clients to protect the attorneys who are responsible for these crimes. An ethic of the American Bar Association is to never say anything bad about another lawyer. Additionally, attorneys fear retribution of losing their license for being honest. This multi-billion-dollar-a-year racket is the elephant in the room when discussing the American judicial system.

ACTIVIST ATTORNEY'S LICENSE CANCELLED AFTER EXPOSING COURT'S 'ELDER CLEANSING' CORRUPTION

By: Submitted by knowmore on Sat, 03/29/2014—05:27

In yet another legal maneuver to shut down dissent, the attorney disciplinary board in the State of Illinois has suspended Chicago-based activist attorney Kenneth Ditkowsky's license to practice law for four years, following a hearing where Ditkowsky's right to speak out against corruption in the courts featured center-stage.

Ditkowsky, who has been practicing law since the early 1960's, came to public attention after he became outspoken against what he calls "elder cleansing," which is taking place in guardianship programs in courts throughout the United States. Ditkowsky has been sending e-mails to public officials, including Attorney General Eric Holder and US Senator Matt Kirk on a regular basis, asking for an "honest and complete investigation" of reported abuses going on under the mantle of adult guardianships.

Ditkowsky has defined "elder cleansing" as a three-step process: First, a court must assert its dominion over an elder person's life and assets by appointing a guardian. Ditkowsky has detailed instances, such as in the

Mary Sykes' guardianship, where legal process was not adhered to. Second, the elder is systematically isolated from concerned family and friends and his assets pilfered by the very guardian who is in place to conserve the estate. The final stage of elder cleansing, according to Ditkowsky, occurs when the elder, now isolated and placed into a facility, is drugged to death.

US Moves to Crush Internal Dissent 03.03. Author: Janet Phelan

In yet another legal maneuver to shut down dissent, the attorney disciplinary board in the State of Illinois has suspended Chicago-based activist attorney Kenneth Ditkowsky's license to practice law for four years, following a hearing where Ditkowsky's right to speak out against corruption in the courts featured center-stage.

Ditkowsky, who has been practicing law since the early 1960s, came to public attention after he became outspoken against what he calls "elder cleansing," which is taking place in guardianship programs in courts throughout the United States. Ditkowsky has been sending e-mails to public officials, including Attorney General Eric Holder and US Senator Matt Kirk on a regular basis, asking for an "honest and complete investigation" of reported abuses going on under the mantle of adult guardianships.

Ditkowsky has defined "elder cleansing" as a three step process: First, a court must assert its dominion over an elder person's life and assets by appointing a guardian. Ditkowsky has detailed instances, such as in the Mary Sykes guardianship, where legal process was not adhered to. Second, the elder is systematically isolated from concerned family and friends and his assets pilfered by the very guardian who is in place to conserve the estate. The final stage of elder cleansing, according to Ditkowsky, occurs when the elder, now isolated and placed into a facility, is drugged to death.

Ditkowsky was placed under disciplinary proceedings by the IARDC (Illinois Attorney Registration and Disciplinary Commission), after his repeated allegations of attorney and judicial misconduct in the guardianship of Mary G. Sykes, Alice Gore and others began to apparently become an irritant. At one point, Ditkowsky was asked by IARDC attorney Leah Black if he were not "sorry" for his e-mails asking for an investigation into these cases.

Mary G. Sykes has been isolated from family and friends for several years. A number of valuable assets, including old gold and silver coins, have reportedly disappeared during the tenure of the guardianship. In another guardianship matter, Alice Gore had her teeth mined for gold fillings, which were removed on order of the guardian.

Ditkowsky has pledged to continue on the fight against elder cleansing. In another one of his widely disseminated e-mails following his receipt of notice of suspension from the practice of law, Ditkowsky stated the following....

"henceforth my full time efforts will be directed toward the fight to prevent 'elder cleansing' and the WAR AGAINST THE ELDERLY AND THE DISABLED that our miscreant abusive guardians and those who work in concert with them—i.e. the political royals, Jerome Larkin and the IARDC, etc. The Supreme Court of Illinois affirmed the IARDC and ruled that the First Amendment to the Illinois Constitution has been abrogated."

The State of Illinois appears to have adopted a "take no prisoners" policy against dissident attorneys. However, the very IARDC attorneys who prosecuted Ditkowsky's license have failed to file their mandated financial disclosure forms. These forms are to be filed to ensure that those in government are not receiving bribes and payoffs in return for their official duties. In other words, the law of the State of Illinois apparently does not apply to those working for government.

In concert with another Illinois attorney, JoAnne Denison, Ken Ditkowsky has filed a civil rights lawsuit in federal court, alleging that his First Amendment rights have been breached. JoAnne **Denison is also on trial for her bar license for the act of running a blog—marygsykes.**

com—which is critical of judges and other legal professionals as relates to the practice of elder law and guardianship.

Ken Ditkowsky's writings have been regularly featured on Denison's blog. Denison has also filed a copyright infringement suit, based on what she alleges to be improper dominion by the IARDC over the blog.

At stake here is more than the individual careers of a couple of attorneys. When individuals are censured for what is considered to be Constitutionally protected speech, the public at large suffers, as well. Writes JoAnne Denison,

"As you are aware, the greatest weapons in this country counter to a dictatorship and tyranny are undoubtedly the right to petition freely and openly our government for redress, and when that fails, our right to take unresolved grievances to be aired in the media.

In one fell swoop, the IARDC takes away these rights.

As attorneys, we cannot call a spade a spade, a pig with lipstick becomes a lady, and words such as "corrupt," "tortfeasor," civil and human rights violations, theft, conversion, embezzlement, false imprisonment are swiftly taken away from our blogs, then the public is not warned.

At the time of going to press, blogger Roger Shuler has been sitting in jail for five months in Alabama, due to a "prior restraint" issue. Moveon. org is being sued by the Governor of Louisianna, Bobby Jindal, for a billboard which states that Jindal's acts as Governor resulted in the denial of Medicaid coverage for 242,000 people. Yet another arrest warrant has been issued for an outspoken probate court victim, this time out in Logan County, Ohio. The arrest warrant for Rosanna Miller is for failure to pay a couple of grand in court costs. However, the law prohibits jailing someone for a debt in Ohio.

A large reaper appears to be at play, cutting down and silencing activists, attorneys and non- attorneys alike. Anyone who speaks out appears to be at risk. The use of the legal system as an instrument of (domestic) war has resulted in the coining of a new word, "lawfare," which aptly describes the sorts of assaults on rights and freedoms such as noted herein.

As summed up by Ken Ditkowsky, **"According to our brethren who regulate Attorney conduct noticing the 'elder cleansing' is unethical, and if you speak concerning it you are a danger to the profession and you will be suspended or disbarred."**

And in an impassioned moment, JoAnne Denison writes comparing the guardianship programs with the T-4 program in Hitler's Germany:

It was not until late in the T4 program and by then the concentration camp program that a German Cardinal finally read aloud a letter protesting forced euthanasia and reaffirming the sanctity of life that protests began among German Catholics and the letter was read aloud in all the German churches eventually and protests in German started to take off. But by then it was simply too late. A deeply entrenched machine had already flourished for years. Jews and other undesirables were already being sent to their deaths by the bus loads.

Only the end of the war would stop this machine.

So I stand here today, and I will trash my law license so that this T4 program with grandma and grandpa will go no further. Many have gone to the ARDC, the federal and state authorities with credible cases and plenty of evidence and were completely ignored. T4 was implemented, condoned and covered up by attorneys in the Drabik and Gore cases. Remember, T4 started with infants. Our seniors are just as vulnerable.

Just say NO to T4 in the United States. Say NO to involuntary euthanasia for elders. Say NO to elder cleansing and elder trafficking. Whatever you call it, it's just plain wrong and people, and especially attorneys must blog and must protest.

Neither Jim Grogan, the press spokesman for the IARDC, nor Jim Tyrbor, press contact for the Illinois Supreme Court, responded to queries from this reporter as to why the ARDC attorneys had not filed their financial disclosure forms.

Janet C. Phelan, investigative journalist and human rights defender, has traveled pretty extensively over the Asian region, exclusively for the online magazine New Eastern Outlook.

Attorney Teddy Moore lost his license to practice law for writing "The Fixer" regarding corrupt courts throughout the U.S. court system.

"THE FIXER" TACKLES CORRUPTION OF US JUDICIARY
Re: Teddy Moore

NEW YORK—The United States legal system is built to be corrupt and not to make justice.

So says Teddy Moore, author of the book *"The Fixer,"* a book which chronicles what he says is the most-kept secret in US history—extreme corruption of the US Judiciary.

A television interview with Moore will air on cable on Tuesday, Dec. 6 at 6.30:00 p.m. on Channel 56 in Brooklyn and Manhattan, and on Dec. 20 at 3.30:00 p.m. on Channel 34.

For those who cannot watch it in New York, the interview can be accessed via the Internet at http://www.cinemazo.com/TheFixer.wmv Moore was an attorney admitted to the New York Bar and the federal courts in New York for nine years. Most of his work was concentrated in appellate review of state and federal courts, including the United States. Supreme court.

The interview addresses major issues plaguing the judiciary, the court of appeals, lack of supervision by the congress. Moore offers his opinions as to how to overhaul the system.

Moore says the main problem with the legal system as he sees it is that the legal system doesn't admit to the obvious which is that the legal system is corrupt. "You don't know about the corruption because the media doesn't report it," Moore says. "They call it a single bad apple but the bad apples are everywhere...on the top of the barrel, in the middle, on the bottom...everywhere...they refuse to report it for what it is."

The legal system is built to be corrupt and not to make justice. Moore says. "This is the uniqueness of the United States legal system. **The US legal system created a system to make money for attorneys and judges. In order to do so, they created a kind of extortion of attorneys... an extortable attorney. An extortable attorney to the judge has to comply with everything the judge asks him to do and can only be explained as the extreme means of greed of the judiciary."**

"Attorneys fear the judiciary because the system is built in this way...so they can be easily be extortable to the judge....the judge can

easily accept money from the other parties for the extortion. People who believe that they come to court to decide their case based on the facts and the law are terribly mistaken. It's a mecca of just siphoning money to the judges," Moore asserts in his book.

He says that Congress is part of the problem. "*Most of the Congresspeople are attorneys that are afraid of the judiciary, afraid to be disbarred and sanctioned, look forward for the time they are out of Congress and join the corruption and make a buck for themselves. Therefore they cannot be part of the solution.*"

The Court of Appeals allows the corruption to continue and money to flow, he says.

"The Court of Appeals is a phony show in the United States. The outcome of an appeal is well known. The only one who doesn't know the outcome of an appeal is the client who paid the money for the phony show. Had he known it was a phony show, he wouldn't have paid the money." Moore says.

"The facts in my book suggest that the legal system in the United States is terribly corrupt because the hypocrisy of the United States, the rich and powerful are interested in the system giving them the judgment they want for the price they can afford."

"The US Supreme Court supervises the racket of extortion, bribes and extreme corruption." The author claims that the United States judiciary is liable for more damage and injuries to US people then the Nazis.

CHAPTER 2

Guardianship Fraud Schemes

• • •

The first article in this section explains what to look for if you believe you're involved in a fraudulent guardianship/conservatorship. Dr. Woodhull gives an excellent description of the general method used by perpetrators throughout the United States to put this crime into action.

HOW A FRAUDULENT GUARDIANSHIP/CONSERVATORSHIP COMMENCES AND CONTINUES
By: Angela V. Woodhull, Ph.D.

ORIGINALLY PUBLISHED IN *PPJJ GAZETTE* © 2010–2011, Angela V. Woodhull, Ph.D.
Used with permission of the author December 23, 2015

• • •

This essay examines conditions in Florida, but the same problems exist in many states.

STEP ONE: EMINENT DANGER—THE INITIAL COURT PETITION
The professional guardian [or conservator], with the assistance of her attorneys, commences the embezzlement process by filing an emergency

petition in the probate courts to become the *"emergency"* *"temporary"* guardian.

Florida guardianship statutes (Chapter 744), like many states, require that there be an *"eminent danger"* in order for the petitioner to become the *"emergency temporary guardian."*

The guardian oftentimes fabricates the *"eminent danger"* by stating that there is a neighbor or relative or stranger who is taking advantage of the elderly person. In some cases, this may be a somewhat true statement, albeit an exaggerated claim. In most cases, upon further investigation, there has been no *"eminent danger"* whatsoever.

Step One takes away all of the victim's civil rights and therefore gives the guardian and her attorneys full control over the victim and his or her assets.

• • •

STEP TWO: THE EXAMINING COMMITTEE

Once the professional guardian has taken control of the victim on a temporary basis (the emergency temporary guardianship order expires in 60 days [in Florida]) an examining committee of three medical *"professionals"* steps in to verify the allegation of mental incapacity. Oftentimes, the victim is administered a cocktail of psychotropic drugs to enhance the claims that he or she is incompetent.

"Ward" Elizabeth Faye Arnold, for instance, stated, *"They put me on drugs that made me feel very drunk. I couldn't even remember my name. Now that they have all my money, they don't medicate me that way anymore."* One of the three medical professionals must be a psychiatrist and the victim is generally always found to be mentally incapacitated. The guardian usually has her own set of medical professionals that she utilizes on a regular basis. For instance, one professional guardian is married to a medical doctor and therefore has an entire fleet of medical professional associates available to her.

Back in the courtroom, soon after the three medical professionals file their reports, there is a capacity hearing. The victim seldom is permitted to attend this hearing. The judge quickly scans the medical examinations that *"verify"* that the victim is *"mentally and/or physically incapacitated."* The judge then signs an order that gives the professional guardian full and permanent legal authority over the victim's person and property.

• • •

STEP THREE: THE "FEAST" BEGINS

Property is sold for below market value and the deeds switch and switch several times. (kick backs are suspected). Bank accounts, annuities, stocks, and Certificates of Deposit are liquidated into one big guardianship account.

Out of this large bank account, the guardian is expected to pay all the victim's, but bills oftentimes go unpaid.

• • •

HOW THE VICTIM'S MONEY IS SPENT

1. **Attorney's fees and guardianship fees for "services rendered to 'Benefit' the 'Ward'"**

   A large part of the victim's money is spent on attorney's fees and guardian's fees. As long as there is ample money in the victim's guardianship account, the guardian and her attorney cohorts will file motion upon motion after motion to the courts, such as:

   ◦ A motion to sell the ward's furniture.

   ◦ A motion to liquidate stocks and Certificates of Deposit.

   ◦ A motion to transfer the ward to a different nursing home.

   > A large part of the victim's money is spent on attorney's/guardian'fees. As long as there is ample money in the victim's account, the guardian and her attorney cohorts will file motion upon motion after motion to the courts

* A motion to sell the ward's homesteaded house.
* A motion to open up a safety deposit box.

Each motion can cost the *"ward"* in excess of $2,000 because the motion must be written, researched, filed, and then a hearing is scheduled. Oftentimes, the motions cost more than what is being petitioned for.

2. **Puffing the monthly budget**

   The guardian frequently doubles the monthly expenses then keeps the remainder.

3. **Selling the "Ward's" personal belongings for below market value then pocketing the difference**

   The guardian underestimates the amount of the sale of personal items, such as jewelry, paintings, and antiques, for the purpose of the court record inventories, then is free to keep the difference. There is little and often no court oversight.

4. **Bills are simply not paid**

   Oftentimes, the bills of the *"ward"* are not even paid. When the *"ward"* dies, the guardian simply places an ad in an obscure newspaper, if there is money left for an estate to be probated. Assuming creditors do not see the ad and file a claim against the estate within 30 days, their claims are forever barred and so the guardian was able to fool creditors and abscond with the money and not have to pay any of the bills. If she is caught, she simply pays the bills of the creditors who caught her. This frequently includes Medicaid.

5. **Accounting is not accurate**

   The guardian can claim a much lower amount of liquid assets than what the victim is actually worth and then pocket the rest.

   Examples:

   * Julie Sweeten–$400,000.00 estate with an alleged $80,000.00 remaining when Sweeten died. More than $300,000.00 was spent in three years.
   * Louise A. Falvo started off with approximately $800,000.00. Two months into the guardianship, her guardian filed an accounting

with the court stating that Falvo was worth only $672,000.00. Shortly thereafter, a bank statement from Bank of America stated that Falvo now had $449,000 after all accounts had been liquidated. So, approximately $200,000 turned up missing.

6. **Fake wills**

   In this scenario, the guardian claimed that Julie Sweeten desired to leave her estate to her bank. A forged will was entered into the record. Wachovia Bank trustee was then given $80,000 from the uncontested, probated estate.

• • •

STEP FOUR: THE MYSTERIOUS DEATHS

Once the funds have been spent, the *"ward"* oftentimes suddenly dies.

or

The *"ward"* dies when there is still plenty of money—if a huge probate battle can commence, thereby further enriching the attorneys and guardian.

Examples:

- Carlisle Bosworth died soon after his $250,000 had been spent.
- James Deaton — $5 million, three years in probate — $3 million in attorney's fees with a pittance finally paid out to his family members.
- Louise A. Falvo—suspected morphine sulfate overdose as cause of death; huge probate battle to enrich attorneys ensued even though her bank accounts were all Pay On Death/In Trust For (POD/ITF) to her daughter, so probate should have been completely unnecessary.

NASGA, National Association to Stop Guardianship Abuse, has adopted a three part theme to succinctly describe the legally sanctioned exploitative guardianship process:

"Isolate, Medicate, Take the Estate"

• • •

Predatory guardians: How courts are allowing professional guardians/conservators to rob your assets

Examples:

* Marie Long was worth $1.3 million when she suffered a stroke and came under the *"protection"* of a professional guardian. Three short years later, she is penniless and subsisting off of a meager social security pension and Medicaid.
* Louise A. Falvo, 91 had accumulated nearly one million dollars when she was placed under a guardianship that was commenced with a forgery of her daughter's signature by a probate attorney. Within three months, Louise A. Falvo was dead. Two and a half years later, the guardianship remains open. The guardian and her attorneys have, to date, been awarded by the judge more than $350,000.00 of Falvo's estate—*"to benefit the 'ward'"*—who is deceased.
* Corretta Brown was placed under guardianship when the Department of Children and Families discovered that her home was uninhabitable. Today, Brown is deceased, her assets have disappeared (more than $100,000), and all of her debts—totaling more than $75,000 in nursing home costs, remain unpaid. The professional guardian, it was discovered, was not licensed and has since fled the state of Florida with Brown's assets.
* Marie Sandusky signed a power of attorney to guarantee that her beloved daughter, and not her rejected son, would manage her financial affairs and health care directives. Today, Sandusky has a court-appointed guardian who has spent more than $300,000 of Sandusky's money in attorney's fees. The reason? Sandusky's

rebuked son hired an attorney and together they made false allegations against Sandusky's beloved daughter. As the *"wheels of justice"* move forward, Sandusky's money is legally used to fund the frivolous feud.

* Debra Duffield, 58, has been under the control of a professional guardian for the last four years. She was only 54-years old when an involuntary guardianship was petitioned against her by a professional guardian who gleefully discovered (tipped off by a social worker) Duffield's substantive worth when Duffield was hospitalized for anorexia and a broken hip. During the last four years, the vast majority of her assets have been converted to attorney and guardian fees. Duffield, who was diagnosed as merely bipolar, had allegedly been financially exploited by a friend — hence, the rationale for the guardianship. She is confined to a nursing home without rehabilitation. She sits in a bed, smelling of urine and fecal matter, watching television. The guardian and her attorney regularly and steadfastly bill her account for merely *"reading her file"* or checking on the latest whereabouts of her former girlfriend. Soon, Duffield, who once owned a fabulous house complete with expensive antiques, valuable imported rugs and fine paintings, will be penniless.

When you hear the word *"professional guardian,"* what do you think? Do you think of someone who protects the elderly? Assists them with their daily needs? Guarantees they are protected from financial exploitation and physical neglect?

Think again.

The pristine image of professional court-appointed guardians who allegedly protect the elderly is being challenged. Grass root organizations, such as the **National Association to Stop Guardian Abuse (N.A.S.G.A.)** and **Advocates for National Guardianship Ethics and Reform (A.N.G.E.R.)** are claiming that professional guardians, their attorneys—and even judges—need to be watched.

* May 25, 2010. Latifa Ring of Elder Abuse Victims Advocates addressed the Committee on the Judiciary, Subcommittee on Crime, Terrorism and Homeland Security stating, "*...exploitation in guardianships is rampant. It is largely kept out of the public eye under the guise of 'protection.'*"

  "*Family members are portrayed as 'Osama Bin Laden' or the devil incarnate,*" David Newman said, a guardian reform advocate.

These "*unproven and often false allegations*" commence a flurry of legal activity that can only be likened to Charles Dickinson's Bleak House. While family members are forced to spend thousands of dollars defending themselves against the false accusations, these same accusers—oftentimes, the professional guardians—handsomely profit from the legal havoc they create.

THE GUARDIANS NEED TO BE WATCHED

Take, for example, the recently widely publicized case of **Clay Greene and Harold Scull,** a gay couple who had cogently cohabitated together for more than twenty years, rendering mutual durable powers of attorney, wills, and other legal declarations upon one another. When Scull, 89, unexpectedly fell onto a stone patio, paramedics were called and the local sheriff department hastily alleged that Greene had intentionally shoved Scull to the ground. Yet, despite the fact that all charges were subsequently dropped, the public guardianship office for Sonoma County used the already disproved physical abuse allegation to commence an involuntary guardianship against Scull. Scull was removed to a nursing home, isolated him from Greene, and the couple's jointly owned property which included valuable paintings, expensive Persian rugs, antiques, silverware, jewelry, and real estate—was sold for far less than appraised value—at least according to the court records. It was later discovered that the items had been sold for far more by the public guardianship office.

These types of guardianship irregularities have sparked a guardianship task force **Special Committee on Aging,** which reported, "*...guardianship...has the potential of harming older adults rather than protecting them...*

*The…continuing reports of the failure of courts…to prevent [financial] exploita-
tion of incapacitated adults by their guardians have long been of concern to this
Committee."*

Greene sued the public guardianship office who settled with him
for approximately $600,000.00 just days before trial. Amy Todd-Gher,
Greene's attorney, stated:

"This victory sends an unmistakable message that all elders must
be treated with respect and dignity…and that those who mistreat
elders must be held accountable. [But] Even as we celebrate this
victory…we are deeply troubled that the Sonoma [County] continues to refuse to take responsibility for their egregious misconduct…We urge every citizen…to demand more oversight of the
Public Guardian's office. They need to be watched."

AN ALARMINGLY COMMON PRACTICE

Is elder financial exploitation by professional guardians and their attorneys a commonplace occurrence? According to John Caravella, a former
detective and office manager for **Seniors vs. Crime,** a special project of
the Florida Attorney General's Office, Gainesville, Florida, the answer is
"Yes."

Caravella became simultaneously intrigued and disturbed by the
court-sanctioned practices of professional guardians on their *"wards"* (the
legal term dubbed to those who have lost all of their civil rights under
court-mandated guardianship) when one of his neighbors mysteriously
disappeared shortly after receiving an inheritance of more than a quarter
of a million dollars. The neighbor, referred to as *"Adelle"* in Caravella's
book, **Marked for Destruction,** had been falsely induced by a stock broker, whom she had consulted about her fledgling inheritance money, to
sign papers that authorized a professional guardian and her attorney to
manage Adele's finances—if she should become mentally incapacitated.
Within a few weeks, the guardian and her attorney petitioned the court
alleging that Adele was not competent to manage her own affairs. The

court authorized that she be stripped of all of her civil rights and placed in a nursing home. Soon thereafter, Adele's recently acquired $250,000+ was quickly consumed by the attorney and guardian for *"professional services"* fees. And Adele soon passed away.

• • •

How it all begins – GUARDIANS PLAYBOOK

Isolate Ward From Family	Eliminate Family Obstacles to Total Control	Seize All Personal Assets Quickly
Replace all caregivers and Vendors	Retain Counsel Initiate Costly Endless Litigation	Hire Crony Consultants
Medicate the Ward	Void Prior Documents	Break All Trusts

BILL ENDLESSLY WITH ASSURANCE OF COURT APPROVAL

Kevin Gallagher had a trusted, longstanding pact with his beloved parents: When the time was *"right,"* he would make arrangements for their safe return to Maine where they would reside in assisted living. That *"right time"* came unexpectedly one day after Sunday services when Robert and Elsa Gallagher became slightly disoriented in traffic when they happen chanced upon orange cones in a road detour. Kevin and Lisa, delighted to hear that their parents were ready to journey home, began making all of the necessary arrangements. Kevin even phoned his estranged Orlando-based sister, Lori, and asked if she would simply *"telephone"* Mom and Dad during the interim. The sister, however, consulted the Yellow Pages and telephoned a company, **Geriatric Care Management,** that specializes in elder care.

THE SHERIFFS ARRIVE

Within 48 hours a professional guardian, and owner of the elder care company, arrived at the Gallagher's doorstep with a court order and two deputy sheriffs. She had hastily petitioned to become the couple's *"emergency temporary guardian"* after learning of their substantive assets. Upon her arrival, the couple were forcefully removed from their home and placed in separate nursing home facilities. Mrs. Gallagher, hysterical, secretly phoned her daughter-in-law, her speech slurred, crying for help. She had been forcibly administered psychotropic drugs. Three medical professionals quickly examined her while under the influence of the narcotics, and declared both she and her husband simultaneously 100 percent mentally incapacitated. The temporary guardian was then quickly appointed the permanent, plenary guardian.

The guardian's first move was to encumber all of the couple's assets.

THE LEGAL CONTEST COMMENCES

Instead of making arrangements for their safe return home, Kevin Gallagher suddenly found himself furiously searching for Florida attorneys. Meanwhile, the guardian's legal counsel quickly filed papers to block Kevin's attempts at removing his parents from Florida to Maine. A hotly contested guardianship soon commenced with attorneys from both sides legally authorized to generously pay themselves from the Gallaghers' assets.

"The story is always the same," states Newman, a guardianship reform advocate. *"A family member fights the guardianship; then the family member later 'wins' the contest—when all the assets have been spent in attorneys' fees."*

Three years passed. Kevin found himself switching attorneys four times in an attempt to get the legal nightmare to stop Then, suddenly, it did stop. Kevin was declared the winner of the contest.

ALL OF THE ASSETS HAD BEEN SPENT.

"They then placed my parents on an airplane with a single suitcase with a broken zipper," Kevin stated. *"Inside the suitcase were tattered clothes that had the*

names of other people in Magic Marker inside the clothes. Everything they had owned—even their clothes—had been sold or trashed by the guardian."

Both Elsa and Robert died shortly after returning to Maine.

FAMILY FEUD—OR—AN OPEN INVITATION FOR FRAUD?

Corrine Branson, 82, had been happily living in Miami Beach with the daily assistance of a CNA when her grandson secretly petitioned the court to become his grandmother's guardian. When Branson learned that she was to be moved into a nursing home, she quickly phoned her beloved daughter, aunt to the grandson, who had been granted a springing power of attorney many years before. Bonnie Reiter, with little knowledge of guardianships or guardianship law, quickly hired an attorney who suggested that a *"professional guardian"* be appointed during the interim legal contest.

It turned out that the guardian he suggested works with him on a regular basis. Reiter fired her attorney, hired another, and then moved for a court hearing which her mother planned to attend.

"Two weeks prior to the hearing, my mother ended up mysteriously dead," Reiter stated.

The guardianship remained open after Branson's death with Reiter, alone, having spent $130,000.00 in attorneys' fees.

"They took more than $800,000 of my mother's money in attorneys' fees. The guardianship, in which my mother had never even been declared mentally incapacitated, lasted less than three months. This is a racketeering scheme that needs to be investigated. The F.B.I. should step in."

DIFFERENT NAMES, SAME STORY

* An Orange County court auditor discovered $50,000.00 missing three days before the ward died. The judge ordered an *"Order to Show Cause."* Prior to the hearing, the guardian and her attorney

simply brought back the missing money and placed it back with the court. The judge dropped the scheduled hearing.

* Court records show that the guardian received $12,000 a month to pay the nursing home bills for Carlisle Bosworth. However, the skilled nursing home facility where he was placed charges only $6,000 a month. No investigation has ever been conducted regarding what happened to the extra $6,000 per month. Bosworth died shortly after all of his money had been spent.

* Marion Copley was placed on Medicaid—even though her guardian sold her home for more than $250,000.

* In another case a professional guardian petitioned the court to become an elderly woman's guardian when she discovered the woman had no living relatives. She told the judge that the woman, who was still living independently in her home, had *"bats flying all over the inside of the house."* The allegation resulted in a guardianship and the victim was removed from her home. Neighbors later stated that they had never seen *"bats flying all over the house."*

* In yet another case a professional guardian obtained a guardianship over Christian Van Beekum stating that neighbors had exploited him. A quick search of the property records showed that the neighbors who had allegedly exploited Van Beekum had actually sold their home and moved to another state six years prior.

* James Deaton had owned an extensive coin collection, an expensive baseball card collection, and his deceased mother's diamond rings and pearl necklaces, according to relatives. None of these items were ever listed on the guardian's inventory report.

* *The Denver Post* has several times (**2010, 2011**) published investigative reports exposing the problems with the probate court there.

* In July 2012 *World News* **posted a video** by Lisa Flurie and story about what has been done to her brother Mark in Florida probate courts. Links to many other stories of guardianship/conservatorship fraud are available there as well.

Law enforcement agents, social workers, and judges have been trained to maintain a watchful eye over exploitative family members. Yet no one seems to be guarding the guardians. Family members have complained to local law enforcement, the state attorneys' office, and even the F.B.I.without any significant action being taken.

The problems grow worse with time as the courts become ever more dysfunctional.

• • •

ABOUT THE AUTHOR

Dr. Angela V. Woodhull, a licensed private investigator, spent more than two and a half years investigating court records in Seminole and Orange Counties, Florida, and interviewing family members and victims in order to compose this story. All court records that verify the contents of this article were submitted as attachments to the editor of the F.B.I. journal as verification of accuracy. Dr. Woodhull can be reached at (352) 327–3665 or (352) 682–9033, or write her at PO Box 14423, Gainesville, Florida 32604–2423, or e-mail her at *chachaangelina@yahoo.com*.

Dr. Woodhull is a licensed private investigator and the author of *Police Communication in Traffic Stops* and *Private Investigation Strategies and Techniques*.

• • •

REFERENCES AND RESOURCES

Advocates for National Guardianship Ethics and Reform (ANGER)
Elder Abuse Victims Advocates_— For National Guardianship reform
General Accounting Office (GAO) report on **Guardianships: Cases of Financial Exploitation, Neglect, and Abuse of Seniors**
CNN Report: **Probe shows court-appointed guardians often not screened or monitored**
National Association to Stop Guardian Abuse (NASGA)

*This next article illustrates the description given by Dr. Woodhull in a case summary of a sixty-four-year-old man who filed for divorce and had just been to his neurologist and received a clean health report. The woman he was trying to divorce chemically restrained him to prevent him from leaving the state. With the help of a non-conclusive psych report written at the wife's instructions, a corrupt guardianship firm, corrupt attorneys, and a corrupt court commissioner, he became a Non Person in a matter of a few weeks. He had inherited millions of dollars from his parents. He believed his wife was a sociopath. He finally had the courage to leave her. He sent warning emails to friends seeking help, but the story was almost too unbelievable. The friends who tried to help were sued. As part of the "Order for Protection – Vulnerable Adult," the attorney for the guardian firm wrote into its margin that the **respondent was also restrained from going to " law enforcement and government agencies"** with information about the case.*

SEATTLE CASE SUMMARY OF GUARDIANSHIP FRAUD
By: Anthony Domanico   2017 NJ

• • •

This case summary is chiefly written by attorneys Leslie Garrison and David Zuckerman of Seattle, Washington regarding Case No. 11-2-13154-3SEA and taken from their brief to the King County Court of Appeals. The case illustrates the description given by Dr. Woodhull in her article: "How a Fraudulent Guardianship/Conservatorship Commences and Continues."

Edward O Mott was a sixty-three-year-old man when he filed for divorce 1/11 and received a clean health report from his neurologist 2/11. He purchased a plane ticket 3/11 to leave Washington prior to the divorce from his wife, Carolyn Knick. When she found out Mott was going to Arizona to rent a home pending the divorce, it is believed Ms. Knick chemically restrained Mott to prevent him from leaving the state and to gain custody over his entire estate.

With the help of a non-conclusive (junk) psych report written at the wife's instructions 5/11, a corrupt guardianship firm, corrupt attorneys, and a corrupt court commissioner, **Ed Mott became a Non Person in a matter of a few weeks** 6/11. Mott had inherited millions of dollars from his parents. Mott believed his wife was a sociopath, and he finally had the courage to leave.

When Ed Mott suspected something was wrong, Mott sent warning emails 4/11 to friends seeking help, but the story was almost too unbelievable. The friends who tried to help were sued. As part of the "Order for Protection – Vulnerable Adult," the attorney for the guardian wrote into its margin that the respondent was restrained from going to " **law enforcement and government agencies" with information about the case** since she had worked as a District Court Clerk, Investigator for Defense Attorneys, the U.S. Attorney's Office, and had damning information against all parties regarding possible drugging, kidnapping, robbing, and torturing of Ed Mott.

The following is a synopsis as a way of illustrating to the reader: *How A Fraudulent Guardianship/ Conservatorship Commences and Continues* by Angela V.Woodhull, Ph.D..

This is one case example out of millions committed by coldblooded guardianship firms, judges and attorneys that use the process to commit guardianship fraud as outlined by Dr. Woodhull.

When I found Woodhull's article, I realized it was a match for the same proceedings used against the victim's friends, Jerry and Janet Pipes, who were trying to save Ed Mott.

Step One: Eminent Danger—The Initial Court Petition. In this case the initial court petition was against the friend who had the most documentation. She knew that the victim was afraid of his wife and experienced panic attacks caused by childhood abuse, had filed for divorce, had purchased a plane ticket to move out-of-state pending the divorce, and had a recent clean-bill-of-health from his neurologist, had inherited millions of dollars from his parents, and she also knew that he told his regular physician that he thought his wife was a sociopath.

Step Two: The Examining Committee. In this case the victim was taken for a "psych exam" that was inconclusive with the wife present who made contradictory statements and had no input from the victim's physician. Because of the number of witnesses and the fact that the victim's wife and her friend Holmstrom had made an attempt to take his assets prior to his becoming a ward of the state and prior to the "psych exam," the victim was administered psychotropic drugs by the wife to enhance the claims that he was incompetent. The victim Ed Mott was noted as being "almost immobile" at his vulnerable adult hearing by the respondent's attorney.

Step Three: The "Feast" Begins. This victim's home was worth between $700,000 to $900,000. His father had owned a manufacturing facility that was sold and the proceeds from that sale invested in CDs in approximately six banks. The victim's wife had asked him to marry her in 2002. He was a lonely man and this was his third wife and her first husband. The week after they married the wife, Carolyn Knick, told Ed Mott that "God didn't think they should have sex" according to court records.

The friends who were sued probably lost a quarter of a million dollars in fighting the false claims and continued lawsuits in attorney fees and bogus fees imposed by the Commissioner. Having someone to sue allows the attorneys to drain the victim's funds that much more quickly according to Dr. Woodhull.

Step Four: The Mysterious Deaths. Ed Mott was kept isolated and medicated while his assets were taken over by the court appointed guardian and wife he was trying to divorce. As Dr. Woodhull states, "Once the funds have been spent, the 'ward' oftentimes suddenly dies."

This was quick and relatively easy for the unscrupulous professionals involved in this guardianship fraud scam, and they made millions with little effort and with little public awareness. The public appears to shy away from believing that there are lawyers who lie, cheat, steal and murder, which keeps this crime under the wire. Other lawyers, such as the ones for the respondent in this case appear to think they are being ethical by protecting their fellow attorneys and refusing to go to the prosecutor as their client requested. Psychologists would probably call these lawyers enablers, and the rest of us call them accomplices.

> *Once judged incompetent and placed under a conservatorship [or guardianship], a citizen becomes a nonperson, with fewer rights than a convicted felon in a penitentiary.* — **Robert Casey, editor, Bloomberg Wealth Manager**

Appellate Brief Summary:

From the onset of this case petitioner attorneys knowingly and willfully brought misleading and false charges to promote their cause, when as examples:

1. Ms. Barbara West, attorney for Godfrey Holmstrom, brought the original petition against the Pipes that falsely stated Mr. Mott had been diagnosed with dementia for several years knowing the diagnoses was done the day prior to the hearing.
2. Ms. Janet Somers, attorney for GSS, threatened the Pipes to sign the CR2A in September 2011 knowing that she was denying the Pipes of their Constitutional rights to go to law enforcement or

government agencies. The CR2A is all the more a concern since the it came on the heels of Ms. Walker's report to Janet Somers and subsequently to Commissioner Velategui regarding the suspicious psyche exam used to declare Mr. Mott a vulnerable adult that contained no sustaining documentation of dementia from his physician.

3. Ms. Somers made false statements about Mr. Mott and Ms. Pipes to the Guardianship Court to obtain confidential documents that pertained to the request to Adult Protective Services to have Mr. Mott's circumstances investigated.

4. Ms. Somers falsely claimed to the Court that Ms. Pipes was a "stalker" and was behind the emails and mailings sent out by others.

5. Ms. Somers filed a case of Contempt of Court against the Pipes with Commissioner Velategui rather than with the King County Prosecutor. Commissioner Velategui consistently ignored the declarations of those who stated that they believe Mr. Mott was competent shortly prior to his vulnerable adult hearing or have stated that Mr. Mott warned them that he was fearful of his wife Carolyn Knick; Commissioner Velategui ignored the fact that *both GSS and Ms. Knick breached the CR2A by Ms. Knick going to the Bellevue Police to harass witnesses and by GSS making false statements to the Guardianship Court and not abiding by the guidelines of the CR2A by giving six month reports on Mr. Mott*; and Commissioner Velategui made several errors in the current judgments as noted in the Pipes' brief to the Court of Appeals when:

    a. <u>Finding the Pipes in contempt of court without identifying which act(s) the Pipes committed to warrant the finding and instead making a contempt finding based on inference and the conduct of third parties;</u>

    b. Awarding $28,800 in attorneys' fees against the Pipes that are unreasonable and excessive;

    c. <u>Sanctioning the Pipes $20,000 when such sanction is punitive and imposed in violation of RCW 7.21.030(2);</u>

    d. Awarding $30,000.00 in damages without a showing of actual damages incurred since the court issued its order in June 2012 and with no showing that any injury was proximately caused by the Pipes' conduct;

    e. Relying on the court's inherent contempt authority to impose punitive sanctions without making specific findings that the remedial remedies available under the statute are inadequate to insure compliance.

    f. <u>Imposing restrictions of the Pipes that amount to an unconstitutional prior restraint on speech in violation of the first amendment.</u>

6. Ms. Karolyn Hicks, attorney for Carolyn Knick, falsely claimed to the Court that Ms. Pipes was responsible for defamation comments about Ms. Knick when these comments were clearly made by Mr. Mott to others who wrote declarative statements of this fact that are part of Court record.

In addition, it was reported that the Governor's Office, FBI, King County Sheriff all had requests that this matter needed investigation that were filtered to the **Bellevue Police Department** (BPD) when:

1. Major witnesses report that they have not been contacted for an interview of the facts of this matter concerning their declarations to the court which were sent to BPD.

2. Detective Thompson of BPD called Bill Kennamer and told him the false statement that Janet Pipes was the sole recipient of the Will Mr. Mott requested her to draft to protect his children. According to Mr. Kennamer, Detective Thompson had no interest regarding the statements Mr. Mott made to Mr. Kennamer in Mr. Mott's request for help from this friend of many years.

3. Detective Thompson called Ms. Pipes to harass her without any knowledge of this case and without any desire to know more about what occurred even though Ms. Pipes wrote to the Bellevue Police

from the onset seeking help for Mr. Mott and included the names of witnesses to contact.

4. Detective Thompson stated to Ms. Pipes that he was involved in reports from Ms. Knick regarding her belief she was being harassed, which was in direct conflict to the CR2A for Ms. Knick to go to law enforcement.

5. Chief Pillo of BPD responded to Cindy Walker's request for an investigation by stating her department was not going to investigate this matter and referred her to Adult Protective Services.

Adult Protective Services (APS) case worker Marie Alexander responded to Cindy Walker's October 31, 2011 request for an investigation when:

1. On February 9, 2012 (3 months later) she saw Mr. Mott with Ms. Knick present and reported that all Mr. Mott could say was "Yes" or "No" and that in her opinion Mr. Mott had severe dementia. This was eight days after Mr. Mott was seen by Dr. Werner who reported that Mr. Mott got up to greet him, they talked, and Mr. Mott correctly identified the Governor of Washington and that Mr. Mott needed stimulation.

2. Ms. Alexander called Ms. Pipes and told her that she thought all of the emails sent to her by Mr. Mott were bogus and that all of the emails and letters in the file were bogus. When Ms. Alexander was asked if she had called any of the witnesses, Ms. Alexander responded that it was none of her business. When asked if she would verify that all of the emails were truthful by calling her attorney, Ms. Alexander said that the case she was investigating was harassment against Ms. Knick.

3. Ms. Alexander called Mr. Kennamer and told him that he must be lying about what Mr. Mott said to him because Mr. Mott was "not allowed to talk to anyone," which clearly violates the Standards of Practice as set out by the National Guardianship Association and should have been investigated rigorously by APS.

4. None of the witnesses who have written declarations in behalf of Ms. Pipes/Mr. Mott have been called for interviews by APS.

There has been a callous pursuit against the Pipes in court by petitioners in opposition to RCW 74.34.200 (2) which states that: "it is in the intent of the legislature, however, that where there is a dispute about the care or treatment of a vulnerable adult, the parties should use the least formal means available to try to resolve the dispute," thus costing the Pipes massive attorney fees.

As a case history the original petitioners filed a motion for a VAPA order based on a May 2011 medical report that appears to have been done for the purpose of filing the original VAPA motion and for a Guardianship Petition of Mr. Mott. The baseline psych evaluation was done May 5, 2011. The factual wording of the psych exam states that Mr. Mott could have metabolic or psychological dementia caused by stress, depression or PTSD. It states that Mr. Mott does not have Alzheimer's. There are contradictory statements by Ms. Knick regarding Mr. Mott in the report. There was no input by Mr. Mott's long term physician Dr. Kinnish which additionally raised questions about this report. **These matters were ignored by Commissioner Velategui.**

There were misstatements of fact in the original petition which included the assertion that Mr. Mott suffered from dementia for a number of years; that Ms. Pipes took advantage of him by drafting up new wills in which she was the *sole* beneficiary; and Ms. Pipes opened a joint bank account implying that she did so to take Mr. Mott's money – omitting the amount of Ms. Pipes own money she deposited and requiring Ms. Pipes attorney to facilitate the return of her deposit.

The original petitioners had Mr. Mott sign new legal documents transferring all his personal and financial interests over to Ms. Knick and Mr. Holmstrom when he was purportedly suffering from dementia and allegedly lacked the capacity to have signed the previous wills dated sometime earlier. **This fact was ignored by Commissioner Velategui.**

Thus, the credibility of Ms. Knick and Mr. Holmstrom are without merit. Ms. West should have known this. Unfortunately there have been additional misrepresentations in this case, including:

In the *Petition for Order Directing Adult Protective Services to Release Investigation File and Identify Complainant* presented by attorney Janet Somers states these two **false statements**:

> *Despite Mr. Mott having been diagnosed with dementia several years prior, Ms. Pipes has engaged in an extramarital affair with Mr. Mott. During the course of that affair, inter alia, she drafted a Will for Mr. Mott's signature appointing her both Personal Representative and sole beneficiary. See O'Brien Decl., Paragraph 4.*

Declaration of Tom O'Brien In Support of Guardian's Petition for Order Directing Adult Protective Services to Release Investigation File and Identify Complainant again states the same **false statements**:

> 5. *Mrs. Pipes is known to have carried on an extramarital affair with Mr. Mott, in spite of his diagnosis with dementia. During the course of her relationship with Mr. Mott, among other things, Mrs. Pipes drafted a Will for Mr. Mott to execute in which she named herself both Personal Representative and sole beneficiary of Mr. Mott's Estate.*

The court records show that **William Kennamer previously sent an email to a number of people regarding Mr. Mott's welfare and the fact that none of his friend's had access to him**. Mr. Kennamer was contacted by Det. Thompson on behalf of Ms. Knick and given false statements about Ms. Pipes. Ms. Alexander of APS told Mr. Kennamer that she did not believe his story that Mr. Mott asked for help and wanted out of his house since Mr. Mott was not allowed to talk to anyone. **Not allowing Mr. Mott to talk and visit with friends violates the Standards of Practice as set down by the Certified Professional**

Guardian Standards of Practice. Commissioner Velategui ignored the Standards of Practice.

Additionally, there are records in this case that Mr. Mott sent many people information about his dissatisfaction with his marriage and his desire to get divorced. This information has been filed by GSS in the court file and made available to the public and also sent to the Arizona Board of Nursing in their efforts to punish Ms. Walker. This information has been made available to Detective Thompson via the Bellevue Police Department by Janet Pipes and Cindy Walker.

As Examples:

a. **Mr. Mott stated in his letter to Dr. Kinnish that he thought his wife was a sociopath** and that he thought she had slept with a large number of Bellevue Police. This letter was additionally sent to the Holmstroms in 2010 who acknowledged the letter. A signed copy along with a copy of *the Will naming both Mr. Holmstrom and Ms. Pipes as representatives and Mr. Mott's children beneficiaries of their grandparent's CDs* and a copy of Ms. Pipes' Durable Power of Attorney was sent in a sealed envelope to Mr. Holmstrom. Mr. Holmstrom used Ms. Pipes' Durable Power of Attorney to take her money without her knowledge.

b. **Mr. Mott filed for divorce from Ms. Knick in January 2011 on his own accord.** Presumably, had his attorney Mr. Matthew Cooper thought Mr. Mott had dementia and unable to make decisions on his own it would have interfered with his ability to file Mr. Mott's petition for dissolution as he did.

c. Ms. Benish, a close friend of Mr. Mott since childhood, states in her declaration that she asked Mr. Mott why he didn't just divorce his wife. According to Ms. Benish, **Mr. Mott replied, "I don't dare. I don't know what she'd do, but it wouldn't be pretty."**

d. Ms. Konitzer states in her declaration that when she spoke with Mr. Mott on the phone regarding her experiences with her husband, Mr. Mott replied with statements that lead her to believe he had experienced something similar, "I told Ed about my experiences and the sensation I had that things were unreal, that I couldn't defend myself, and that I felt emotionally unstable. Each time I made a point about my own experiences, Ed's comment and tone of voice indicated that his wife was treating him the way I had been treated by my ex-husband. For example, I described to Ed how my ex-husband would accuse me of being the crazy one, and how I started believing he was right. **Ed responded, 'I already know that.' When I described how sociopaths have a tendency to twist your words to use against you, Ed responded 'she does that.'"**

e. Mr. Mott was sent a letter by Ms. Pipes addressed to Mary Mott, his first wife. Mr. Mott told Ms. Pipes that he did not trust her and was afraid that she would send the letter to Godfrey Holmstrom. Mr. Mott sent this letter asking for help to several of his friends. Those friends included Joe Austin, Marian Benish, Sheila Evans and friends from the San Juan Islands who contacted Ms. Pipes. In this letter were numerous statements that Mr. Mott had made to Ms. Pipes regarding his wife Carolyn Knick. When Ms. Benish contacted Ms. Pipes following the first hearing, ***Ms. Benish told Ms. Pipes that Mr. Mott had told her all of the same things about his wife reflected in that letter.*** **One of the statements in this letter found in the Kane email was that Ms. Knick had sex with the guide when Mr. Mott took his wife on an African safari.**

f. In the document prepared by Mr. Holmstrom's attorney, Barbara West, entitled *Joinder and Declaration in re Petition for Immediate Temporary Order of Protection for a Vulnerable Adult*, Mr. Mott crossed out the words "and do not intend to divorce Carolyn."

g. The GAL found it was necessary to appoint a professional Guardian for Mr. Mott and neither Mr. Holmstrom nor Ms. Knick as originally petitioned.

Commissioner Velategui ignored these declarations and ruled in favor of Ms. Knick.

There have been multiple irregularities in this case which run the gamut from misinformation provided by Ms. West regarding Mr. Mott's own actions prior to his wife and neighbor taking over his life such as telling Ms. Pipes that Mr. Mott was seeing multiple women (at the same time alleging he had dementia), to information by Ms. Somers to Ms. Pipes' first attorney, Kristina Selset regarding Mr. Mott's wealth and Mr. Mott's health updates (Ms. Selset noted Mr. Mott was almost non-responsive at the first hearing, several months later it was reported to her that his physical health was again good but he had almost no cognitive skills, to several months later reporting that Mr. Mott easily got up to greet Dr. Werner, they talked and Mr. Mott correctly identified the Governor of Washington). **The records show that shortly before the VAPA petition was initially filed, Mr. Mott was capably living alone, driving without difficulty, and able to care for himself. This includes Mr. Mott's preparations to voluntarily move to Arizona; filing for divorce; and letting David Culbertson and others know that he was excited about moving to Arizona. A declaration informed the court that Joyce McBride visited Mr. Mott in his home in April 2011 when Mr. Mott was still living alone and driving. Ms. McBride reports she did not see any evidence of dementia.** The first psych exam was done May 5, 2011. The first hearing was May 6, 2011. Commissioner Velategui was advised at the hearing that the psych exam noted in the petition stating it was done several years ago was instead done the day prior to the hearing.

Ms. Pipes has repeatedly been falsely characterized as a "stalker" in court hearings and court documents by Ms. Somers. Not only is that a legal misuse of the term, but it is untrue. Declarations filed in this case state that in January 2011 when Ms. Pipes went to Seattle to visit friends, including Mr. Mott, *Mr. Mott called Ms. Pipes* to tell her that his wife had taken his car keys and was taking him to a bogus doctor appointment (Mr. Mott's words). Mr. Mott gave Ms. Pipes the address of the doctor's office, the time of his appointment, and asked her to meet him there. Had Mr. Mott not contacted Ms. Pipes, she would have had no way of knowing about this appointment. It was due to Ms. Knick's reaction to this meeting where she told Ms. Pipes that her husband had Alzheimer's and dementia that Mr. Mott realized what his wife was planning and told her he wanted a divorce.

The file reflects that Ms. Benish was never contacted by the Bellevue Police, and that she sent information about her perception of GSS and Ms. Knick to her and Mr. Mott's mutual former classmates in an email in early Fall 2012. Additionally, the emails from Mr. Kennamer, Mr. Kane and other friends of Mr. Mott contained factual information available in the public court file. Ms. Pipes has been falsely accused of being the sole person behind this correspondence, when in fact this information is public and has been presented to the Court numerous times by GSS.

The fact that GSS was appointed Guardian instead of Ms. Knick and has since allowed Ms. Knick to act as gatekeeper to Mr. Mott is troubling, to say the least, and at most signals that GSS may have violated the Standards of Practice as set down by the Certified Professional Guardian Standards of Practice. It is additionally troubling that Detective Thompson has harassed and made false statements to those involved trying to help Mr. Mott.

GSS filed a complaint with the Arizona Board of Nursing requesting an investigation of the nurse Cindy Walker after threatening her to sign a document that her letters of warning to agencies were instigated by Janet Pipes. Upon Ms. Walker's refusal to commit perjury by signing the document, the complaint to the Arizona Nursing Board was filed by GSS.

Commissioner Velategui ignored this evidence.

The following legal arguments prepared for this case by Pipes' counsel for the court of appeals also pose questions **regarding First Amendment rights denied the Pipes**.

FIRST AMENDMENT:

The protection order entered in this case violates two provisions of the First Amendment: the right to free speech and the right to petition the government for redress of grievances. One provision of the order states that Ms. Pipes cannot have any contact with the vulnerable adult by any means "including without limitation filing of legal or administrative actions regarding the vulnerable adult." Added in the margin and adopted by the court "and law enforcement and government agencies." Another paragraph includes this provision: "In the event additional reports alleging abuse, neglect or exploitation of the Vulnerable Adult are filed by Respondent(s) or their agents without reasonable cause with any governmental, legal or administrative agency in the future, Respondent shall be liable for any costs, including reasonable attorneys' fees, etc."

The protection order is a prior restraint on speech. A prior restraint is an administrative or judicial order forbidding in advance certain communications. Alexander v. United States, 509 U.S. 544, 550, 113 S.Ct. 2766, 125 L.Ed.2d 441 (1993). "Temporary restraining orders and permanent injunctions—i.e., court orders that actually forbid speech activities—are classic examples of prior restraints." Id. Prior restraints carry a heavy presumption of unconstitutionality. Bantam Books, Inc. v. Sullivan, 372 U.S. 58, 70, 83 S.Ct. 631, 9 L.Ed.2d 584 (1963). They are permissible only in exceptional cases such as war, obscenity, and "incitements to acts of violence and the overthrow by force of orderly government. Near v. Minnesota ex rel. Olson, 283 U.S. 697, 716, 51 S.Ct. 625, 75 L.Ed. 1357 (1931). "An order issued in the area of First Amendment rights must be couched in the narrowest terms that will accomplish the pin-pointed objective permitted by constitutional mandate and the essential needs of the public order." Carroll v. President & Commissioners of Princess Anne, 393 U.S. 175, 183, 89 S.Ct. 347, 21 L.Ed.2 325 (1968).

While an order prohibiting the Pipes from contacting Ed Mott directly might be upheld, the superior court's order defines "contact" far more broadly. It includes "filing of legal or administrative actions regarding [Mott]"including those addressed to "law enforcement and government agencies." Clearly this is not merely a restriction on "contact." An agency could handle a complaint concerning Mr. Mott's treatment without passing on the content of the complaint to Mott himself. The Court's order severely chills Pipe's right to free speech and to redress of grievances by threatening – and as it turns out, imposing – substantial financial sanctions. This is a classic prior restraint of First Amendment rights.

WAS EDWARD MOTT MURDERED?

The Pipes withdrew from their case with the Court of Appeals due to their inability to finance this cumbersome and expensive process. By this time they had lost their life savings trying to save their friend's life. They had to pay attorney fees to the other attorneys as well as their own, and they were saddled with an $80,000 threat that if any further information came out about this case prior to July 2017, they would be have to pay this amount additionally. In addition to writing APS, the nurse who reviewed the junk psych report on Ed Mott also wrote to Bellevue Chief of Police Linda Pillo asking for an investigation of this matter. Following Pillo's written response stating that her department would not investigate this matter, Guardian Services of Seattle (GSS) attorney Janet Somers falsely told Pipes attorney Leslie Garrison that the Bellevue Police Department had already done an investigation and found nothing wrong, not realizing that a letter had been sent out to the contrary. It is interesting to note that a new out-of-state Chief of Police was installed in Bellevue shortly thereafter, and Linda Pillo is now Senior Vice President with The Mercer Group, Inc.

Ed Mott was well-known by law enforcement throughout the State of Washington. Mott had been featured on 20-20, he was an instructor at Bellevue Community College in the Criminal Justice Program, Mott wrote professional manuals such as: "Detectives Homicide Crime Scene Investigations Checklist" that was adopted by the FBI, and "Homicide Manual: Death Investigation" that was also adopted by the FBI, and a Washington State Training Manual for Fire Personnel responding to crime scenes that was adopted by all Washington State Fire Departments. Mott served on major crime task forces such as the Green River Killer. Mott appeared on *"Cross Fire"* televised in Canada regarding two Canadian citizens in the Rafay multiple murder investigation. Mott was featured on the Discovery Channel *"New Detective"* regarding the George Russell serial murder investigation.

The Pipes received numerous emails from people who knew Ed Mott and believed that this case had too many red flags. The Pipes requested that nothing be done since it would only result in their being sued again. As more information was sent to the Pipes, the Pipes realized that this case matched the mantra of "Medicate, Isolate, and Take the Estate" set out by *Americans Against Abusive Probate Guardianship* www.AAAPG.net.

In late October, 2015, the Pipes received an unusual phone call from a lady who sounded as though English was a second language. She told the Pipes that she wanted to find Ed Mott because friends who worked for Synergy Home Health Care told her that Ed Mott had basically been kept a prisoner in his own home by GSS and his wife Carolyn Knick prior to being put into a nursing home. She said she was going to visit nursing homes until she found him. The end of November, she called a second time to report that she had gone every Thursday on her day off to over 25 nursing homes in and around Bellevue and surrounding areas, but she was unable to find Ed Mott. The Pipes asked her to please stop looking.

Early 2016, the Pipes were informed that Ed Mott died December 3, 2015 at the Bridle Manor Adult Family Home in Kirkland, Washington, a fews days after the November search. He was 68 years old. The Pipes believe Ed was probably murdered to keep anyone from finding him.

King County Deputy Sheriff Bill Kennamer, son of William Kennamer who tried to save Ed's life in early 2012 and sent out an explosive email that Ed Mott told Bill Kennamer he wanted help, gave the Pipes the court documents regarding Mott that Deputy Kennamer found in his parents' home following their deaths in January and February 2016. Deputy Sheriff Bill Kennamer placed Mott's obituary in the **Seattle Times**. Deputy Kennamer had Mott as a law enforcement instructor at Bellevue Community College. The obituary appeared March 27, 2016, which would have been Mott's 69th birthday had he lived.

The Pipes were informed in April 2017 by a Washington State Advocate against the crime of professional guardianship fraud that the case of Ed Mott was sealed. The reason given was that Janet Pipes was too "dangerous." Janet Pipes worked as a District Court Clerk, CASA Volunteer, Investigator for Criminal Defense Attorneys in Seattle, and at the U.S. Attorney's Office in Tucson, Arizona. Perhaps she was called 'dangerous' because she has **documents attesting to judicial, legal, guardian, APS, and law enforcement misconduct and perjury that are the standard fare in this massive underreported crime of professional guardianship fraud.** This case sorely needs an **Honest Investigation**.

The next two articles will educate you on how easily judges, lawyers, andj Guardians can take everything you or your loved one owns.

ESTATE LOOTING 101: HOW THE GOODS ARE GOTTEN WHEN THE WILL GETS IN THE WAY
By: Lou Ann Anderson   5:08 p.m. MST

The looting of estate assets, also known as Involuntary Redistribution of Assets (IRA), can occur through the use of various probate instruments—wills, trusts, guardianships, powers of attorney—and with the actual acts configured in different ways. Guardianships or powers of attorney can provide for estate looting while a person is alive, but asset diversion can be perpetrated posthumously via wills or trusts. Whether these acts are instigated by greedy lawyers, disgruntled family members or wannabe heirs (or often a combination), the sad reality is that death doesn't necessarily bring the closure one might expect. Death, even with the most meticulous of estate plans, in no way ensures the honoring of a decedent's wishes or heirs' avoidance of IRA.

In December 2006, Austin American-Statesman reporter Tony Plohetski wrote a special report entitled Breach of Trust. In this article, Plohetski detailed how "Texas estate laws make stealing from the dead a relatively easy crime." These are nothing more than cases of postmortem IRA. He described not only the estate theft activities of Austin attorney Terry Erwin Stork, but Plohetski also pointed out how Texas probate laws do little to ensure that people's belongings reach those designated in the decedent's will. The article also depicted a loose approach to oversight on the part of some probate judges.

The Statesman report prompted law makers to introduce several reform-oriented bills during the 80th Texas Legislative session. Effective September 1, 2007, S.B. 593, as per the Texas Senate Research Center, requires the personal representative of a decedent's estate, within a certain time period of an order admitting a will to probate, to give notice to each beneficiary named in the will whose identity is known or, through reasonable diligence, can be ascertained, and to file an affidavit with the court listing the beneficiaries notified. The bill also sets out what the notice must contain which is a good thing as estate administrators previously having been on the "honor system" didn't seem to workout so well. This legislation can seem (and might be) a helpful "first step," but as IRA practitioners routinely ignore laws and bypass normal business/legal courtesies, more than an assumption of compliance is needed.

Stork ultimately plead guilty to three counts of felony theft and in September 2008, was sentenced to fifteen years in jail. Attempts to reconcile what's due to each estate continue, but heirs will likely recover few of the assets left to them.

It is important to note the inaccuracy of believing these type situations only occur with high dollar estates. The three estates from which Stork stole had a combined value of less than $1 million. Another misconception to dispel is the absolute protection provided by "proper estate planning." The estates outlined in the Austin American-Statesman article belonged to people who took the proper steps to ensure the orderly distribution of their assets. They, however, fell victim to IRA due to a betrayal by the attorney they trusted for assistance.

The legal industry won't tell you this, but an estate executor can basically do anything they want with an estate. Realistically, judicial oversight is minimal—most judges believe what attorneys tell them and perform little or no independent follow-up. Heirs believing something is amiss must mount their own challenge. The Stork case was unique in that it was prosecuted as a criminal case, but most heirs pursuing "justice" in an estate dispute are relegated to the civil court system which is a pay-to-play venue open only to those willing and capable of expending significant sums of money for an eye-opening, but rarely confidence-inspiring experience. Steal $250,000 from a bank, people get excited. Steal the same from an estate, it's hard to get law enforcement or any other officials to care. These points are never lost on today's grave robbers or other property poachers while an unsuspecting heir has no idea the web of deceit and gamesmanship into which they are entering with a civil estate dispute case.

Dishonest estate administrators sometimes use under-handed tactics to draw legitimate heirs or beneficiaries into litigation of which their participation is self-funded while the administrator/executor can use the dispute as justification for additional billing against the estate of his/her time along with legal or other applicable professional services.

The threat of legal action can also be used to pressure heirs into forfeiting or sharing rightful bequests rather than risk being the target of a contrived dispute. It's been called an inheritance litigation tax, but extortion when defined as "illegal use of one's official position or powers to obtain property, funds, or patronage" also sounds familiar. Either spend time and money fighting or get out—it's that simple, it's that ugly.

As people's entitlement mentality grows, probate has become an excellent venue for weaponization of the legal system by grave robbers, property poachers, asset looters and walker stalkers looking to divert assets in a manner contrary to the stated intentions of honest, hard-working Americans. Losing the ability to determine the final distribution of one's assets is a tragedy for Americans individually, as families and for us as a country in that the intergenerational transfer of assets has historically helped to strengthen our social and economic fabric.

Reform in this area will be difficult as the legal industry is powerful. However, the stories of estate abuse and probate corruption seem to increase almost weekly and as they do, a generally unsuspecting public is starting to awaken to the growing threat to their property rights and to their heirs' rights of inheritance.

Forewarned is forearmed.

HERE'S HOW THE GREAT $41 TRILLION GENERATIONAL WEALTH TRANSFER IS INTERCEPTED BY PROBATE PIRATES

By: Juliette Fairley Apr 23, 2015 10:13 a.m. EDT NEW YORK (*MainStreet*) —

It used to be that Theresa Lyons bartered with the elderly relatives in her family.

"My aging mother and her sister were helping me pay the rent, gas and electricity bills and I would take them out to eat and drive them around to where they needed to go," said the single mother of three children.

That was until 2011 when Blanca Tozzo, Lyons's aunt, passed away and her mother, Carmen Hernandez Tozzo, was placed in a retirement home in Florida once the Department of Children and Families (DCF) stepped in.

"I have no access to my mom's finances," Lyons told *MainStreet*. "The only way I can get any money is through a subpoena and blessings from the probate judge."

Once Tozzo became a ward of the state under a professional guardian, Lyons said most of her mother's $100,000 in retirement savings was drained.

"The guardian isolated and drugged my mom, placed her in a lock down area with mentally ill and psychotic patients where she suffered dozens of falls, cuts, bruises and was almost killed by one of the male residents," said Lyons, who is in her 50s. "When I complained, my visitation was taken away."

Lyons's mother is among the senior citizens losing some $36.48 billion each year to elder financial abuse, according to a True Link study called Friendly Grandparent Syndrome.

"These numbers indicate how the guardianship industry destroys the legitimate inter-generational transfer of wealth and in the process irreparably damages entire generations of innocent families," said Dr. Sam Sugar, founder of the Americans Against Abusive Probate Guardianship (AAAPG) in Miami.

That's 12 times more than the previously reported $2.9 billion, because elders are ashamed and humiliated and in some cases drugged while residing in a retirement home.

"They often refuse to report this crime," said Jack Halpern, CEO of My Elder Advocate, a franchise that works with families to solve elder care-related crises. "Elder financial abuse is probably the most unreported crime in the country."

Some $16.9 billion of these losses a year comes from deceptive but technically legal tactics designed specifically to take advantage of older Americans, according to the 2015 True Link Report on Financial Elder

Abuse. "This crime is shielded from public view because the criminal is most often a lawyer in probate court," said Kristi Hood, author of the book *Probate Pirates* (JKH Publishing, 2015). "The probate pirate attorney either directly or indirectly finds a way to pick the pockets of the elderly ward of the state, taking money that should be used to care for the person or charging their adult children exorbitant legal fees for help."

Uncannily similar to organized crime defined in the Racketeer Influenced and Corrupt Organizations Act of 1970 (RICO), probate piracy can involve the involuntary redistribution of assets, which is also known as property poaching, with the elderly person becoming the enterprise that is defrauded.

"Unscrupulous charities, probate courts, home repair scammers, retirement homes, neighbors and even distant family members know that a friendly senior with cognitive issues is a potential gold mine," said Kai Stinchcombe, CEO and founder of True Link.

Baby Boomers and Gen X-ers are reportedly expected to be the recipients of some $41 million from their World War 2 generation parents as they pass away.

"The transfer of wealth is going to last for the next 30 to 40 years," said Dan McElwee, certified financial planner and executive vice president with Ventura Wealth Management.

But an elderly adult who is extremely friendly is four times more likely to fall victim to high amounts of senior financial fraud.

"Those of us working in the field have long known that the United States is in the throes of an elder financial abuse epidemic," said Shawna Reeves, director of elder abuse prevention at the Institute of Aging.

Adult millennial and Gen X children who find their elderly Boomer and World War II-generation parents have been targeted with legal tactics designed to rob them can report the fraud to their local district attorney's office, consumer protection agency, the state attorney general and even the local FBI office.

"We are all affected by these scams," Halpern told *MainStreet*. "When an elder loses their assets to scam and they need care, they will have to look to welfare and Medicaid."

In this fifth article, Lt. James Weiskoph testified before the Nevada State, Clark County Commissioners, stating that, "There are no criminal penalties for the for-hire guardians who exploit their elderly or disabled wards." This is why legislation is desperately needed, but why it is not happening. This article illustrates an example of how corruption takes place between judges, lawyers and guardians. Parts of Lt. Weiskoph's testimony to the Clark County Commissioners was shown on KTNV, channel 13, NBC News on 12/26/15

POLICE LT. EXPLAINS HOW FAMILY COURT STEALS FROM WARDS

By: Steve Miller, Las Vegas

Lack of legislation and the considerable profit in this crime is described by Lt. James Weiskoph as the Perfect Crime.

LVMPD Abuse and Neglect Lt. James Weiskoph testified before the Clark County Commission.

The Lieutenant on Tuesday, April 21, told the Board of Commissioners that there are NO criminal penalties for the for-hire guardians who exploit their elderly or disabled wards.

The NRS Chapter 159 Guardianship statutes he cited detail only what and how guardians are to operate. What these statutes purposefully do not include, as most NRS statutes do, is any description of penalties, fines, or reference to how the guardians can be prosecuted or made accountable criminally for not following the statutes.

That's the catch. NRS 159 does say the "court" can have the guardian "cited," but that's it!

As the Lieutenant said to the commissioners, it's all in the "court's jurisdiction," and he is correct. However, the Family Court is obviously controlled by several crooked guardians, and people like Judges Charles Hostin, William Voy, Art Ritchie, and Commissioner Jon Norhiem have proven to ALWAYS side with the guardians and their attorneys, and won't punish them under ANY circumstances.

Also, to discourage family members from taking their court appointed guardian to court, NRS 159 allows the judges or Norheim to force the family to pay the guardian's exorbitant attorney fees if the judge or commissioner rules that the family's complaint had no merit.

How was NRS 159 enacted without penalties?

Jared Shafer owns hundreds of A-frame political advertising signs placed on vacant lots during elections. As an ex-politician, I can personally attest that you Nevada state assemblyman and senators need these signs to stay in office, and for this reason many have voted to weaken laws that could have put people like Jared Shafer behind bars many times over.

It's as though Shafer and his cronies have found a way to commit the perfect crime.

Jared Shafer's Lawyer Elyse Tyrell Capitalizing Off Appointment To Nevada Supreme Court Guardianship Commission

Guardianship attorneys Patricia Trent and Elyse Tyrell, who often represent for-hire "guardian" Jared E. Shafer in Family Court disputes against his "wards" and their families, are the Registered Agents for Shafer's political sign company, Signs of Nevada, LLC.

Shafer's office manager/secretary/bookkeeper, Amy Viggiano Deittrick, is listed as his sign company's manager by the Secretary of State, and uses Shafer's guardianship business address on Pecos Road to rent or donate signs to candidates for Clark County Family Court, and District Court judgeships.

The effectiveness of the signs was so evident that soon after Shafer bought the sign company in 2003, the Clark County Family Court bench was filled with judges who used Shafer's signs to get elected, then as pay back made Shafer and his firm their choice when it came to awarding lucrative guardianships over the persons and assets of wealthy retirees, most deemed mentally incompetent by persons without credentials to make such a determination. Based on these court appointments, Shafer and his attorneys made obscene profits by gaining complete power of attorney over their court appointed ward's estates, and converting the assets for their own use (Tyrell charges wards $500 per hour).

Jared Shafer *illegally commingles funds* from his sign company with funds from his "wards" in his Professional Fiduciary Services of Nevada, Inc. (PFSN) bank account. Commingling of ward's funds is a violation of NRS 159.073 (III) (IV).

The portable A-frame political signs are allegedly the reason local judges and the District Attorney do not go after Shafer for allegedly bilking the elderly and disabled, and blatantly violating NRS 159.073 (III) (IV), and other Nevada laws.

BACKGROUND:

http://www.stevemiller4lasvegas.com/ShaferFinancialRecords2.html

CHAPTER 3

The Racketeering Enterprise of Professional Guardianship Fraud

• • •

These 14 articles are a small selection of cases that describe various ways these criminals commit their racketeering and corruption enterprises to steal your money.

DIRTY SECRETS OF PERSONS WHO PUT ON BLACK ROBES AND PRETEND TO BE "PROBATE JUDGES" BUT INSTEAD ARE RUNNING A HUMAN TRAFFICKING, MONEY LAUNDERING FULLY FLEDGED RACKETEERING OPERATION UNDER COVER OF THE STATE COURTS

By: National Alliance For the Dissolution of Guardianship

The black robed persons and their accomplices who operate in an area of the Circuit courthouses called probate don't want you to know it houses a cartel who represent themselves as guardians, attorneys and judges but are not engaged in legal matters. The Courthouse is their headquarters for human trafficking and money laundering where immoral acts of physical, emotional and mental terror, abuse, financial fraud and vicious retaliation are committed against vulnerable defenseless elderly disabled persons and their families. The fraud scheme works in this manner:

1. A senior citizen/disabled person is railroaded into "guardianship" where their rights are completely stripped and turned over to an

unlicensed person with fabricated "credentials" who takes ownership of them.

2. **The usual scenario is for the guardian and their attorney to
    file fabricated statements against family members falsely al-
    leging "misdeeds" with a colluding judge (usually accusations
    of "agitation" that the abusive guardians cause themselves by
    administering contraindicated medications with dangerous
    side effects) in order to obtain a fraudulent court order iso-
    lating the victim (disabled person) from their family and their
    normal life.**

3. The fraudulent court ordered separation and isolation of their
    prey from their family is a KEY element of this crime against hu-
    manity. It paves the way for the vicious abuse and theft to occur
    in secrecy.

4. **They are drugged, beaten and brutalized to render them
    compliant, sometimes sexually assaulted**. A person who could
    be your parent is being tormented, sexually abused and financially
    exploited by a cartel who operates a human trafficking ring insidi-
    ously in the courthouse.

5. **The victims are denied their right to an attorney once they
    are forced into guardianship**. Thus, their family frantically file
    futile pleadings to seek remedies—removal of the guardian, resto-
    ration of rights, appointment of an attorney and doctor for their
    love one, all of which are ignored or denied. Unbeknownst to the
    family, their pleading are **ALL IN VAIN** as nothing is going to
    detract this racketeering ring from accomplishing their goal—
    draining the assets of their prey. In fact, the petitions only serve to
    facilitate this goal as the cartel bills their prey for their fraudulent
    "response" documents and their court "appearances" that are fixed
    and preordained in advance.

6. The court proceedings are a sham and a pretense where ex parte
    motions and orders, or tenuis proclamations, self-serving "confi-
    dential" reports are exchanged. **A "wired court" is working hand**

and hand with an arsenal of self-dealing attorneys, guardians, judges and judicial officers to disseminate the life savings, possessions, home, car and personal property of their prey.

7. Family members are viciously retaliated for speaking up once they catch on to the crime ring that brazenly operates in Courthouses all over the country. They have been wrongfully arrested, forced to flee the country, threated and endangered, become bankrupt, lose their homes and their livelihood defending their loved ones against slander, fabricated and staged litigation reigned on them forcing them to hire attorneys who take their money, while secretly working in collusion with the other side.

8. The entire proceeding is a fraud devised by a wired judge. There is a pretense that a real court proceeding is occurring under American Law and Rules **but the only thing really happening is the illegal, criminal distribution of the assets of an elderly person to a fully-fledged racketeering crime ring presided over by a wired sham judge wearing a black robe.**

The state "guardian" statutes are a misnomer. They have morphed into a set of vastly conflicting provisions that are utterly ignored. The premise, persons who may have limitations in caring for themselves would be assisted through court oversight, could not be further from the reality. The guardian industry has discovered the obvious: **A statute that allows the removal of constitutional and civil rights of vulnerable citizens, the transfer of their assets pre-death to a stranger with no license or substantiated credentials and bans them from having their own attorney is <u>unconstitutional</u>.** No other industry is solely regulated by the court—it is not a regulatory agency. No amount of legislation can "fix" an unconstitutional law that allows removal of all natural rights and fails to provide state regulation.

Thus, guardianship has seized on an overbroad, vague, conflicting, unconstitutional statute as a vehicle to establish a covert operation—a racketeering enterprise. A covert operation is defined as one

that is so planned and executed as to conceal the identity of or permit plausible denial by the sponsor. It differs from a clandestine operation as emphasis is placed on concealment of identity of sponsor rather than on concealment of the operation. In this divisive scheme, guardianship is the buzz work for court ordered pillaging of assets of elderly and disabled, theft of their identity and their removal from their former life and family by a judge, the undisclosed sponsor, using the 11th Circuit Court as a shield.

This cartel of judges, attorneys and guardians are engaged in acts of crimes defined by the FBI who has failed to enforce its law enforcement mandate.

We call for their arrest and indictment. We call for impeachment of these judges such as Michael Genden of Dade County Florida, the voiding of his self-serving orders that empower him to enrich his cohorts that are viciously abusing, retaliating and discriminating against the elderly.

Florida has been reported the most corrupt State by Huffington Post. The proclaimed "probate judges" are engaged in heinous crimes that shame the judiciary and are protected by other judges and law enforcement who close ranks in an immoral cloak of secrecy and breach of fiduciary duty.

JUSTICE ARTHUR G. SCOTLAND FEDERAL CRIMES ALLEGED BY SACRAMENTO COUNTY SUPERIOR COURT WHISTLEBLOWERS—COLLUSION WITH TRIAL COURT JUDGES AND SACRAMENTO BAR ASSOCIATION FAMILY LAW SECTION ATTORNEYS—PRO PER CIVIL RIGHTS VIOLATIONS

Published by: M.P. Roberts on Jan 20, 2015

23-Page Crimes Catalog: Justice Arthur Scotland charged with federal crimes by Sacramento Superior Court whistleblowers. Collusion with Sacramento Bar...

23-Page Crimes Catalog: Justice Arthur Scotland charged with federal crimes by Sacramento Superior Court whistleblowers. Collusion with

Sacramento Bar Association Family Law Section attorneys alleged by watchdog group. This archive collection includes hyperlinks to hundreds of additional documents, court records, court reporter transcripts and other documentary evidence in support of the allegations.

Alleged crimes include misprision of felony (18 USC 4), honest services fraud (18 USC 1346), and RICO racketeering (18 USC 1962). Sacramento Superior Court whistleblowers assert that Justice Arthur Scotland and the 3rd District are responsible for concealing systemic civil rights violations, honest services fraud, and RICO racketeering by Sacramento judges and SCBA judge pro tem attorneys against indigent, financially disadvantaged and disabled pro per litigants.

For over fifteen years, Scotland and other 3rd District justices who are former Sacramento Superior Court judges and have ties to Sacramento Superior Court personnel, trial court judges, and Sacramento Bar Association Family Law Section lawyers obstructed, impeded, and dismissed state court appeals implicating the RICO enterprise conspirators. The scale and scope of the corruption rivals that of the Kids for Cash scandal in Luzerne County, PA.

23-Page Crimes Catalog: Justice Arthur Scotland charged with federal crimes by Sacramento Superior Court whistleblowers. Collusion with Sacramento Bar Association Family Law Section attorneys alleged by watchdog group. This archive collection includes hyperlinks to hundreds of additional documents, court records, court reporter transcripts and other documentary evidence in support of the allegations.

This ongoing investigative project was updated in February, 2015.

Sacramento Family Court News is conducting an ongoing investigation of published and unpublished **3rd District Court of Appeal** decisions in trial court cases originating from family courts. This page is regularly updated with our latest news, analysis, and opinion. Our preliminary findings reveal an unsettling link between how an appeal is decided and the political ideology, work history, and family law bar ties of the court of appeal justices assigned to the appeal.

Our investigation indicates that the outcome of an appeal is in large part dependent on the luck of the justice draw. Appeals are assigned to three of ten justices. The background of each appears to play a significant role in how an appeal is decided.

3rd District Court of Appeal watchdogs assert that appeal outcomes are inconsistent, and in large part determined by the work history, and social or professional connections of the three judges assigned to decide an appeal.

For example, **3rd District** unpublished opinions show that **Court of Appeal** justices who were elevated to the appellate court from **Sacramento County Superior Court** will often effectively cover for judicial errors in appeals from the same court.

Third District Justices George Nicholson, Harry E. Hull, Jr., Ronald B. Robie, and Presiding Justice Vance W. Raye previously were trial court judges in **Sacramento County Superior Court**. Each have social and professional ties to family court judges and attorney members of the **Sacramento County Bar Association Family Law Section**. After his retirement in 2011, **3rd District Presiding Justice Arthur Scotland** described the professional and personal relationships he had with attorneys during his career on the bench.

"[I] enjoy friendships...I go to all the county bar events. I do that for two reasons. One, I think it's a responsibility of a judge to be active in the community, and the attorneys appreciate it. But I really like the people.

I really like going to these events. I enjoy friendships and that sort of thing."

To get a sense of the collusive atmosphere in **Sacramento Family Law Court**, we recommend reading our special *Color of Law* series of investigative reports, which document the preferential treatment provided by family court employees and judges to **SCBA Family Law Section** lawyers at the trial court level. Financially disadvantaged, unrepresented litigants who face opposing parties represented by **SCBA** attorneys assert that the collusive collegiality taints appeal proceedings in the appellate court.

Pro per advocates contend that under **Canon 3E(4)(a) and (c)** of the **Code of Judicial Ethics**, Raye, Robie, Hull and Nicholson should disqualify themselves from participating in any appeal originating from **Sacramento Family Law Court**. Advocates argue that the same conflict of interest principles apply to family court appeals that resulted in **the self-recusal**, or removal, of **Vance Raye** from participating in the 2002 **Commission on Judicial Performance** prosecution of family court **Judge Peter McBrien**. To view the 2002 Raye recusal and **CJP** decision against McBrien. The **CJP** has **disciplined judges** for violating the **Code of Judicial Ethics** rules requiring judges to disclose conflicts.

It is a basic principle of law that state appellate justices and federal judges with personal or professional relationships with trial court judges connected to an appeal or federal court action should disqualify themselves to avoid the appearance of partiality.

The conflict disclosure problem infects the Superior Court as well. To the benefit of local family law attorneys who also hold the office of temporary judge in the same court, **Sacramento Family Law Court judges** effectively have **institutionalized** noncompliance with state conflict of interest disclosure laws. For an example of a **Sacramento County** *civil* court trial judge who fully complied with conflict laws. Without oversight or accountability, family court judges routinely—and in violation of state law—ignore the same disclosure requirements.

HISTORY & ORIGINS OF THE CURRENT SACRAMENTO COUNTY FAMILY COURT SYSTEM

TANI CANTIL SAKAUYE WORKED WITH PETER J. MCBRIEN IN SACRAMENTO COUNTY SUPERIOR COURT FROM 1997 TO 2005. In 1991, as a superior court judge, current 3rd District Justice Vance Raye partnered with controversial family court Judge Peter J. McBrien and attorneys from the Sacramento County Bar Association Family Law Section in establishing the current, dysfunctional Sacramento Family Court system, according to the sworn testimony of McBrien at his 2009 judicial misconduct trial before the Commission on Judicial Performance.

Behind closed doors and under oath, the judge provided explicit details about the 1991 origins of the present-day family court structure. The *public* court system was built to the specifications of *private-sector* attorneys from the SCBA Family Law Section Family Law Executive Committee, according to McBrien's testimony. To view McBrien's detailed description of the collusive public-private collaboration, posted online exclusively by SFCN. To view the same, current day collusion.

The 1991 restructuring plan began with a road trip suggested by the family law bar:

"[T]he family law bar, and it was a fairly strong bar here in Sacramento, initiated the concept of a trip to Orange County and San Diego County to pick up some ideas about how their courts were structured. And myself and Judge Ridgeway and two family law attorneys made that trip and came back with various ideas of how to restructure the system," McBrien told the CJP.

But before his sworn 2009 CJP testimony, McBrien gave the public a different account of the road trip and who restructured the family court system in 1991. As reported by the *Daily Journal* legal newspaper McBrien dishonestly implied that the system was conceived and implemented by judges alone after they made a county-paid "statewide tour" of family law courts. The judge omitted from the story the fact that the trip was initiated by the family law bar, and included two private-sector family law attorneys who took the county-paid trip with McBrien and the late **Judge William Ridgeway**.

"[M]cBrien and a few other Sacramento judges went on a statewide tour of family law courts. At the time, there were continual postponements of trials. 'This is how we came up with the system today,' McBrien said. 'It was the best trip Sacramento County ever paid for.' The judges changed the local system so that family law judges presided over both law and motion matters and trials..." the *Daily Journal* reported.

Under oath, McBrien admitted that the private-sector, for-profit family law bar dictated the public court facility restructuring plan—conceived to serve the needs and objectives of **SCBA Family Law Section** member attorneys—which then essentially was rubber-stamped by the bench.

"[T]he Bar culled through the various ideas and options, came up with a plan, presented it to the family law bench. We made what adjustments we felt were appropriate and then presented the whole of it to the full bench," and the plan was approved.

In essence, McBrien disclosed that the current *public* court system was set up by and for local attorneys with little, if any, consideration of the needs of the 70 percent of court users unable to afford counsel. The system also has shown it is designed to repel carpetbagger, outsider attorneys, like **Stephen R. Gianelli** of **San Francisco**, and **Sharon Huddle** of **Roseville**.

"[T]his is a 'juice court' in which counsel outside Sacramento have little chance of prevailing...[the] court has now abandoned even a pretense of being fair to out-of-town counsel," **Gianelli** said.

According to the **Commission on Judicial Performance** - the state agency responsible for oversight and accountability of California judges— the structure is known as a *"two-track system of justice."*

"In this case, we again confront the vice inherent in a two-track system of justice, where favored treatment is afforded friends and other favored few, and which is easily recognized as corruption at the core of our system of impartial equal justice, and...intolerable," the **CJP** said in

a 2005 judicial **discipline decision** involving a Santa Clara County judge. **To view a list of similar CJP decisions.**

According to the gold standard reference on judicial ethics, the *California Judicial Conduct Handbook [pdf]*, published by the **California Judges Association**, providing preferential treatment to local, connected attorneys also is known as "*hometowning*," and is prohibited by the **Code of Judicial Ethics**.

KEEPING NEUTRAL JUDGES OUT-OF-THE-LOOP

One objective of the revamped system was to keep all family court proceedings in-house: within the isolated family relations courthouse. Prior to the change, trials were conducted at the downtown, main courthouse and before judges more likely to have a neutral perspective on a given case, and less likely to have ties to the family law bar.

"*The judges changed the local system so that family law judges presided over both law and motion matters and trials, which used to be sent to a master calendar department and competed with criminal trials for scheduling*," the *Daily Journal* reported.

Family court watchdogs and **whistleblowers** allege that under the system set up by Raye and McBrien, the local family law bar—through the **Family Law Executive Committee** or **FLEC**—now controls for the financial gain of members virtually all aspects of court operations, including local court rules. **A cartel** of local family law "*The judges changed the local system so that family law judges presided over both law and motion matters and trials, which used to be sent to a master calendar department and competed with criminal trials for scheduling*," the *Daily Journal* reported.

Family court watchdogs and **whistleblowers** allege that under the system set up by Raye and McBrien, the local family law bar—through the **Family Law Executive Committee** or **FLEC**—now controls for the financial gain of members virtually all aspects of court operations, including local court rules. **A cartel** of local family law attorneys receive preferential treatment from family court judges and appellate court justices because the lawyers are members of the **Sacramento Bar Association Family Law Section**, hold the **Office of Temporary Judge**, and run the family court settlement conference program, court reform advocates charge.

Court watchdogs have **catalogued and documented** examples of judge pro tem attorney favoritism, and flagrant **bias** against **unrepresented litigants** and **"outsider"** attorneys. Published and unpublished **3rd District** opinions indicate that **Court of Appeal** justices without direct ties to the same superior court are more likely to follow the law, and less likely to whitewash trial court mistakes.

CLARK COUNTY'S PRIVATE GUARDIANS MAY PROTECT — OR JUST STEAL AND ABUSE
By: Colton Lochhead LAS VEGAS REVIEW-JOURNAL

APTOS, Calif. — Guadalupe Olvera sits in his tall green chair, blowing a familiar tune on his harmonica as a baseball game plays on his television. The harmony echoes off the walls of his daughter's 1960s-era home, filling the air with an enticing melody.

Although slowed by age at 95, the World War II veteran regularly attends Veterans of Foreign Wars barbecues in Aptos, where he easily remembers the names and family details of those he meets. Life in the lush green hills near Santa Cruz is peaceful for Olvera and his family.

That wasn't the case a few years ago, when he was isolated and alone, a prisoner in his Henderson home — a ward of Clark County, surrounded by people he didn't know who were supposed to protect him, but who ended up with more than $420,000 of his money, most of his estate.

No longer a ward of any state, he's settled in the home of the daughter who had to "kidnap" him when all else failed.

A Fateful Choice

Olvera and his wife, Carmela, moved from California to Henderson to retire in 2002. They enjoyed warm weather and quickly became active members of their new Sun City Anthem community. Life was serene for the Olveras.

In 2007, Carmela took a step that would later prove costly. At a financial planner's behest, she became her husband's guardian.

The couple's daughter, Rebecca Schultz, said Carmela already handled the couples' finances, so Guadalupe never questioned the move.

But after Camela's sudden death in fall 2009, he needed a new guardian. Schultz wasn't an option because state law says a guardian must live in Nevada.

"I didn't understand it," Schultz said of the guardianship system. "I knew nothing about what that term meant, legally."

Schultz called the office of the guardianship commissioner, who at any one time supervises 8,500 such cases for Clark County Family Court.

"I thought these people were going to help me," Schultz said.

A court clerk told her she needed to see Jared Shafer, who for 24 years handled estate administration and guardianships as Clark County public administrator before starting Professional Fiduciary Services of Nevada, a guardianship company for hire, in 2003.

Shafer told Schultz he would act as a temporary guardian until conservatorship could be transferred to California, which should have taken about six months. She assumed the transfer would go quickly with such an experienced guardian involved.

In a few months she realized she was wrong.

Rather than making an easy move to California, Olvera was stuck in Nevada while his family was forced to watch him lose everything.

"My father had a 3,000-square-foot house with a huge master bedroom and two guest bedrooms and they (his court-appointed guardians) wouldn't let us stay there when we first visited," Schultz said. Later visits were limited to a maximum of four days.

"That's the first sign I saw that 'OK, something's wrong,'" she said.

A month after he was granted temporary guardianship, Shafer petitioned the court to make it permanent — a legal move that tethered Olvera and his money to Nevada.

Schultz and her father became increasingly suspicious of Shafer and the people he assigned to work with Olvera — people such as Shafer's case manager, Patience Bristol, and his bookkeeper, Amy Deittrick.

Deittrick runs AViD Business Services, a bookkeeping company with ties to Shafer.

In February 2010, just three months after Shafer became guardian, Olvera's Wells Fargo trust was billed $39,297.

More than $8,700 went to Bristol. AViD received $5,760 for charges ranging from $40 to $125 to pay a bill.

Shafer's then-attorney, Elyse Tyrell, was paid $5,919.

Shafer's bill alone was $15,000.

Only $3,080 went to KeepYou Company, a health care provider that took care of Olvera in his home. A representative of the now-defunct company said it had no business relationship with Shafer beyond caring for Olvera.

Neither Shafer nor Deittrick responded to requests for comment for this article. Bristol could not be reached for comment, for good reason. After leaving Shafer's office to start her own business she was convicted of stealing at least $200,000 from her wards and is now serving a prison term.

Still mourning the death of his wife, Olvera began to change, Schultz said. Once a cheerful joker, he became withdrawn — a shell of his former self, she said.

"He wasn't happy being there with somebody that wasn't his family," Schultz said. "He had no friends there. No relatives. He was fearful."

Watching costs mount and fearing her father was being exploited, she tried to have Shafer removed as guardian, hoping to eventually move Olvera to California.

That set in motion a long, costly legal battle that resulted in a warrant for her arrest.

HARD TO FIGHT

Schultz learned quickly that Nevada law and Family Court favor the guardian. She couldn't even go to court unless a Nevada resident would act as a co-petitioner. A friend from Las Vegas agreed to help, and they hired local attorney Brian Boggess.

Shafer responded by filing court papers claiming Schultz was an estranged daughter who had no contact with her parents after they left California, and thus should not be allowed to care for her father.

"They said that I had no relationship at all with my parents, which I found kind of strange since a year and a half before my mom's death I had been there taking care of her when she broke her hip," Schultz said. "I'm the one who taught my mother, at her late age, how to use a computer."

Jon Norheim is an attorney appointed by the Clark County Commission to serve as guardianship commissioner. His clerk was the one who suggested Shafer to Schultz.

Although not a judge, Norheim's decisions carry the weight of one. His ruling can be appealed to higher courts, but seldom are because of the cost. Attorneys familiar with the process say an appeal to District Court and the state Supreme Court would run about $50,000, too much for most estates to bear.

In response to Shafer's claims, Schultz tried to show her relationship with her parents to the court. She provided a stack of handwritten letters that spoke of recent visits and dozens of emails between her and her mother.

Norheim wasn't moved. He observed that Olvera enjoyed having Shafer as his guardian, and didn't want to move to California.

But that's not what the old soldier said.

In the one time he was allowed to speak in court, Olvera said, "I would like to live in California. I don't need that man. I don't need Jared."

Boggess, meanwhile, argued that Shafer was improperly draining Olvera's estate with excessive charges, and challenged the legality of Shafer's appointment as guardian, citing state and federal laws that say guardians for military veterans are limited to having only five wards at any one time. Shafer had dozens of wards at the time of his appointment.

The same law also limits how much guardians can charge wards to 5 percent of the ward's annual income. Boggess argued that Shafer's billings far exceeded that limit.

Again, Norheim was unmoved. According to a hearing transcript, he called the law regarding veterans "nice and clear," but not enough to justify "a major upsetting of the apple cart" for Shafer and other private guardians.

"All these private guardians have more than five wards," Norheim said in court. "You couldn't stay in business if you only had a couple of wards."

Olvera would stay Shafer's ward in Nevada, Norheim ruled later.

Boggess said he thought Norheim was more concerned about the effect on Shafer's business than the law's aim of assuring proper attention to the needs of veterans.

"That should be the last conceivable thing that a judge or commissioner thinks about — how it will upset somebody else's business," Boggess said.

In a recent interview, Norheim told the Las Vegas Review-Journal that statutes regarding veterans "could be read harmoniously, and not in conflict."

And Olvera was inconsistent about wanting to return to California, he said.

"They totally ignored him," Schultz said. "In my opinion, it's a kangaroo court, at least concerning Shafer's cases. Your attorneys can spend an enormous amount of time researching and filing and writing ... and you don't get anywhere."

Days after the hearing, Olvera and his daughter took what they saw as their only option.

"The only way to solve the problem was to get my dad out of there," Schultz said.

Olvera packed a few belongings and they drove to her home in Aptos.

"He left of his own volition," Schultz said. "He wanted to go. He was afraid."

Boggess said he didn't tell Schultz to run, but he understands why she did.

"If I was in Becky's shoes, and I could see that I wasn't going to get a fair shake, I'm not sure I would have made a different choice," Boggess said.

In subsequent Guardian Court hearings, Shafer's lawyers accused Schultz of kidnapping her father.

No such charges were ever filed, but Norheim did issue a bench warrant for Schultz's arrest after she and her father ignored his order to return for a court appearance.

"This was considered a kidnapping because he's incapacitated. And (Schultz) took him in violation of Nevada law, and we can't allow that to happen," Norheim recently told the Review-Journal. "There has to be enforcement of the statutes."

FOLLOWING THE DOLLARS

Although Olvera made it out of Nevada, his money did not. For years after Schultz and Olvera fled to California, Shafer continued an expensive court fight to maintain his status as the old soldier's guardian.

Olvera paid for all of it — about $240,000 in legal costs over five years, all billed to the estate Shafer still controlled.

More than $130,000 of the charges went to lawyers representing Bristol and Shafer, Solomon Dwiggins and Freer, Clark & Trevithick in Henderson, and the Grunksy Law Firm in California.

Shafer himself charged $250 per hour to send emails or make phone calls related to the case. Often he and his lawyers would discuss matters over the telephone, with each billing Olvera's account separately for their time, according to invoices obtained by the Review-Journal.

Clark County District Judge Charles Hoskin, who supervises the guardianship program, said he doesn't see a problem with Shafer's rates or billing practices.

"Given his background and experience, I think that's a reasonable number," Hoskin told the Review-Journal.

Lawyers fighting Shafer on Olvera's behalf also were paid from his estate, but their bills amounted to just about $60,000.

All told, over about 3½ years Olvera's estate had been tapped for at least $420,000, Boggess said in a U.S. District Court lawsuit filed last fall in Las Vegas.

In the lawsuit, Boggess accuses Shafer of inflating bills, submitting false charges and embezzlement.

"They were robbing me of my money," Olvera said.

In Nevada, guardians are allowed to use their ward's estate to pay for services and other fees, including attorney fees. But many involved in the guardianship world warn that the practice is easily abused by those in power.

"When people aren't using their own money to fight the war, the disincentives aren't as present," said David Hardy, chief judge of District Court in Washoe County and an advocate for reforming the guardianship system. "Those numbers add up very, very quickly."

In late 2012 the legal case was transferred to a Superior Court in California, where on Aug. 21, 2013, a judge terminated Olvera's guardianship, restoring his ability to manage his own affairs. Shafer withdrew his accusations of kidnapping, and the bench warrant for Schultz was dismissed.

The judge in California did not respond to interview requests, but in court he cited Olvera's improved condition thanks partly to being home with family.

"I never felt that my father needed a guardian," Schultz said. "He just needed someone to assist him for his disabilities."

Olvera still struggles with a bum knee, a sore shoulder and back, and permanent frostbite damage from his wartime service. But those injuries don't slow him as much as they used to, thanks in part to electric chair lifts the Veterans Administration installed in Schultz's two-story house. The VA also gave him a motorized scooter.

When the old soldier was a ward in Nevada, no one bothered to ask the VA to help improve his quality of life, Schultz said.

"None of my dad's benefits were really utilized, because Shafer really didn't care," Schultz said. "I believe that if I'd left him there that he would be dead now.

"He's healthier, heavier and happier than when he was down there," Schultz said. "He's in his comfort zone."

Olvera and his son-in-law seldom miss a VFW post meeting, barbecue or parade. That VA-provided scooter gets good use.

No longer surrounded by strangers and left with no say over his own life, Olvera has no complaints.

Family and friends "treat me real fine," he said. "They feed me anything I want … They know what I like."

Contact Colton Lochhead at clochhead@reviewjournal.com or 702-383-4638. Find him on Twitter: @coltonlochhead

GUARDIANSHIP CASE PLAYS OUT IN NEVADA, CALIFORNIA
By: Fred Couzens September 9, 2009 *Las Vegas Tribune*

Calif. Agency Investigating DuDeck "Abduction" Case
Charles Pascal of Marina Del Rey, Calif., the son-in-law of Marcy DuDeck who was allegedly taken without permission from her third-floor living quarters at the Sunrise Senior Assisted Living facility in the Los Angeles beach community of Playa Vista, Calif. three weeks ago while under the guardianship of former Clark County Public Administrator Jared Shafer, said last week that the Adult Protective Services Program of the Los Angeles County Community and Senior Services has begun an investigation into DuDeck's August 4 "abduction."

"After analyzing information (from the Las Vegas Tribune August 19 article about DuDeck's guardianship story), the agency feels it has enough (information) to open a case," Pascal wrote in an August 20 e-mail. "My attorney, John Guy in Los Angeles, said it is very rare for them to open a case."

An August 21 call to Adult Protective Services in Los Angeles revealed Las Vegas Tribune article stirs interest in elder abuse officials indirectly that a case had been opened.

Without coming out and confirming or denying the question, Patricia Senette-Holt, the public information officer for Los Angeles County Community and Senior Services did say, "We can not comment on that because by law we need to protect a client's privacy."

According to Pascal, who filed the complaint on behalf of his 91-year-old mother-in-law, said he was told by the chief administrator of Adult Protective Services that the case would be assigned to a social worker in the agency's west side office for investigation.

"It was all because of your article," Pascal told Las Vegas Tribune on August 20. "I emailed them your story and this is what happened."

DuDeck's disappearance in early August from the facility that opened in 2006 is wrapped up in a mysterious scenario filled with intrigue and possible civil or criminal action, which Pascal related in telephone conversations that comprised much of the Aug. 19 article.

On August 6, "…according to Jason Malone, the director of Sunrise (at Playa Vista), he told me… that he had gotten a call from Patience Bristol, an employee of Jared Shafer, who told him Lance (DuDeck, Marcy's 56-year-old son) was coming into town and would be taking his mother outside of Sunrise for extended periods of time," Charles said. "Jason said 'you can't do that because… (the California conservator, Winnie Weshler) …had put an order out that no one was to take her out. Patience hung up with Jason and, according to Jason, he wouldn't tell me the name, (Patience) made a second call to a staff member stating that… Weshler had ok'd for Lance to take her out, but that the staff member said 'no, you can't do it.' That was about, according to Jason, 10:30 on the morning of August 4. As best we can see it, Lance came in about 1 p.m. on that day and Sunrise had done a very strange thing. They told the receptionist named Stephanie to take the day off and they brought down the third-floor supervisor at 12 o'clock on that day to run the reception desk. The third floor is where Marcy stayed.

It's called the Reminiscence Floor that Sunrise uses for Alzheimer's. So she's on the desk, Lance comes in and all of a sudden out of a secure facility Marcy is whisked away and now she's in Vegas."

According to Pascal, the senior living facility is supposed to maintain written orders for all activities of its residents, but in Marcy's case, there are no such orders allowing her to be taken on August 4.

"They claim in their handbook that they require written orders, but in this case there is no written order," Pascal said. "Now here comes the bomb. The logs for August 4, according to Stephanie, have completely disappeared. No one can find them. They have Monday of the week, Wednesday of the week, Thursday and Friday of the week, but for some reason or another, Tuesday went into the Twilight Zone. Tuesday is gone. Goodbye Ruby Tuesday. So, we wondered about that because that's the day Lance took her."

Meanwhile, DuDeck is here in Nevada and is being cared for until the day in the not-too-distant future when she can return to Southern California where her daughter, 60-year-old Heidi Pascal, and Charles live.

According to the official state records of Adult Protective Services, a division of California's Health and Human Services Agency, the division worked a monthly average of 14,583 elder abuse cases statewide during the first six months of 2009 while Los Angeles County, the site of the DuDeck case, averaged 3,713 cases a month during the same period.

As for the total number of elder abduction cases from January to June of this year, there were 35 in California with five of them determined to be confirmed cases. Los Angeles County accounted for six of the state's 35 elder abduction cases, but all of the five confirmed abduction cases in California were recorded outside the county.

Guardianship Nightmare Ending for California Couple
Former Public Administrator Jared Shafer Implicated in Plot
Fred Couzens Las Vegas Tribune August 19, 2009

Heidi Pascal of Marina Del Rey, Calif.wants nothing more for her mother, Marcy DuDeck, a ward of Clark County Family Court, than to let her live out the rest of her life in the peace and sanctity of a place where she'll be safe and cared for.

But the past three years have been a living nightmare, a legal Hell if you will, for the daughter and her husband, Charles Pascal, who have tried to achieve that goal for the 91-year-old widow suffering from mild dementia.

It's not enough, as Heidi found out disappointingly, that she tries to do as much as she can to become her mom's guardian so she can effectively and judiciously administer the estate's trust account because to do so, as she also discovered, you have to be a resident of Nevada regardless of how close you live to the ward.

That means a ward of the court can be living in Laughlin and the guardian can be located in Denio, Nev., 710 miles to the north and everything is legal, but if a loved one lived in Bullhead City, Ariz. – a stone's throw across the Colorado River – they could not be the ward's guardian.

"This was an issue when it first came up because the Nevada statute won't allow the court to appoint someone a guardian of a person unless they're a Nevada resident," said Vincent Kostiw, the Pascal's attorney in Las Vegas. "So that was a problem with Heidi, initially, that she was a California resident. So they had a friend who lived here in town and they were petitioning the court to be co-guardians; to have a local guardian and Heidi be coguardians for Marcy, but it didn't work out. (The court) never accepted that because the statute requires that if you're co-guardians you've got to look at layers of sanguinity. You've got to look at blood first and if blood is exhausted then you start looking at friends and distant relatives."

The reason Heidi's co-guardianship plan got tossed out of court is because her brother, Lance DuDeck, lives in Las Vegas and, because of the blood line, he should have been the co-guardian. The two of them have differences, though, which would have made even a workable co-guardianship unworkable.

But that didn't matter. A report from two Senior Citizens Law Project attorneys appointed as temporary guardians uncovered a number of alleged "human flaws" in both Heidi and Lance that made either one singly, or both collectively, unfit to take part in their mother's guardianship.

As a result of the report, Family Court Commissioner Jon Norheim at a May 1, 2007 evidentiary hearing declared both adult children – Heidi is 60 and Lance is 56 – as "unsuitable to be guardian" of their mother.

With neither Heidi nor Lance being able to take care of their mother's affairs, the court appointed former Clark County Public Administrator Jared Shafer as the sole guardian of Marcy DuDeck and her trust account.

But the DuDeck story started long before that.

Heidi's 59-year-old husband, Charles, who earned a masters degree in counseling from Loyola-Marymount University of Los Angeles and now performs rehabilitation counseling, has kept tabs of every moment, every action in his mother-inlaw's case and paints an informative palette of what has transpired from that family's perspective.

Following the death of Marcy's husband on Mar. 16, 2006, Lance lived with his mom until his live-in girlfriend called Heidi during the summer with disturbing news about Lance.

She told us "...Lance is making methamphetamine in the garage and he's drinking, he sleeps to noon and his mother isn't getting fed and wants us to come over there," Charles Pascal related. "Based on the violence, we did the next best thing and called the cops. Las Vegas Metro went to the house and found the girlfriend had a black eye, she was beat up and so they promptly removed Marcy from (her) home (at 2709 Showcase Drive in Sun City Summerlin) and placed her in a facility called Chancellor Gardens."

Heidi made a couple of visits to the 150-bed adult group care facility for Alzheimer's and dementia patients at The Lakes off West Sahara Avenue before taking her mom to California in mid-November 2006.

"...When we got to... Chancellor (Gardens) we found the conditions were filthy and Marcy said, 'Heidi, I want to come with you to California. Please get me out of here' even though she was placed there by... (Clark County Department of) Social Services," Charles said. "Marcy actually begged Heidi to take her to California... that was in September 2006. We went back again in November and Marcy didn't look well and again she begged us and we went in front of Commissioner Norheim. (He) told us that we could submit a plan, but that he wasn't really going to listen to it. When our attorney asked why, (Norheim) said because we weren't residents of Nevada and therefore we really didn't have any say in the care of Marcy."

A subsequent visit to Norheim's courtroom evoked a similar response.

"This time we saw Marcy had gotten a lot worse; she really looked bad," Charles said. "At that point, Heidi and I took matters into our own hands and Heidi flew back on Nov. 18 and right in the middle of breakfast walked out of Chancellor with Marcy and brought her to Los Angeles. We then put her into Sunrise Senior Assisted Living (in Playa Vista, Calif.), but before we did it we had her checked out by the doctor and we found her weight had dropped, in the care of Chancellor, from 138 to 114 pounds and she could hardly walk. She hadn't had a bath in a long time. She smelled awful. Her hair hadn't been washed for a long time. I'd say weeks or months, but let's just say a very long time."

Taking DuDeck from Nevada to California didn't sit well with the court here, but Marcy won out anyway.

"The courts in Nevada were enraged at what Heidi had done and they had an evidentiary hearing in May 2007…they had issued two court orders to bring Marcy back and we refused on two grounds," Charles continued. "They insisted she be put back in the same place she'd been taken out of, Chancellor Gardens, and they weren't going to do anything to police Lance who had been taking meth and had been yelling and screaming at his mother whenever he was there, so we said she's staying here. The guardians ad litem (who wrote the May 1, 2007 report) came out here and they said they had never seen a place as wonderful as Sunrise. They ruled at the evidentiary hearing that Marcy could stay in California permanently and that Jared Shafer would be appointed to be the guardian of the trust."

But a year later, the Pascals noticed what they thought were irregularities in billings for services by Shafer the guardian.

"… (When) we got the first accounting… we saw well over $80,000 had been taken out of the estate for doing absolutely nothing," Charles claimed. "Charges came out like billing us $60 to get a $20 credit,

$1,500 visits that never took place, phone conversations that never happened with the family with us being named as the people in the phone conversation..."

All of this while Heidi took care of her mom who was living in California at the time.

"Exactly, and he really wasn't doing anything because Heidi was taking her mother to the doctor, Heidi was handling all of the medicine, Heidi was doing everything... he was charging us $225 (an hour) and then he also set up other companies like certain business services. He's got three separate companies that he set up. In California, it's against the law for a guardian to have other companies to bill. What he would do, he would put in his bill for $225 and then add AVID Business Services after that."

A check of both the Nevada Secretary of State's Office and the Clark County Business License database failed to show up a business titled AVID Business Services or Shafer's name attached to such a business. His name is attached to Professional Fiduciary Services of Nevada, Inc. as president and resident agent – a company with origination papers filed in Carson City in mid-September 2002, more than three months before he left public office – while he and his wife, Claire, are named as managing members of JCS1, LLC.

The Pascals objected to more than 210 individual billing charges, most of them under $100, made by Shafer to the court – things like $25 to pick up a court order when $187 had already been paid for the same service or a bank account management fee of $50 when $20.83 had already been paid for the same service – but Commissioner Norheim "...having reviewed the petition and amended objection" nevertheless went along with Shafer's charges and denied the Pascals an evidentiary hearing to look further at the billing.

"The fees and costs incurred by the guardian, and those professionals hired by the guardian, are consistent with what this court anticipated when it appointed (Shafer) to serve as guardian," Norheim found, adding "Although the parties are entitled to an evidentiary hearing this court is concerned that an evidentiary hearing... will be extremely costly to

(Marcy), and therefore finds that... a hearing is not in the best interests of (Marcy.)"

From that court appearance in mid-November 2008, to the summer of 2009, Heidi tried through the California courts to get Shafer out as guardian and get her mom's trust account into the control of Morgan Stanley, the financial services firm where Marcy's husband, Michael, wanted the account before his death.

She succeeded in getting a California conservator (the same as a guardian in Nevada) named, but it didn't include her.

"Well, we started the proceedings and (Chief District Court) Judge (Art) Ritchie (of Clark County) called the California court and started saying that Heidi was no good and Heidi was this," Charles related. "So when we went into court, the California courts listened to Judge Ritchie and put a temporary conservator here in California that took Heidi completely out of the loop even to the point Heidi could no longer take her mom to the doctor, she couldn't take her to lunch, she couldn't take her to the hairdresser, she could do absolutely nothing, no church, no nothing. This guardian named Winnie Weshler was appointed and... she told us point blank in a meeting in February... that she was going to follow the directives of Jared Shafer."

On August 6, Marcy was set to testify in court that she wanted Heidi to be her conservator and take care of her, but according to Charles, Shafer didn't want that to happen.

Mysteriously, two days earlier, Marcy disappeared from her California living facility under suspicious circumstances, only to end up in Las Vegas under the watchful eye of Shafer.

On August 6, "...according to Jason Malone, the director of Sunrise (at Playa Vista), he told me... that he had gotten a call from Patience Bristol, an employee of Jared Shafer, who told him Lance was coming into town and would be taking his mother outside of Sunrise for extended periods of time," Charles said. "Jason said 'you can't do that because... Weshler... had put an order out that no one was to take her out. Patience hung up with Jason and, according to Jason, he wouldn't tell me the name,

(Patience) made a second call to a staff member stating that…Weshler had ok'd for Lance to take her out, but that the staff member said 'no, you can't do it.' That was about, according to Jason, 10:30 on the morning of August 4. As best we can see it, Lance came in about 1 p.m. on that day and Sunrise had done a very strange thing. They told the receptionist named Stephanie to take the day off and they brought down the third-floor supervisor at 12 o'clock on that day to run the reception desk. The third floor is where Marcy stayed. It's called the Reminiscence Floor that Sunrise uses for Alzheimer's. So she's on the desk, Lance comes in and all of a sudden out of a secure facility Marcy is whisked away and now she's in Vegas."

According to Pascal, the senior living facility is supposed to maintain written orders for all activities of its residents, but in Marcy's case, there are no such orders allowing her to be taken on August 4.

"They claim in their handbook that they require written orders, but in this case there is no written order," Pascal said. "Now here comes the bomb. The logs for August 4, according to Stephanie, have completely disappeared. No one can find them. They have Monday of the week, Wednesday of the week, Thursday and Friday of the week, but for some reason or another, Tuesday went into the Twilight Zone. Tuesday is gone. Goodbye Ruby Tuesday. So, we wondered about that because that's the day Lance took her. So now, as of (August 10), there was an order issued in the court that Heidi or Lance can not call, contact, visit or see the mother in Vegas. We know where she's at right now; at Jump for Joy Care No. 3 located at 7881 Rainshower Dr.) in Las Vegas. Heidi is now banned so she can't find out how her mother is. Her mother's been in dementia, but the one thing the mother knows is that Heidi talked to her every day. Heidi always brought her a nut bar, watched TV with her, spent an hour to two hours with her every single day for the last three years and that has just been taken away."

Last week at a hearing before Commissioner Norheim, he agreed Marcy should be in California. He set a September 9 hearing to see how things are progressing.

"A California judge wants Marcy back and the Nevada judge would like her back if she can travel safely, so we're looking into whether she can travel safely and, in the alternative, looking to put her in the best possible facility here in Nevada," Kostiw, Heidi's attorney, said after the hearing. "The commissioner does want her to see her kids, but under some restrictions because both children (have because both children (have made it) a tug of war."

When the Pascals got word of the decision, they were ecstatic.

"When we heard Marcy was coming back, I let out a big whoop you could hear for miles and Heidi started to laugh and then she started to cry and then she jumped up and down; she was that delighted to know her mom was going to be returning and she was going to safe," Charles said the night of Norheim's decision. "So, in that part of the battle we're happy, but one of the other things I'll tell you is this is one battle in a long war because basically Shafer is still taking money from the estate for doing absolutely nothing and we're going to have to try to fight that in the California proceedings."

Attorney Cathy Mazzeo, who has represented Shafer in recent court proceedings, wasn't able to shed any light on her client's actions. "Unfortunately, my client and I cannot comment on claims or allegations that have not been presented in the form of actual litigation," Mazzeo wrote in an August 14 e-mail. "Due to HIPAA regulations we are also unable to comment on matters relating to Ms. DuDeck's health, which was the focal point of Wednesday's hearing. However, in an effort to share with you the history in this case, I am attaching a couple of the Court's previous orders."

The Pascals have yet another court date September 8 before California District Court Commissioner Reva Goetz, the same judge who ruled in the Britney Spears custody case last year, to get Shafer off and Heidi on as Marcy's guardian as well as get the trust account transferred to Morgan Stanley.

"So that's the battle we're fighting right now and then, of course, as far as Shafer is concerned, we're looking at our options… in terms of what horrible things he's done to the estate and we're looking to investigate Sunrise's culpability," Charles added. "Weshler may decide to put (Marcy) back in Sunrise (Senior Living at Playa Vista) and if she does, we are definitely violently opposed to it; we'll vehemently protest it because their security was breached. We don't know if it will be breached again so that's our other concern. All in all, when we take a look at it from the hilltop, the fact that Marcy is going to be safe and out of the hands of where she is, is very, very delightful to us."

Former Public Official Defends His Actions After Term

July 25, 2007

KVBC/News 3 (Las Vegas)

Ignorance of the law is typically not a defense, but that's what a former public official is using as his defense today in a hearing before the state ethics commission. News 3 Investigators have been digging deeper into allegations of misuse of public office.

Jared Shafer served as Clark County Public Administrator for more than 20 years. His job was to handle estates when someone died and had no known relatives who could do so. Although Shafer's been out of that public office for two and a half years, what he did at the end of his term is still plaguing him today.

Money is said to be the root of all evil, and today it's the root of a contentious case before the state ethics panel. At issue is whether former Public Administrator Jared Shafer misused his office to get a lucrative contract. "To get money from the wrongful death suit."

Terry Williams's father, Charles, died in November 2002, allegedly as a result of nursing home negligence. He left a will, in which he gives all his assets to his daughter Terry, making no provisions for any of his other children. "They just weren't close. They were never close. My brother didn't even want to visit my dad."

But it's her brother who lived in Texas, who initiated the wrongful death lawsuit, and had Jared Shafer appointed co-administrator of an estate to which the brother legally had no right. "My dad is probably just mad, I mean, just beyond belief. He would never want to see me have to fight all of these people this way."

The part of that fight that brought her here today has to do with timing. When Shafer left public office, and when he signed on to co-administer Charles Williams' estate. "He was retiring from office and the documents seemingly were signed and prepared prior to that, but then filed the day after he left office, so it just was troubling."

Mark Hutchison is the State Ethics Commissioner. "Is there any question that at the time you signed the petition on January 2, 2003, you were acting in a private capacity, but you were still a public officer?"

"Yes, I agree with that."

Shafer agrees, but says he didn't know he was still in public office, mistaking when his term really ended. "I've been fed so many inconsistencies, I can't begin to understand." Shafer also fed the ethics commission inconsistencies. When asked what he'd planned to do when he left the public administrator position, he said, "I was going to kick back a little bit. I told all my friends that had asked that if you needed help, I would be available. I didn't have any plans to do anything."

But in fact, three months prior to leaving office, he opened a bank account and set up a private fiduciary corporation to handle cases just like that of Charles Williams. "This was no opportunity. This was helping somebody out. The word opportunity indicates you're going to make money. There was no money to be made in this thing."

There was according to a petition he filed with the court several weeks after leaving office. In it, he asks for compensation at the rate of $200 per hour. "The documents scream for themselves." The News 3 Investigators have also obtained documents suggesting further impropriety, showing Jared Shafer still personally holds real estate that was put in his name in his official capacity as public administrator.

Clark County Judges take Guardianship Oversight Away from Embattled Judge, Hearing Master

Clark County Family Court Commissioner Jon Norheim during an interview at Clark County Family Court on Friday March 13, 2015. Private professional guardians have been abusing the system and causing elderly wards in Clark County to lose their life's savings worth hundreds of thousands of dollars. (Jeff Scheid/Las Vegas Review-Journal)

By: Colton Lochhead LAS VEGAS REVIEW-JOURNAL March, 2015

The judge and hearing master who presided over the troubled Clark County guardianship court will no longer hear those cases, the court announced Thursday.

For over a decade, guardianship cases were heard by Commissioner Jon Norheim. District Court Judge Charles Hoskin handled any appeals or disputes between parties. Those cases will be transferred to Judge Dianne Steel, District Court's longest-serving judge, effective June 1, according to a statement released Thursday.

The changes at the court coincided with the filing of a petition with the Nevada Supreme Court Thursday to create a commission to review the process and examine the creation of guardianships, monitoring of cases, court documentation and judicial training.

Long-running problems with the system that handles about 8,500 adult guardianship cases each year were exposed in a series of Review-Journal articles published in April. Cases highlighted by the newspaper showed a lack of oversight by the courts, such as failing to require guardians to file annual accounts of a ward's finances even though it is required by state law.

Swift changes have come since.

After hearing concerns raised by the newspaper and from dozens of people who felt wronged by the system, County Commissioners began discussing the problems last month.

Chief Judge David Barker has asked the commissioners to approve funding for two court investigators and two compliance officers that he hopes will increase the level of monitoring of guardianship cases and protect wards, who are people under guardianship. Barker also help set up a hotline for people to lodge guardianship complaints by calling 702-671-4614 or sending an e-mail to guardianshipcompliance@clarkcounty-courts.us.

Clark County commissioners quickly moved to establish a Blue Ribbon Panel to analyze and recommend fixes to the court. But when Chief Justice James Hardesty of the Nevada Supreme Court expressed interest in creating a larger, state-wide panel, the commissioners gladly obliged.

Hardesty, along with Barker and Washoe County Chief Judge David Hardy, filed the motion to create the commission Thursday afternoon.

"There are several critical problems facing Nevada's courts as a result of an increase in the number of elderly and vulnerable persons who require guardianships or conservatorships," said Hardesty said. "We recognize the need to address these problems statewide and identify the resources necessary to assist the court system to meet Nevada's needs."

Handling guardianship cases will not exactly be foreign to Steel, who has been a judge since 1997. She heard minor guardianship cases from 2007 to 2011.

"I am committed to the court's goal to protect those impacted by intellectual disabilities and diseases associated with aging," Steel said in the release. "Through experience, I know how difficult these cases are for families, and I will work hard to ensure that the court is handling these cases in a manner in accordance with the laws established to protect families dealing with guardianship."

The court did not specify any exact reasons for the change, saying only that the change comes after talks with "state and nationally respected judicial experts." The court did not say what Norheim would be reassigned to after the changes become official next month.

FORMER CLARK COUNTY FAMILY COURT JUDGE STEVEN JONES SENTENCED TO MORE THAN TWO YEARS IN PRISON FOR INVESTMENT FRAUD SCHEME

•

U.S. Attorney's Office   District of Nevada (703) 388-6336
February 25, 2015

LAS VEGAS, NV—Former Clark County Family Court Judge Steven E. Jones was sentenced today by US. District Judge Jennifer A. Dorsey to 26 months in prison, three years of supervised release, and ordered to pay approximately $2.9 million in restitution for participating in an investment fraud that bilked over 50 investor victims out of millions in cash for almost a decade, announced US. Attorney Daniel G. Bogden for the District of Nevada and Laura Bucheit, Special Agent in Charge of the FBI for Nevada.

Jones, 57, of Henderson, Nev., who served for almost 20 years as a family court judge in Clark County, pleaded guilty in September to one count of conspiracy to commit wire fraud. He was permitted to self-surrender to federal prison by May 25, 2015. Jones' sentence was enhanced for violating his position of trust, and because the loss amount was over $200,000 and there were more than 10 victims. Jones resigned his position as judge and surrendered his Nevada law license in September as one of the conditions of his plea agreement.

"Former Judge Steven Jones played an integral part in this investment fraud scheme and was the most prominent and indispensable member," said US. Attorney Bogden. "This crime was not a "one-off" for Jones, but a calculated and deliberate decision that he replicated for years. He knew right from wrong, but engaged in the conduct anyway because he could."

"This sentencing reaffirms to the public that the FBI will continue to make certain that no one is above the law, and when public corruption is identified, it will be aggressively investigated and prosecuted," said Special Agent in Charge Bucheit.

All of the co-conspirators charged in the fraud scheme have also pleaded guilty. Thomas A. Cecrle Jr., 57, of Henderson, Nev., and Constance C. Fenton, 70, of Gig Harbor, Wash., are scheduled to be sentenced on March 2. Terry J. Wolfe, 59, of Henderson, was sentenced on Feb. 19, to time served, three years of supervised release, and ordered to pay approximately $2.9 million in restitution. Mark L. Hansen, 56, of Corvallis, Ore., was sentenced on Jan. 27, 2015, to four months in prison, three years of supervised release, and ordered to pay approximately $2.9 million in restitution. Ashlee M. Martin, 31, of Las Vegas, Nev., entered into a 12-month pretrial diversion agreement with the government.

According to the plea memoranda, defendants lured victims into a fraud scheme by falsely telling them that Cecrle worked as a contractor for the US Department of Homeland Security, purchasing and selling water rights worth millions of dollars as part of a secret government program. The co-conspirators then solicited money by falsely claiming that Cecrle needed short-term cash loans to complete his phantom water deals, loans he promised to repay in short order along with a very large return. Cecrle and his co-conspirators concocted a similar story involving a land deal on the Las Vegas Strip where Cecrle needed short-term loans to supposedly close a deal with Sir Richard Branson. In truth, however, Cecrle held no position with the federal government and there were no land or water rights deals.

Using his office as an elected state court judge, defendant Jones knowingly vouched for Cecrle and the legitimacy of the deals to potential investors when he knew the deals were, in fact, scams. According to the plea memorandum, Jones continued to further the conspiracy by receiving money from a victim in the parking lot of the Family Division Courthouse, meeting with at least one potential investor in his chambers and elsewhere in the courthouse to discuss the investment, obtaining an "Own Recognizance" bond to release Cecrle from custody after he was arrested for bad checks he had passed to a victim, and opening and maintaining a joint checking account with Cecrle, through which flowed over $260,000 in illegal proceeds. During the entire conspiracy, which lasted from about September 2002 to October 2012, the defendants defrauded at least 22 victims of more than $2.6 million, money they quickly converted to their own use.

The case was investigated by the FBI and prosecuted by First Assistant US Attorney Steven W. Myhre and Assistant US Attorney Daniel R. Schiess of the US Attorney's Office for the District of Nevada.

This prosecution is part of efforts underway by President Barack Obama's Financial Fraud Enforcement Task Force. President Obama established the interagency Financial Fraud Enforcement Task Force to wage an aggressive, coordinated and proactive effort to investigate and prosecute financial crimes. The task force includes representatives from a broad range of federal agencies, regulatory authorities, inspectors general and state and local law enforcement who, working together, bring to bear a powerful array of criminal and civil enforcement resources. The task force is working to improve efforts across the federal executive branch, and with state and local partners, to investigate and prosecute significant financial crimes, ensure just and effective punishment for those who perpetrate financial crimes, combat discrimination in the lending and financial markets and recover proceeds for victims of financial crimes. For more information about the task force visit: www. stopfraud.com.

This content has been reproduced from its original source.

COUNTY COMMISSION PROBING 'FRIGHTENING' ABUSES IN GUARDIANSHIP SYSTEM

Steve Marcus

Elizabeth Indig speaks during a commission meeting at the Clark County Government Center Tuesday, April 21, 2015. Commissioners called for a blue ribbon panel to investigate the professional guardianship system...

By: Conor Shine   Tuesday, April 21, 2015 | 6:00 p.m.

COMMISSIONERS TO INVESTIGATE PROFESSIONAL GUARDIANSHIP SYSTEM

Many questions but few concrete answers emerged today as Clark County commissioners probed what they called "frightening" and "appalling" abuses in the private guardian system intended to protect the elderly and infirm.

More than 8,000 people in Clark County are designated wards of court-appointed guardians, who oversee the care and finances of those who aren't mentally or physically fit to care for themselves. In the majority of those cases, the guardian is a family member or friend, District Court Chief Judge David Barker said today, but many are placed under the supervision of for-profit private guardians who charge fees for their services.

It's those private guardians who have come under increasing scrutiny in recent weeks following a story in the Las Vegas Review-Journal that detailed the case of one guardian accused of draining her ward's estate of nearly half a million dollars.

Commission Chairman Steve Sisolak said he's received dozens of calls from residents concerning "unbelievable" stories of private guardians "manipulating the system to drain their (wards') assets."

Commissioners attempted to dig into the system during their meeting today, hearing reports from Barker and other staff about the lax licensing requirements for private guardians and the lack of oversight on the fees they charge to wards.

The guardianship system is run out of Family Court, with the entirety of the caseload being handled by a single hearing master and one Family Court judge.

A person is entered into the guardianship system following a petition by a family member, doctor or someone else in a position of responsibility for that person.

Sisolak said that once a person is deemed in need of a guardian, "it's virtually impossible to get out."

During public testimony, Las Vegas resident Elizabeth Indig shared the story of her 93-year-old mother who was put under the care of a private guardian in 2012. Indig said her mother was entered into the system without Indig's knowledge or consent and that she's been unable to reclaim legal responsibility for her mother since. During that time, Indig said the guardian charged excessive fees to her mother's estate while failing to pay bills like her homeowners association dues, leading to her mother's house being foreclosed upon and forcing her to move to a nursing home.

These concerns were echoed by Metro Police Lt. James Weiskopf, who said he's heard similar complaints during his time at the department's abuse and neglect detail.

"The complaints we're hearing from our agency, the family members aren't even aware that this Family Court is occurring or that a private guardian has been appointed for the estate," Weiskopf said.

He said that when family members petition to take control back from the private guardian, they feel like their testimony is ignored by the court's hearing master.

"The next thing the family knows, the private guardian has total access to the finances of these wards. What the private guardians are doing is charging these fees for all the different services, that gets charged against the ward's estate," he said.

As the ward's estate is depleted, the private guardian goes to Family Court for permission to sell assets like cars, homes or other valuables to continue funding their services, according to complaints Weiskopf received.

"The goal is to create liquid assets so that way these private guardians can continue to charge their fees," he said. "That's the overall gist of the complaints we're getting…that there's no oversight of these private guardians who are charging these ridiculous fees."

Weiskopf said Metro is limited in its ability to investigate these types of complaints because the court is responsible for oversight and there are limited regulations on what types of fees can be charged by private guardians.

Commissioners weren't presented any immediate solutions for solving the perceived problem in the private guardianship system, but they promised to continue looking into the issue in search of abuses and potential fixes.

Sisolak requested that a task force be formed to investigate the system and said the county's audit committee would look to review financial records submitted by guardians to the court.

Barker said one potential fix could be to take the guardianship system out of the hands of a single hearing master and judge and instead spread them around to multiple judges.

Another potential fix could be to add staff to the county's Public Guardian Office. That government office provides similar services as private guardians, but currently only has six employees handling about 300 cases, a fraction of the total number of guardianships in the county.

"If there is private guardian abuse out there, we should go after a couple right away. We don't have to wait for the overall analysis," Commissioner Larry Brown said. "If we can start going after some of the most flagrant abuses, I think we can start to build back the public trust as we…improve the system."

GUARDIANSHIP ABUSE SPREADS TO PENNSYLVANIA
By: Michael Volpe

March 10, 2015
News, Rebel Pundit

As part of an ongoing series on guardianship abuse, Rebel Pundit will present a two part series on Montgomery County, Pennsylvania.

Taisha Lee said her grandmother's guardianship case was Kafkaesque, lacked due process, and one she believes was pre-determined.

Lee said trouble for her grandmother, Jannie Myers started, when her grandfather, Isaiah Myers, was near death and both her grandparents moved in with her and her husband in September 2012.

Lee said prior to her grandfather's death, he changed the will and wrote all his children out, leaving their estate, worth a bit more than $300,000, to Lee and another grandchild.

Her grandparents made Lee their power of attorney at about this time.

Lee's grandfather died in October 2012. On January 11, 2013, Lee's aunt, Gloria Myers filed a petition with the Montgomery County Orphan's Court for her mother to be put into guardianship, alleging she was incapacitated and unable to take care of herself.

A call was left at Bowman's office but was not returned.

Lee said she knew there would be problems right away when the Judge Stanley Ott refused to allow her grandmother to use her own attorney, instead assigned to her Diane Zabowski.

Lee said in August 2013, her then attorney Saul Langsom emerged from a meeting in the judge's chambers with Judge Ott, Bowman, and Zabowski, and an area attorney named Erin McDevitt, who'd be named guardian, and informed Lee that a deal had been made to place her grandmother into guardianship.

"I was shocked," Lee told Rebel Pundit, adding that she expected evidence to be heard before taking away her grandmother's freedom.

Elaine Renoire, of the National Association to Stop Guardianship Abuse (NASGA), said that while such deals are of questionable constitutionality and almost never in the ward's best interest they are common. In the case of her grandmother, her own lawyer made a deal in a bathroom with the judge to put her grandmother into guardianship.

Lee said the deal only fell apart when her aunt objected to Lee being named guardian of the person, a bureaucratic title which would have allowed Lee to make some decisions though the bulk of the decisions would be left to McDevitt.

Lee said a hearing was finally scheduled on September 17, 2013, but before then Zabowski warned her that if she continued to obstruct the court's attempts to guardianize her grandmother that Zabowski would attempt to jail her.

"We'll just say she was always incapacitated," Lee recalled Zabowski telling her, and suggested she'd get the court to say Lee stole money she spent during the previous year as their power of attorney.

According to the transcripts of the hearing, there were several red flags. First, Zabowski asked that the courtroom be cleared of all non-essential individuals forcing Lee's husband and cousin to be removed even though Ms. McDevitt was allowed to stay.

Notes of Testimony 1 for Jannie Myers

Second, Zabowski asked to put the proceeds of the sale of Ms. Myers home into escrow, though it had already started before any decision on guardianship had been made.

Lee told Rebel Pundit that clearing the court was part of a pattern of a lack of transparency on Ott's part as he's sealed most correspondence on the case and she's been barred from looking at the entire file.

Jannie Myers charged that the hearing was designed to take her assets from her: "My daughter have (sic) me her," Myers said according to the transcript. "I heard she want everything I have."

Ms. Myers's concerns that the entire proceeding was done simply to take her assets were never addressed, and Judge Ott simply moved forward with the hearing which would put her into guardianship.

Myers was also clearly uncomfortable with Zabowski representing her. "I seen her," Myers told Judge Ott of Zabowski, "but I don't really know her."

"That's because I appointed her to be your lawyer." Judge Ott responded shortly thereafter. "She's your lawyer."

The main witness at the hearing was Dr. Dominick Galluzzo. Dr. Galluzzo, who not only treated Ms. Myers but her deceased husband, testified that he administered three Mini Mental State Examinations (MMSE), one in October 2012, and two in 2013. While the first test, Ms. Myers scored a 14 out of 30, she subsequently scored a 26 and 27 out of 30 on the last two tests.

Dr. Galluzzo explained that the low test score in the first instance was because of major depression suffered by Ms. Myers in the aftermath of her husband's death; she married at eighteen years old and was married for sixty-seven years.

Though these test scores indicate a person able to function on her own Zabowski, later on in Dr. Galluzzo's testimony, Zabowski read off the Pennsylvania code for an incapacitated person: "An incapacitated person means an adult whose ability to receive and evaluate information effectively and communicate decisions in any way is impaired in any way to such a significant extent that her or she is partially or totally unable to manage his or her financial resources or to meet essential requirements for his or her physical health and safety."

Dr. Galluzzo then said according to that definition he considered Myers impaired.

While that reading of the statute is accurate, there is another portion which Zabowski left out which should also have been considered: "The need for guardianship services, if any, in light of such factors as the availability of family, friends and other supports to assist the individual in making decisions and in light of the existence, if any, of advance directives such as durable powers of attorney or trusts."

At the time of the hearing, Ms. Myers had been living with her granddaughter Taisha Lee and her granddaughter was made a power of attorney, and in fact, during his testimony Dr. Galluzzo said, "She (Jannie Myers) was quite content living with her granddaughter."

Elaine Renoire, who examined the statute, believes the clear intent is to make guardianship a last resort and to cede to family members if they are willing and able to take care of the potential ward as was the case with Ms. Myers; she said the presence of the POA should have been even more evidence that guardianship was unnecessary.

Furthermore, Zabowski had previously sent Dr. Galluzzo a letter which suggested that she wanted to receive the answer he gave that day. On March 28, 2013, Zabowski sent Dr. Galluzo a letter in which she stated, "Your answers will form the medical basis for the medical opinion which Judge Ott will need in order to enter a decree that Ms. Myers is an incapacitated person."

Worse yet, the letter included a check for $250. Renoire called the letter itself and the payment wholly inappropriate, after examining it for Rebel Pundit.

Myers fate was sealed when Judge Ott acted not only as a judge but as a physician: "I am not a physician; I am not trained, however I handle about a hundred of these cases and I have for the last twenty years so I guess that makes me an amateur physician." Ott stated in court. "If I were to characterize her level of dementia, I would say it's moderate. I would not call it mild."

He also stated Ms. Myers "has a great deal of confusion and memory loss". Myers was placed in guardianship and forced into a nursing home.

Lee said her grandmother slowly withdrew and became less and less responsive until she had a stroke in December 2014. Lee said she might have lived however it took the guardian, Erin McDevitt, eight days to approve her to be taken to the hospital for treatment and by then it was too late.

Jannie Myers died on December 16, 2014.

Lee said her grandmother's treatment before and during guardianship was only one part of the problem. She said she's never received a full accounting of the expenses associated with the guardianship was only told to prepare to be shocked by what's left in her grandmother's estate.

This is no small matter as guardianship is ostensibly done to protect the ward financially from themselves and it appears most if not all of the estate has gone to costs associated with guardianship itself.

Lee was able to secure invoices from all three lawyers associated with this case and all, including Bowman whose job it was to put her into guardianship, was paid from her estate.

An examination of each of these reveals several more questionable and dubious charges. Erin McDevitt charged $5,747.50 for 64.9 hours of work from September to November 2013, however many of the line items appear inflated including: she charged 12 minutes to mail a US Postal Service change of address form, she charged for six minutes worth of work to send a fax, another occasion she charged for twelve minutes worth of work to send another fax, she repeatedly charged for six minutes worth of work to print faxes, and she charged for twelve minutes worth of work to write and mail a check.

Also, a close examination of all their invoices shows several discrepancies in telephone calls. For instance, one line item from Zabowski's invoice has a telephone call lasting twelve minutes on November 7, 2013, to McDevitt however McDevitt has no such line item for this call. Rebel Pundit found numerous instances where calls didn't match up.

Even when they did, the times didn't always match up as well. In April 2, 2013 phone call between Bowman and Zabowski, Bowman lists the line item as lasting .2 hours while Zabowski lists the line item as lasting .32 hours.

Renoire said billing fraud and other forms of overbilling are also far too common during guardianship and she added they are rarely prosecuted or corrected. Lee told Rebel Pundit that while she was able to reduce some of the fees the costs incurred to her to pay for a lawyer to challenge the fees wound up costing as much as what she saved her grandmother in fees.

Lee has spoken to nine other victims of the combination of Zabowski and Judge Ott and part two of this series will identify some of them.

Guardianship Abuse Spreads to Pennsylvania Part 2

By: Michael Volpe

When F. Harvey Whitten was a medic in the Korean War, he held dying soldiers in his arm so they wouldn't die alone, now at the behest of the Montgomery County (Pennsylvania) Orphans Court and its main players- Judge Stanley Ott and Diane Zabowski- Whitten is headed toward that very fate.

Harvey, a long term advertising executive, is worth millions if not tens of millions. Harvey is also gay and was in a long term relationship with Robert Sprau.

In 2010, Harvey Whitten had a stroke and was diagnosed with vascular dementia causing some of Whitten's nieces and nephews to petitioned the court to have Harvey Whitten guardianized and the case wound up in front of Judge Stanley Ott, of the Orphan's Court of Montgomery County. Like in the previous case involving Jannie Myers, Ott eschewed Whitten's request for his own counsel and ordered Diane Zabowski to act as his counsel.

During a fact finding interview with Zabowski, Coz remembers that Zabowski was fixated for most of the duration of the interview on Harvey being gay and at one point remarked that the Whitten family was one of the most dysfunctional she'd known.

In fact, both Mary and Coz say their family is far from dysfunctional and the charge was absurd and provocative.

A long protracted family legal fight was avoided, when Harvey Whitten was declared incapacitated and Coz and Robert Sprau agreed to be the guardian and co-guardian on August 11, 2011. Harvey Whitten went to live with Sprau at his retirement home at the Shannondell in Audobon Pennsylvania. The Shannondell is considered among the most magnificent retirement communities in the country. Univest Bank was made guardian of the estate and their employee Julianna Van Duyne-King was the point person because Judge Ott had worked with her before.

In 2012 Sprau developed an aggressive lung cancer and passed away on September 22, 2012, but not before handpicking the aides who would be with Harvey twenty four hours a day while he continued living in Shannondell.

Zabowski then lobbied to have Deborah Klock, a nurse, to replace Sprau as co-gaurdian on November 16, 2012.

Both Mary and Coz told RebelPundit that Klock exhibited problems right away. Mary Whitten especially has written numerous complaints against Klock in which she alleges: Klock impersonated a family member, made herself the emergency contact, and changed the medication with notifying the family.

The change in medications done behind the family's back, say Mary and Coz, caused Harvey to have a psychotic break at the end of 2012. He began experiencing various ailments and outbursts went from Shannondell to three hospitals in January 2013, before winding up in the Meadows at the beginning of February 2013; the Meadows is a psychiatric unit for especially difficult cases also located within the Shannondell confines only unlike the rest of the place, this portion is much like something from One Flew Over a Cuckoo's Nest.

PRE-MEDITATED MURDER

"Let me first emphasize that the FBI has identified elder fraud and fraud against those suffering from serious illness as two of the most insidious of all white collar crimes being perpetrated by today's modern

and high tech con-man. Many elderly citizens rely on pensions, social security and life savings to support themselves. The losses inflicted by these unscrupulous con men and their organizations are both financially and emotionally devastating to these victims." **Dennis Lormel, former Chief, Financial Crimes Section, FBI**

"Everyone, even the experts, can be taken in, manipulated, conned by them. A good sociopath can play a concerto on anyone's heartstrings. Your best defense is to understand the nature of these human predators." **Dr. Robert Hare, author, "Snakes in Suit: When Psychopaths Go to Work"**

GLYNNIS WALKER, MBA, PH.D.

In 2010, three women stole my mother. This is the story of how I tried to get her back.

Her name was Rosalind, but my dad always called her "Joy" because she was his joy for sixty years. The trio of conspirators that targeted her, and later my family, consisted of a lawyer, a neighbor and a part-time supermarket checker.

Two of them were motivated, in part, by an overwhelming need to control and manipulate others. All of them were enticed by the prospect of easy money. During their association with my mother, they abused her, defrauded her, changed her will, stole her identity, and mine.

My mother was an easy target. She was a sweet, naive woman who belonged to a generation when women were brought up to be trusting and compliant. She also had recently been diagnosed with Alzheimer's. It was not difficult for them to take over her life, isolate her from her family, empty her bank accounts, use her credit cards, and later, when the time was right for them, arrange for her to die so they could profit from the bogus will they created.

Unfortunately, though what happened to my mother is perhaps one of the worst examples of elder fraud, experts in the field agree that it was hardly a rare series of events. Fraud and abuse happen every day to millions of seniors, and the numbers are escalating.

Susan Warren, MA, LPC, LIAC, NCC, CHT

In 2004 I went to see a new GYN who referred me to her gay male friend, Terry, to be a caretaker for my mother. He worked for us from July—Dec and in that time my mother, who was diabetic and always overweight, lost 50 lb. so he must have been giving her something as she was dining out daily.

He turned her against her 5 physicians (she never saw the GYN), her friends, and at the end against me when I became her financial POA. He took her to our bank and the bank mistakenly allowed her to withdraw all her money and she deposited it in his bank. His plan was to take her to Vegas with all of his gay friends and marry her, as he convinced her he wasn't gay. He had an appointment with an attorney for when they returned with a list of her assets and was sure she would sign everything over to him as he had convinced her I was going to put her in a nursing home.

The bank, on realizing what had happened, called Adult Protective Services and the Judge had me evict him. I had to get an attorney, the State appointed my mother an attorney, and my mother was declared incompetent and I became her Guardian. We spent the next two years in court because my attorney wasn't ethical. In 2007 I changed attorneys and all the insanity stopped. I agreed to let the Tucson police interview me for their show on "predators of the elderly/incompetent" if they would investigate the GYN and caregiver as there was never an investigation after I got my mother's money back. They said they would but never did. But they said this is one of the biggest scams going in this country.

Teresa Tozzo-Lyles, Ph.D., CHES, June 2015

My mom, under guardianship since June 2011, just passed away less than 1 month ago. There are several things that I have not seen brought to the forefront, and I am hoping it will come as time goes by, that regards my mom. First, she did not have freedom of religion, which is one of the BASIC rights in our constitution. Regardless of your mental status, EVERY US citizen has the right to worship where and when they want. This is ALSO taken away from these individuals under guardianship.

Secondly, is the concept of premeditated murder. These guardians INTENTIONALLY allow their wards to be harmed, drugged, isolated. Any and all medical research on elders show that medicating with anti-psychotic drugs, including anti-depressants and pain medications, which causes PERMANENT neurological damage to the elder. These meds speed up the process of confusion and forgetfulness, which is one of the reasons they can't speak for themselves.

Here in Florida, and across the nation, they have tried to push for mini-cams on police officers b/c of the violence. I think that we HAVE to push for legislation to have these in nursing home facilities as well...24 HOURS a day/7 days a week!!!

It is also a LAW that regardless of capacity, the individual giving the medication to the elder has to let them know what they are taking. I have witnessed SO MANY times, where the person just gave me the meds and said, "give this to her" and walked away.

I fought four years to even be able to see my mom FOUR hours a week. I consider myself lucky to have this. Now, I am dealing with so much other stuff and the grief of losing her.

Thank you for reading.

Teresa

UP TO 80 PER CENT OF DEMENTIA PATIENTS IN AGED CARE FACILITIES RESTRAINED WITH PSYCHOTROPIC DRUGS: REPORT

By: Steve Cannane Updated Wed 26 Mar 2014, 6:10 p.m. AEDT Lateline

A new study produced by Alzheimer's Australia suggests up to 80 per cent of dementia patients in aged care facilities are being treated with psycho-tropic drugs.

The report, to be released today, suggests only one in five dementia patients receive any benefit from taking such medication.

Alzheimer's Australia says the use of drugs in nursing homes is excessive and it has called for reform of the sector.

Lateline previously revealed that up to 6,000 elderly Australians could be dying prematurely each year because of the misuse of psychotropic drugs in aged care facilities.

Psychotropic drugs are psychiatric medicines that alter chemical levels in the brain, affecting mood and behaviour.

Anti-depressants, anti-anxiety medications and ADHA drugs are some examples.

Alzheimer's Australia chief executive Glenn Rees says about 140,000 nursing home residents are being sedated and restrained with psychotropic drugs.

"For people with dementia in residential care—and remember that people with dementia account for 50 per cent of residents—about 80 per cent will be on restraint at some time or other," he said.

"Restraint can be necessary and as an organisation we accept that physical restraint in some circumstances and medical restraint are necessary, but we think it should be the last resort, not the first resort."

But the aged care industry argues it has been following the advice of medical professionals.

"It's not the aged care facility that does the diagnosis nor prescribes the medication," said Patrick Reid, the chief executive of Leading Age Services Australia.

"They're acting on the...information from the clinical pathway, from a doctor."

But Mr. Rees says there are alternatives to medication.

"There are a number of things that can be done to reduce restraint," he said.

"One is to adapt the physical environment so it's less confusing and less noisy. Another is to give a person activities and a sense of purpose in life, whether it's rehabilitation, social activities, physical recreation.

"Another is to adopt person-centred care approaches so that the care staff can relate better to the individual and know their personal histories."

Mr. Reid says the industry is open to change.

"Any changes to environment, whether it be the built environment, the culture and other things, are important," he said.

"Certainly many of the refurbishments we are seeing in aged care, about 60 per cent of new buildings are around improving that environment. So I think it is a positive.

"My members do embrace those approaches and are trying very hard to make sure everyone is treated as well as they can be, and with their dignity and respect."

A Senate committee has been hearing evidence about the overuse of psychotropic drugs in aged care facilities.

Nursing Home and Drug Abuse of an Elderly Man
SUNDAY, MARCH 15, 2015   T.S. Radio: Gerald's Story

Patrice Gilgan joins us this evening to expose the abuse and drugging of her father at the hands of doctors and nursing home workers in two different facilities in Orange County, California.

The first instance of abuse both physical and with drugs occurred at Irvin Cottage Board and Care where Gerald had been sent to recover from brain surgery. Gerald was drugged within 24 hours of admittance to the home with massive doses of Haldol, Seroqel and overdosed on morphine. There was no prescription for the morphine. Cottage Board and Care is operated by St Joseph Hospice, a Catholic enterprise.

At a second facility, Villa Valencia Skilled Nursing (a St Michael Hospice and another Catholic owned enterprise), Gerald was given 7 different drugs. None of these drugs were to be used on brain injured or individuals suffering from dementia. When Gerald was finally freed from this facility and hospitalized again, it took more than two weeks for him to respond due to the massive drug overload in his system.

Videos of Gerald, and of some of the abuse he endured are available on the you tube channel; Ireland Dallas.

Gerald Gilgan was a retired New York City Fire Fighter.

This man did not deserve this callous treatment. No one does. Yet it happens to the elderly every day here in the United States.

How New York's Elderly Lose Their Homes to Guardianship

By: Michael Volpe October 29, 2014   News, *Rebel Pundit*

A prominent New York attorney is caught in the middle of apparent abuses of the elderly and allegedly pilfers their estate during the guardianship process, according to relatives of victims who hope to bring exposure that will stop her actions.

Mary Giordano is a partner with the New York State law firm, Franchina and Giordano, and among her duties is that Giordano is routinely chosen by the Nassau County Superior Court system to be a guardian for elderly guardianship cases.

But two relatives involved in cases in which Giordano was a guardian say their relatives were forcibly removed from their homes, their assets plundered, and their family members had the life sucked out of them until they died depressed and isolated.

Diane Wilson found her mother Dorothy Wilson lying on the floor at her home on December 8, 2008. Advised due to long standing family disputes to enter her mother into guardianship, Wilson said by March, 2009, at the order of then Nassau Supreme Court Judge Joel Asarch was removed as guardian and instead Asarch appointed Giordano as the court appointed guardian.

As Wilson's guardian, Giordano was given power over nearly every decision in Wilson's life including how her money was spent, where she lived, and her medical care.

Giordano ordered a reverse mortgage be placed on Dorothy Wilson's home which netted about $275,000 and along with Wilson's pension of about $2,300 month, Judge Asarch claimed in court the money would last for five years. But it only lasted two years, and Diane Wilson told *Rebel Pundit* that proper accounting of the expenses were never provided by Giordano.

Worse yet, in November 2010, Wilson was tricked and forced to move out of her home and into a nursing home. "Dorothy Wilson is currently placed in the Bristal, an assisted living facility in Massapequa. She was taken there on November 3, 2010, on the pretense of having lunch, by her daughter, Candice Bruder," Diane Wilson said in a complaint to the New York State Unified Court Grievance Committee. "After she was there, she was told she was moving in there and her clothes were brought later that same day. She is not allowed to leave the Bristal at all, including Thanksgiving. The family is only permitted to go there and visit."

The elder Wilson, who was 87 at the beginning of the process, was miserable and felt like a prisoner her entire time at Bristal. "On November 15 (2010), after placing three phone calls during a 3½ hour period, I was finally able to speak with my mother. During the entire phone call her "caseworker," Tracy, sat next to her while my mother begged me to come and pick her up and take her home. She had no privacy. When I went to visit her in the evening, she cried the entire time, begging me to take her home, asking me over and over again why I never came, why no one visited her, why no one called," Diane Wilson said the same complaint. Wilson was force to stay in the facility for thirty days at a cost of $53,000, and Giordano never provided a line by line breakdown of why the costs were so high.

On August 22, 2011, on the direction of Giordano, Dorothy Wilson was again moved to Meadowbrook Care Nursing Home in Freeport, New York again against her will. On September 2, 2011, Giordano again moved Wilson into another nursing home Maria Regina Nursing Home in Brentwood, NY. Giordano also attempted to sell Wilson's house.

What followed was a series of furious court maneuvers until on October 18, 2011, Giordano resigned as guardian but still Judge Asarch kept Dorothy Wilson in the nursing home. She died there on October 23, 2011. Throughout the process Dorothy Wilson sent a series of letters to the judge begging to be allowed to be cared for by her daughter.

"It's very strange that my daughter Diane is not allowed to go into my house." Dorothy Wilson said in a letter dated October 20, 2011. "She is the only one I trust." Dorothy Wilson also made a series of You Tube videos begging to be released. "I hate it here. I want to go home." Dorothy

Wilson said while holding back tears in one You Tube video. "I feel like I'm locked up in a jail."

A call to Giordano's law firm was left unreturned. Kevin Kelly told Rebel Pundit he experienced something very similar with the guardianship of his grandfather, Richard Maass, which also started when a family dispute introduced guardianship directed again by the combination of Judge Asarch and Mary Giordano.

Kelly said his story started in 2008 when he was living in a home his grandparents owned since 1951, and helping to take care of his grandfather who had Alzheimer's after his grandmother's death in 1998. After a dispute between Kelly and one of his cousins, Judge Asarch brought in Giordano to be Maass's guardian, and the nightmare began, Kelly told Rebel Pundit.

Asarch decided that Kelly wasn't "immediate family" and forced him to move out of the home which Kelly did moving to an apartment near the home in March 2009.

In September 2009, without telling Kelly, Giordano had Maass moved out of his home and into a nursing home. Kelly said that Giordano never produced an inventory of Maass's personal property and personal items were missing in the days immediately following Maass's forced removal from his home. Kelly said in a follow up visit he noticed items missing: all of the artwork on the walls, grandfather clock, the entire crystal and china collection, two antique end tables, all of Maass's clothing, an air conditioner wall unit, a mattress, lamps, a therapeutic massage recliner and most of the assorted knickknacks accumulated by his grandparents over six decades.

Kelly said Maass was forced to live out the rest of his life in a nursing home for Jewish people even though he was Christian. He said his grandfather repeatedly expressed a desire to move back into his home but that Giordano never allowed it. According to court documents, Maass's estate was in excess of $600,000 at the time guardianship began, however at the time of his death on February 28, 2011, Kelly never received a final accounting of his grandfather's assets and he isn't sure how much if any money was left.

Worse yet, Giordano changed the date of Maass's funeral at the last minute forcing the family to scramble as many people were coming in from all over the country. A former employee, Janet Bergen, who assisted Giordano with Wilson's case, died in her forties of cancer in 2012.

Another former employee of the firm who asked to remain anonymous said that Bergen repeatedly asked to be taken off the case and felt extremely stressed over the way it was being handled. *Rebel Pundit* has confirmed that Giordano is currently being investigated for her handling of the estate of Joan Bebry, a wealthy woman who died in March 2014.

According to David Brooks spokesperson for the New York State Unified Court System discipline is done by that entity's Grievance Committee and he was unaware of any malfeasance by Giordano.

Diane Wilson filed a formal complaint with the Tenth District's Grievance Committee. According to a representative of the Grievance Committee, Giordano hasn't been disciplined. Giordano's law partner, Emily Franchina, has been on the Grievance Committee in that district since 2000.

Judge Asarch died suddenly at 60 in 2013, and according to the New York State Judicial Commission, which is in charge of discipline for judges, Judge Asarch's record is also clean, though Wilson also filed a formal complaint with the New York State Judicial Commission. Giordano continues to assign guardians.

FBI RAIDS RESIDENCE OF NURSING HOME CEO
By: Madeline Buckley, The Indianapolis Star 3:19 p.m. EDT September 15, 2015

CARMEL, Ind. —A cadre of agents, including personnel from the FBI, IRS and the Office of the Inspector General, raided the home of an executive of a chain of nursing homes Tuesday morning.

The home is owned by James G. Burkhart, the CEO of American Senior Communities, according to Hamilton County property records.

"The FBI is conducting an investigation into criminal activity in the Carmel area," FBI spokeswoman Wendy Osborne told *The Indianapolis Star.* She declined to provided any details.

An FBI truck was parked in the front drive of the red-brick, 9,000-square-foot house in the Claybridge at Springmill subdivision of million-dollar homes. A Carmel Police Department vehicle sat in front of the home.

Investigators from multiple agencies, including the FBI, Office of the Inspector General and the Internal Revenue Service, worked inside and outside of the home, carrying papers and folders between the residence and the truck late Tuesday morning.

The subdivision is full of sprawling, stately homes, set far back from the residential streets. The neighborhood was mostly quiet Tuesday, with a few walkers and joggers occasionally passing and looking on curiously.

The Office of Inspector General for the US Department of Health and Human Services participated in Tuesday's raid, but a spokeswoman said she could not provide any details about the raid or what might have been seized. The office investigates allegations or suspicions of fraud, waste and abuse in federal health care programs like Medicare and Medicaid.

The Southside Indianapolis headquarters of American Senior Communities was open Tuesday, with FBI investigators at the facility, according to WXIN-TV, Indianapolis.

A receptionist took down phone numbers, but declined to comment. No comment has come from American Senior Communities officials.

American Senior Communities has nearly 100 facilities, with many located in Central Indiana. The company's frequent television ads salute the accomplishments of elderly nursing home residents.

Burkhart and his wife, Angela, have been contributors to Republican and Democratic candidates, according to campaign records. He is a member of the Eskenazi Health Foundation Board and a trustee at Brebeuf Jesuit Preparatory School.

In 2010, American Senior Communities agreed to pay $376,432 in penalties to settle a complaint that it employed seven workers who were ineligible under federal rules for reasons including the loss of licenses and a criminal conviction.

American Senior Communities operates a chain of nursing homes owned by Marion County Health and Hospital Corp.

Indiana Health Care Association, which represents nursing homes in Indiana, released a statement Tuesday, saying they were still gathering information on the raid. "Right now, our most important priority is the care of the Hoosiers in our 330 member centers across the state," the statement read.

ATLANTIC COUNTY LAWYER, BUSINESS WOMAN STOLE MONEY FROM ELDERLY, BOUGHT LUXURIOUS CARS, CONDO: ATTORNEY GENERAL

By: Jessica Beym | *South Jersey Times*

March 20, 2014 at 12:02 p.m., updated March 20, 2014 at 1:34 p.m.

Express Times photo

A prominent Atlantic County lawyer and the owner of an in-home senior care company are among four women accused of stealing millions of dollars from elderly clients.

Attorney Barbara Lieberman, 62, of Northfield, and Jan Van Holt, 57, of Linwood allegedly stole more than $2 million from at least 10 victims. They are charged with money laundering, conspiracy and theft by deception, authorities said.

Lieberman was arrested at her home on Northwood Court. Search warrants were executed there and at her Northfield law office. Bail was set at $300,000 full cash and about $5 million in her assets was frozen.

Holt, the owner of "A Better Choice," a company that claimed to offer seniors "custom designed life care and legal financial planning," was arrested at her home on West Vernon Avenue. Bail was set at $300,000 full cash.

Sondra Steen, 58, of Linwood and Susan Hamlett, 55, of Egg Harbor Township were each charged with theft by deception in connection with the alleged scheme.

Steen is Van Holt's sister, and Hamlett worked for "A Better Choice" as an aide for elderly clients, Acting New Jersey Attorney General John J. Hoffman said.

Authorities allege the women targeted elderly clients with substantial assets who typically did not have any immediate family, offering them non-medical care and assistance, including financial and legal services. They allegedly forged a power of attorney, added their names to the victims' bank accounts or transferred the victims' funds into new accounts they controlled. Holt then used that money to buy two Mercedes, a condo in Florida, pool supplies and health care for her pets. Lieberman allegedly used the money to pay off credit card debt.

The women allegedly went so far as to handle the wills of the elderly in order to continue to steal from their estates after they died.

Nine of the 10 victims have died since the scheme began, Hoffman said.

"These women allegedly preyed ruthlessly on elderly clients, most of whom were facing the end of life without family and with only their savings to ensure they would be cared for properly," Hoffman said. "We're supposed to honor our elders, but these women heartlessly exploited them, allegedly stripping them of their life savings and their ability to live out their final days in comfort, peace and dignity."

Hoffman added that anyone who thinks a loved one has been victimized by the four accused should call the state Division of Criminal Justice toll-free tipline at **1-866-TIPS-4CJ**.

The investigation of the alleged thefts is ongoing, the Attorney General said.

CHAPTER 4

How to Extricate yourself from the Racket

• • •

Trust, wills, durable power of attorney and other legal documents gen-erally associated with protecting an individual and/or family can easily be circumvented by corrupt judges and your entire estate can be looted as noted in earlier articles. Samples of these documents are provided for your review with family and professional servers to have safeguards inserted into standard wording. When family members are in disagree-ment about inheritance, the risks are greater that a family member will sabotage the estate by seeking guardianship through legal professionals who are more than willing to help as long as they get their share of the loot.

REVOCABLE LIVING TRUST AGREEMENT

Known as_____

This Living Trust agreement is made and executed this_____d a y
of _____
20_____ in the (city)_____
State of _____
By and between
Name_____
Address_____
And

Name_____

Address_____

(Hereinafter referred to as "Grantors"), and

Name_____

Address_____

Name_____

Address_____

(hereinafter referred to as "Trustees").

If the above-named Trustees should be unable to serve due to death or incapacity, Grantors name as Successor Trustee _____

Residing at_____

With all the rights and duties as stated herein.

BENEFICIARY(s)

Except as otherwise provided herein, upon the death of the Grantors, the beneficiaries of the Trust are the following:

Name of Beneficiaries   Name of Beneficiaries

_____   _____

_____   _____

2. ASSETS OF THE TRUST

All rights, titles, and interest in and to all real and personal property, tangible or intangible, financial accounts, and securities listed on the attached Schedule A are hereby assigned, conveyed and delivered to the Trustees for inclusion in this Trust.

After death of the Grantors, all assets of the Trust must be distributed among the Beneficiaries of this Trust in accordance with Schedule B of this Trust Agreement. Additional property may be conveyed to the Trust at any time.

3. AUTHORITY, RIGHTS AND POWER OF GRANTORS

The Grantors of the Trust shall have the following authority, rights and power:

(a) The Grantor reserves unto himself (herself) the authority and right to revoke, amend or modify this Trust at any time. No prior notice to or consent of any Beneficiary or the Trustee shall be required.

(b) The Grantor may at any time appoint, substitute or otherwise change the Trustee or Successor Trustee under the Trust hereby created. No prior notice to or consent of any such Trustee or Beneficiary is required.

(c) The Grantor may at any time designate a new beneficiary, without prior notice or consent of a previous Beneficiary.

(d) During the lifetime of the Grantor, the Trustee shall pay exclusively to the Grantor all the income accrued from the Trust property.

(e) During his (her) lifetime, the Grantor may at any time withdraw all or any part of the principal of this Trust, free of Trust, by delivering an instrument in writing duly signed by him/her to the Trustee, describing the property or portion thereof desired to be withdrawn. Upon receipt of such instrument, the Trustee shall thereupon convey and deliver to the Grantor the property described in the instrument.

(f) The Grantor, in his/her capacity as Trustee, shall be empowered with the discretionary authority to mortgage, or encumber with a lien or in any other way, all or any part of the Trust property.

(g) The interests of the Grantor shall be considered primary and superior to the interests of any Beneficiary.

(h)

4. POWERS OF TRUSTEES

In the administration of any property, real or personal, at any time forming a part of this trust estate, including accumulated income, and in the administration of any trust created hereunder, the Trustee(s) shall have all discretionary powers deemed necessary and appropriate to administer this Trust, including, but not limited to, the power to buy, sell, trade, encumber, deal, mortgage, pledge, lease or improve the Trust property.

Additional powers of Trustee(s) are listed next.

5. PAYMENTS OF DEBTS

Upon the death of the grantor, the Trustee may pay from the principal of the Trust Estate the amount of any estate or death taxes imposed under the laws of any jurisdiction by reason of the Grantor's death, whether in respect of property passing under this Agreement or the Grantor's last will and testament or otherwise, and the amount of all debts which the Grantor's estate must pay, the expenses of his illness and funeral, as well as expenses of administering his estate.

6. DISTRIBUTIONS TO MINORS OR INCOMPETENTS

In THE EVENT THAT THE Trustees are authorized or directed by any provision of this Agreement to pay or distribute income or principal to any person who is a minor or incompetent, the Trustees, at their discretion and authorization, may pay or dispense all or any part of such income or principal to such minor or incompetent personally (specific directions given).

7. DISABILITY OF GRANTOR

In the event that the Grantor, in his capacity as Trustee, has become disabled, and is unable or incompetent to properly manage his affairs due to his illness or mental or physical disability, the surviving co-trustee shall continue as the sole Trustee with full authority to exercise all of the powers and rights accorded to a Trustee under this Trust.

8. AUTHORITY OF SUCCESSOR TRUSTEE

The Successor Trustee, upon either the death or Grantors, or the death of surviving Trustee, or incapacity of Co-Trustees, shall assume the active administration of this Trust. Successor Trustee may pay or apply so much or all of the net income and the principal of the Trust Estate as the Successor Trustee deems necessary or advisable for the health, education, maintenance or support of the Grantors and their children, in such amounts and proportions as the Successor Trustee may determine. The Successor Trustee also may pay any gift taxes and income taxes incurred by the Grantors, whether caused by the sale of any assets of the Trust Estate or otherwise. Any income not so paid or applied shall be accumulated and added to the principal of this trust at least quarter-annually.

The successor Trustee's authority and power may be subsequently terminated by the Grantors without prior notice to Successor Trustee, when the Grantors are sufficiently recovered from the medical o mental condition that had prevented them from administering the Trust.

Additional sections of a Revocable Living Trust Agreement are as follows:

9. AUTHORITY OF SUCCESSOR TRUSTEE TO CONTINUE TRUST
10. INALIENABILITY OF BENEFICIARY'S INTEREST IN TRUST
11. BENEFICIARY'S PROPORTIONATE LIABILITY FOR ESTATE TAXES
12. SAVING CLAUSE
13. CONSTRUCTION (where the parties certify, sign, have witnessed and acknowledged by a notary)

The Trust contains Schedules—each section requires that it be acknowledged by a notary.:

A. SCHEDULE OF ASSETS
B. SCHEDULE OF BENEFICIARIES AND DISTRIBUTIVE ASSETS
   Deed of Realty to Trust
   Financial Account(s) Transfer to Trust
   Securities Transfer to Trust (Stocks, Bonds, other)
   Business Interest Transfer to Trust
   Chattel Transfer to Trust

AMENDMENT TO TRUST

LAST WILL AND TESTAMENT OF

_____

I, _____, of the City of _____, _____ County
and State of_____, being of full age, sound mind and memory, and
under no restraint, do hereby publish this, my Last Will and Testament,
revoking all others heretofore made by me.

I.

I hereby order and direct that all of my just debts and funeral expenses be
paid as soon as is practicable after my death. I wish to be _____
and my remains taken to _____

II.

I give, devise and bequeath my entire estate, whether real, personal or
mixed, of every kind, nature and description whatsoever and wheresoever
situated, which I may now own or hereinafter acquire, or have the right
to dispose of at the time of my decease, to _____,
absolutely and in fee simple.

III.

Should, however, _____ predecease me in point of time,
then in any of such events, Item II of this, my Last Will and Testament,
shall fail and become inoperative, and in that event, I give, devise and
bequeath my entire estate, both real and personal, as follows: _____
_____.

IV.

I hereby nominate and appoint _____, as Executor
of this, my Last Will and Testament, and require that no bond be giv-
en by him/her. If he/she does not so act, for any reason, I direct that
_____ take the position of Executor and be so appoint-
ed. I hereby direct that no bond be required of either of said persons in
that capacity.

V.

I empower personal representatives of this will or successors in that capacity to sell, lease or mortgage any property, real or personal, publicly or privately, without an order of the Court or without notice to anyone, upon such terms and conditions as shall seem best to said personal representative and without liability on the part of any purchaser, tenant, or mortgagee to see to the application of the consideration, permit any of the beneficiaries named herein to enjoy the use in kind, during probate of this will, of any tangible personal property without liability on the part of said personal representative for any injury to, consumption of, or loss of any such property so used; and to settle, compromise, or pay any claims, including taxes, asserted in favor of or against me or my estate. The beneficiaries or their personal representatives shall not be liable for any unintentional, non-negligent injury to, consumption of, or loss of any such property so used; and to settle, compromise, or pay any claims, including taxes, asserted in favor of or against me or my estate. The beneficiaries or their personal representatives shall not be liable for any unintentional, non-negligent injury to, consumption of, or loss of any property used as provided herein.

Name:_____

In witness whereof, I have hereunto set my hand at

_____, this_____

day of _____20 _____.

_____

Notary

_____   _____

Witness   Date

_____   _____

Witness   Date

DURABLE GENERAL POWER OF ATTORNEY

I, the undersigned principal, _____, currently residing at _____, hereby appoint _____ _____ (Agent), currently residing in _____, as my attorney-in-fact, hereby granting the Agent full power and authority, as though the Agent were the absolute owner of my assets and liabilities, to perform those acts for me and in my name, place, and stead as expressly provided below as fully as I could perform if personally present and not disabled, incapacitated or incompetent.

This power shall include, but not be limited to the power to ask, demand, sue for, recover, collect and receive all sums of money, debts, accounts, legacies, bequests, interests, dividends, annuities owing and payable or belonging to me, and to take all lawful means for the recovery thereof, and further to lease, let, demise, bargain, sell, release, convey, mortgage and/or hypothecate real and/or personal property, upon such terms and conditions as said attorney-in-fact shall deem advisable, and to make assignments, hypothecations or pledges thereof, and to make, execute, or exercise in my behalf any disclaimers of property in whole or in part, and to do any other acts or execute any other instruments as may be necessary or proper in the premises.

The laws of the State of _____ shall govern this power of attorney in all respects, and I hereby state that this power of attorney shall not be affected by my mental or physical disability.

Furthermore, the agent attorney-in-fact named herein shall have full power to provide for my support, maintenance and health in the event of such disability or incapacity.

My agent attorney-in-fact shall have the authority regarding my person to make all decisions that a court-appointed guardian of the person would have authority to make under the laws of the State of _____, to make all decisions relating to the nature of my health care and to provide informed consent, if required, for such health care decisions on my behalf.

I hereby expressly grant to _____, residing in _____, as an alternative attorney-in-fact, the same powers granted to _____, such powers to be exercised by him in the event that _____, waives or relinquishes such powers hereunder or is unable to act as such attorney-in-fact.

All persons dealing with my agent, attorney-in-fact, are entitled to rely on the apparent authority of the attorney-in-fact, unless they have actual knowledge of invalidity in the execution or the revocation of this Power, or of the termination of this Power by my death.

Dated this _____ day of _____, 20_____

Name_____

SUBSCRIBED AND SWORN TO before me this _____ day of _____, 20_____

_____

NOTARY PUBLIC in and for the State of,

_____

residing at_____.

My commission expires_____.

This is one attorney's explanation of how people can avoid guardianship problems if they have their durable power of attorney, will and trust in order.

This is not always true as indicated in the article that follows.

Avoiding the Guardianship Nightmare

By: Donna Ennis, Elder Law Assistant   May 20, 2014

Let's explore the facts about guardianship and ways to avoid this nightmare for ourselves and our loved ones.

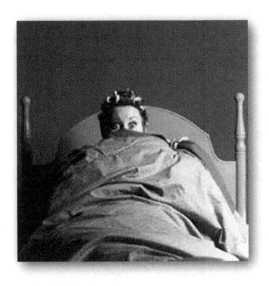

INCAPACITY AND GUARDIANSHIP

The term incapacity, according to the laws of most states means, "an adult whose ability to receive and evaluate information and to communicate decisions in any way is impaired to such a significant extent that he is partially or totally unable to manage his financial resources or to meet essential requirements for his physical health and safety. *Note:* a person can make foolish or irresponsible decisions and not be deemed Incapacitated; they must be incapable of making sound decisions. When an adult is deemed to be an *Incapacitated Person,* (sometimes referred to as *the Ward*), and that person has not previously appointed an agent to manage their affairs by way of legal documents including Durable Financial Powers of Attorney and/or Health Care Durable Powers of Attorney (or Health Care Proxies as referred to in some states), a court must be enlisted to appoint a substitute decision maker called a *Guardian,* (in some states called a *Conservator*).

Such a Guardian is only appointed after the *Petitioner* (a person who wishes to have the Guardianship established) institutes a court proceeding wherein expert witnesses testify as to the alleged Incapacitated Adult's capacity. Most states will ensure that the alleged incapacitated person also has an attorney representing their interests since the loss of independence is taken seriously by the courts. If they cannot afford to hire an attorney the court will have one appointed.

Who Can Be a Guardian?

The guardian can be any competent adult—a member of the incapacitated person's family, a friend or even a professional guardian (an unrelated person who has received special training). The guardian need not be a person at all—it can be a non-profit agency or a public or private corporation. In naming someone to serve as a guardian, courts will usually try to choose close family members—people who know the incapacitated person well and are aware of and sensitive to the incapacitated person's needs and preferences. If two individuals wish to share guardianship duties, courts can name co-guardians.

What is the Guardian's Role?

Once appointed, the Guardian has the legal responsibility to take care of the affairs of the incapacitated person in accordance with the court order establishing the guardianship. The court order can authorize the Guardian to make legal, financial, and health care decisions for the Incapacitated person. This may include where the Incapacitated person should reside and what medical care he or she should receive. Since every incapacitated person has varying levels of capacity a court will generally favor *limited guardianships* where only specified areas of decision making are granted to the Guardian. In other words, the guardian may exercise only those rights that have been removed from the Incapacitated person and delegated to the guardian. If the Guardian seeks to make any decision not authorized in the initial court order, the guardian must return to court for approval of these decisions.

Guardians are expected to act in the best interests of the Incapacitated person, but **given the guardian's often broad authority, there is the potential for abuse.** For this reason, courts hold guardians accountable for their actions to ensure that they don't take advantage of or neglect the Incapacitated person.

REPORTING REQUIREMENTS

One of the ways the courts hold Guardian's accountable is by requiring annual reporting. A Guardian of the property must marshal the Incapacitated person's property, use prudence in investing the Incapacitated person's funds so that they can be used for the Incapacitated person's support, and file regular, detailed reports (usually annually) with the court. Many states also require Guardians to report on the incapacitated person's status. Guardians must provide details about the incapacitated person's residential arrangements, health care and treatment, social activities and educational and training programs. Guardians who do not adequately care for the incapacitated person may be removed and replaced by the court.

ALTERNATIVES TO GUARDIANSHIP

As mentioned earlier, because guardianship involves a profound loss of independence, state laws require that guardianship be imposed only when less restrictive alternatives are lacking. Less restrictive alternatives that should be considered before pursuing guardianship include:

1. ***Durable Financial Powers of Attorney:*** A document granting legal rights and powers by a person (the principal) to another (the agent or attorney-in-fact). The attorney-in-fact, in effect, stands in the shoes of the principal and acts for him or her on financial and business matters. In most cases, even when the power of attorney is immediately effective, the principal does not intend for it to be used unless and until he or she becomes incapacitated. **Note: this document would have to be prepared and signed by the incapacitated person prior to becoming incapacitated.**

2. ***Health Care Durable Powers of Attorney (or Health Care Proxy):*** A document granting a person (the principal) to another (the agent or attorney-in-fact) to act for him or her on medical matters and treatment decisions. **Note that this document would have to be prepared and signed by the incapacitated person prior to becoming incapacitated.**

3. ***Representative or Protective Payee:*** A person appointed to manage Social Security, Veterans' Administration, Railroad Retirement, welfare or other state or federal benefits or entitlement program payments on behalf of an individual.

4. ***Conservatorship:*** In some states this proceeding can be voluntary, where the person needing assistance with finances petitions the probate court to appoint a specific person (the conservator) to manage his or her financial affairs. The court must determine that the conservatee is unable to manage his or her own financial affairs, but nevertheless has the capacity to make the decision to have a conservator appointed to handle his or her affairs.

5. ***Revocable Trust:*** *In some states, and under some specific circumstances,* a revocable or *living* trust is a tool set up to hold an older person's assets, with a relative, friend or financial institution serving as trustee. Alternatively, the older person can be a co-trustee of the trust with another individual who will take over the duties of trustee should the older person become incapacitated.

So, as you can see, not having the appropriate documents in place before a person becomes incapacitated can lead to a nightmare situation for his loved ones if they are suddenly faced with having to put a Guardian in place all of a sudden.

SACRAMENTO ELDER LAW ATTORNEY DELBERT JOE MODLIN CHARGED WITH FINANCIAL ELDER ABUSE
By: Marjie Lundstrom

A Sacramento attorney whose website extols his expertise in "championing the elderly and ensuring they are not taken advantage of" was arraigned

Thursday on felony charges of financial elder abuse, grand theft and securities fraud.

Attorney Delbert Joe Modlin, 63, who was being held on $500,000 bail since his arrest Tuesday, agreed to stop practicing law and seeing clients until the criminal proceedings are complete. In exchange, bail was reduced to $100,000 for the attorney, who has been licensed to practice law in California since 1987.

Modlin's appearance in an orange jumpsuit in Sacramento Superior Court, and his identification as a lawyer, drew gasps and whispered comments from audience members. He did not enter a plea Thursday.

Modlin already faces criminal charges in Placer County, where he was accused in 2011 of defrauding a frail, elderly couple from Auburn and selling their home and assets without their approval.

Both criminal cases were filed by the California attorney general's Bureau of Medi-Cal Fraud and Elder Abuse.

Prosecutor Steven Muni said after the hearing that his boss, Attorney General Kamala Harris, is committed to "protecting elderly victims, who are some of our most vulnerable citizens.

"There are many ways to commit elder abuse," said Muni. "But no one, not even an attorney, is exempt."

This article helps explain to the reader how these types of crimes can be easily done by sociopaths. Go back to the Salem Witch Trials, which is another classic way of taking someone's property. Guardianship was used on the American Indians to take their property. Nazi Germany used excuses to take property from Jews and others. We know from "Operation Paperclip" millions of Nazis came into the United States by using fake IDs. The syndicated crime of professional guardianship fraud needs people who know how to fence jewelry, fine art, cars and to help in the sale of business assets, homes, land, stocks, etc. This is organized crime in its most venal state.

INSIDE THE MIND OF A SOCIOPATH

This excerpt is from: "The Sociopath Next Door: The Ruthless vs. the Rest of Us" by Martha Stout Ph.D. (Broadway Books, New York, 2005, ISBN 0-7679-1581-X). Martha Stout is a clinical instructor at Harvard Medical School and elaborates on the tales of ruthlessness in everyday life based on her 25 years of practice as a specialist in the treatment of psychological trauma survivors.

Imagine - if you can - not having a conscience, none at all, no feelings of guilt or remorse no matter what you do, no limiting sense of concern of the well-being of strangers, friends, or even family members. Imagine no struggles with shame, not a single one in your whole life, no matter what kind of selfish, lazy, harmful, or immoral action you had taken. And pretend that the concept of responsibility is unknown to you, except as a burden others seem to accept without question, like gullible fools. Now add to this strange fantasy the ability to conceal from other people that your psychological makeup is radically different from theirs. Since everyone simply assumes that conscience is universal among human beings, hiding the fact that you are conscience-free is nearly effortless. You are not held back from any of your desires by guilt or shame, and you are never confronted by others for your cold-bloodedness. The ice water in your veins is so bizarre, so completely outside of their personal experience that they seldom even guess at your condition.

In other words, you are completely free of internal restraints, and your unhampered liberty to do just as you please, with no pangs of conscience, is conveniently invisible to the world. ***You can do anything at all***, and still your strange advantage over the majority of people, who are kept in line by their consciences, will most likely remain undiscovered.

How will you live your life? What will you do with your huge and secret advantage, and with the corresponding handicap of other people (conscience)? The answer will depend largely on just what your desires happen to be, because people are not all the same. Even the profoundly unscrupulous are not all the same. Some people - whether they have a conscience or not - favor the ease of inertia, while others are filled with dreams and wild ambitions. Some human beings are brilliant and talented, some are dull-witted, and most, conscience or not, are somewhere in between. There are violent people and non-violent ones, individuals who are motivated by blood lust and those who have no such appetites.

Maybe you are someone who craves money and power, and though you have no vestige of conscience, you do have a magnificent IQ. You have the driving nature and the intellectual capacity to pursue tremendous wealth and influence, and you are in no way moved by the nagging voice of conscience that prevents other people from doing everything and anything they have to do to succeed. You choose business, politics, the law, banking or international development, or any of a broad array of other power professions, and you pursue your career with a cold passion that tolerates none of the usual moral or legal encumbrances. When it is expedient, you doctor the accounting and shred the evidence, you stab your employees and your clients (or your constituency) in the back, marry for money, tell lethal premeditated lies to people who trust you, attempt to ruin colleagues who are powerful or eloquent, and simply steamroll over groups who are dependent and voiceless. And all of this you do with the exquisite freedom that results from having no conscience whatsoever.

You become unimaginably, unassailably, and maybe even globally successful. Why not? With your big brain, and no conscience to rein in your schemes, *you can do anything at all.*

Or no - let us say you are not quite such a person. You are ambitious, yes, and in the name of success you are willing to do all manner of things that people with conscience would never consider, but you are not an intellectually gifted individual. Your intelligence is above average perhaps, and people think of you as smart, maybe even very smart. But you know in your heart of hearts that you do not have the cognitive wherewithal, or the creativity, to reach the careening heights of power you secretly dreams about, and this makes you resentful of the world at large, and envious of the people around you.

As this sort of person, you ensconce yourself in a niche, or maybe a series of niches, in which you can have some amount of control over small numbers of people. These situations satisfy a little of your desire for power, although you are chronically aggravated at not having more. It chafes to be so free of the ridiculous inner voices that inhibit others from achieving great power, without having enough talent to pursue the ultimate successes yourself. Sometimes you fall into sulky, rageful moods caused by a frustration that no one but you understands.

But you do enjoy jobs that afford you a certain undersupervised control over a few individuals or small groups, preferably people and groups who are relatively helpless or in some way vulnerable. You are a teacher or a psychotherapist, a divorce lawyer or a high school coach. Or maybe you are a consultant of some kind, a broker or a gallery owner or a human services director. Or maybe you do not have a paid position and are instead the president of your condominium association, or a volunteer hospital worker, or a parent. Whatever your job, you manipulate and bully the people who are under your thumb, as often and as outrageously as you can without getting fired or held accountable. You do this for its own sake, even when it serves no purpose except to give you a thrill. Making people jump means you have power - or this is the way you see it - and bullying provides you with an adrenaline rush. It is fun.

Maybe you cannot be a CEO of a multinational corporation, but you can frighten a few people, or cause them to scurry around like chickens, or steal from them, or - maybe, best of all - create situations that cause them to feel bad about themselves. And this is power, especially when the people you manipulate are superior to you in some way. Most invigorating of all is to bring down people who are smarter or more accomplished than you, or perhaps classier, more attractive or popular or morally admirable. This is not only good fun; it is existential vengeance. And without a conscience, it is amazingly easy to do. You quietly lie to the boss or to the boss's boss, cry some crocodile tears, or sabotage a coworker's project, or gaslight a patient (or child), bait people with promises, or provide a little misinformation that will never be traced back to you.

Or now let us say you are a person who has a proclivity for violence or for seeing violence done. You simply murder your coworker, or have her murdered - or your boss, or your ex-spouse, or your wealthy lover's spouse, or anyone else who bothers you. You have to be careful, because if you slip up, you may be caught and punished by the system. But you will never be confronted by your conscience, because you have no conscience. If you decide to kill, the only difficulties will be the external ones. Nothing inside you will ever protest.

Provided you are not forcibly stopped, *you can do anything at all.* If you are born at the right time, with some access to family fortune, and you have a special talent for whipping up other people's hatred and sense of deprivation, you can arrange to kill large numbers of unsuspecting people. With enough money, you can accomplish this from far away, and you can sit back safely and watch in satisfaction. In fact, terrorism (done from a distance) is the ideal occupation for a person who is possessed of blood lust and no conscience, because if you do it just right, you may be able to make a whole nation jump. And if that is not power, what is?

Or let us imagine the opposite extreme: You have no interest in power. To the contrary, you are the sort of person who really does not want much of anything. Your only real ambition is not to have to exert yourself to get by. You do not want to work like everyone else does. Without a conscience, you can nap or pursue your hobbies or watch television or just hang out somewhere all day long. Living a bit on the fringes, and with some handouts from relatives and friends, you can do this indefinitely. People may whisper to one another that you are an underachiever, or that you are depressed, a sad case, or, in contrast, if they get angry, they may grumble that you are lazy. When they get to know you better, and get really angry, they may scream at you and call you a loser, a bum. But it will never occur to them that you literally do not have a conscience, that in such a fundamental way, your very mind is not the same as theirs.

The panicked feeling of a guilty conscience never squeezes at your heart or wakes you in the night. Despite your lifestyle, you never feel irresponsible, neglectful or so much as embarrassed, although for the sake of appearances, sometimes you pretend that you do. For example, if you are a decent observer of people and what they react to, you may adopt a lifeless facial expression, say how ashamed of your life you are, and talk about how rotten you feel. This you do only because it is more convenient to have people think you are depressed than it is to have them shouting at you all the time, or insisting that you get a job.

You notice that people who do have a conscience feel guilty when they harangue someone they believe to be "depressed" or "troubled." As a matter of fact, to you further advantage, they often feel obliged to take care of such a person. If, despite your relative poverty, you can manage to get yourself into a sexual relationship with someone, this person - who does not suspect what you are really like - may feel particularly obligated. And since all you want is not to have to work, your financier does not have to be especially rich, just relatively conscience-bound.

I trust that imagining yourself as any of these people feels insane to you, because such people are insane, dangerously so. Insane but real - they even have a label. Many mental health professionals refer to the condition of little or no conscience as "anti-social personality disorder," a non-correctable disfigurement of character that is now thought to be present in about 4 percent of the population - that is to say, one in twenty-five people. This condition of missing conscience is called by other names, too, most often "sociopathy," or the somewhat more familiar term *psychopathy*. Guiltlessness was in fact the first personality disorder to be recognized by psychiatry, and terms that have been used at times over the past century include *manie sans délire, psychopathic inferiority, moral insanity,* and *moral imbecility*.

The possibility of guardianship fraud is a situation where even the most dysfunctional families have much to gain by pre-planning and making certain that all family members have an awareness and acceptance of inheritance. If one family member seeks guardianship of an elderly parent without other family members' knowledge, it can lead to heartbreaking consequences described in this book.

Experts advise senior citizens in any community to stay close to a group of other retirees for protection, and even this can have drawbacks. Once in guardianship, there is practically no escape except perhaps to have family members bring their whole church or employees in their business or all of the neighbors into the courtroom along with reporters. Do not count on an attorney to be of help; even a close friend who is your attorney may betray you.

Considerations to Avoid the Pitfalls of Guardianship Fraud
By: M Larsen

Judges disregard curable powers of attorneys—the single most important document each of us can create to determine our care should we become incapacitated. Judges ignore our lists of pre-selected surrogate decision-makers. The current system does not work. This reality is most apparent when a wealthy individual falls victim to these involuntary proceedings and his or her wealth becomes a ripe plum to be shared by the Judge's favorites. **– Diane G. Armstrong, Ph.D., excerpt of prepared statement before the US Senate's Special Committee on Aging, February, 2003.**

Here we are in 2016 and nothing has been done; it's only worse if that's possible. You become a *Non Person* under guardianship. Relatives and friends may not be allowed to see you. You may be chemically restrained until all the funds are gone, and then you may be drugged even more. Your family and friends will probably be sued if they try to help. They will be accused of committing evil acts against you, which a Judge will dutifully note on your case records. They may be allowed to see you if they pay extra money to do so and only at a certain time and on a certain day.

You may have a slip-and-fall and while you are resting in the hospital, you may become a ward of the state without your consent, without your family's knowledge, and your house will be sold before anyone knows. Does this really happen you ask? Every day. And the reason it's called

THE PERFECT CRIME is because there is nothing you can do about it—for the most part.

The conversations to avoid the dilemma of guardianship are needed immediately with family and friends. Not that any of this is guaranteed to work, but it does call for talks with family and financial advisors regarding this specific problem. And if you're alone in this world, one suggestion is to talk to a religious society you trust or a charity such as United Ways and indicate that part of your estate will go to them should you have this problem, with the caveat that their attorneys will fight for your life (and of course their share of your estate). Make sure your home is in a trust, recorded at the County Recorder's Office, and for extra safety put the trust into an LLC. Again, a Judge with the wave of his pen can change and undo it all—but it gives you and your family more of a chance to not be "selected."

Baby Boomers need to realize that hundreds are signing up to be guardians all the time; they may be seeking a wave of newfound wealth—YOURS.

Typically, Adult Protective Services (APS) is called when there are allegations of abuse. This can initiate a guardianship that was not intended by a family member. Once the court is involved, the family may be in over their head. Elder Americans need to stay connected to senior centers and family so they are not alone, because isolated individuals fall prey to exploitation. The other side of that is that the elderly are more easily identifiable among profiteers who are increasingly networking to gain new clients.

"They are scouting candidates who are aged 65 and older at senior centers, hospitals, retirement homes, clinics, banks and estate planning offices," said Debby Valdez, president of Guardianship Reform Advocates for the Disabled and Elderly in San Antonio, Texas.

Hospital nurses can best tell you about the dangers of being treated without a caring advocate involved. The psychic exam prepared for the purpose of establishing diminished capacity and the need for a guardian can be written at the request of a family member or even a stranger wanting to do the looting. They can even dictate what they want said in the report, which usually follows the victim being chemically restrained and unable to answer questions themselves.

You may be thinking at this point, "Well, my attorney will protect me." Please think again. Attorneys are "ethically" prohibited by the American Bar Association of saying anything bad about another attorney. Many attorneys who have spoken out against this evil practice have been disbarred. We are talking about attorneys who lie, cheat, steal and murder—will your attorney protect them? You bet, and they know it.

Is there any in-fighting in your family, or are family members estranged? It's worth everything in the world to you, literally it is a life and death matter to you, to do whatever is necessary to heal these wounds. And for those family members who think they can profit by gaining guardianship at the expense of other family members—you don't stand a chance against the professionals!

The National Association to Stop Guardianship Abuse has documented hundreds of cases in which family members are denied any say in their loved ones' care. After the estate is sucked dry, the wards are often dumped onto Medicaid rolls—if they're still alive. Barbara F. Hollingsworth, <u>The Examiner.</u>

In the end, the best guard against this truly evil crime is to spread the word. Write your legislator, congressman, senator, and governor. Discuss this at investment clubs, churches and synagogues, public meetings, neighborhood gatherings, and anywhere else where you encounter other people. Most of all, talk to your professional servers and point blank ask them about this crime. Most people are honest, caring and value their reputation and value your business. On the other hand, one in twenty-five people is a sociopath who believes they have the right to your wealth, and that your life is unimportant.

This article gives instructions that should be part of filling out a Will, Trust, and Durable Power of Attorney.

How To Avoid Probate Court
By: Kristi Hood, Author of *PROBATE PIRATES*

It is extremely important that we do everything we can to protect our loved ones so they will not be taken advantage of by lawyers, judges or professional guardians as well as relatives or neighbors. Many people find their loved ones, especially those who are suffering from dementia or any other illness, being used and abused.

Many family members file lawsuits alleging elder abuse because one of their loved ones may have been tricked into signing an agreement they did not understand. The only way to fight this is pre-active action. There are few things as dangerous to the public as a lawyer seduced by money, and instead of helping clients, rips them off," Los Angeles-based attorney Lori Meloch firmly maintains.

Unfortunately for our elders, all the lawyers that were once referred to as "ambulance chasers" have now gravitated to the new legal money pit, estate and probate law. The reason? 1 in 5 people in America is now over the age of 60. People are living longer and a far greater percentage of the population will need some type of supported decision making and care in their later years.

Make no mistake, in my experience, for most of the probate litigators it is all about the money all the time. It's not about protecting your elders or safeguarding your family money. The game is rigged from the judge to the lawyers, to medical professionals down to the paid professional guardian for the sole purpose of lining their pockets and extracting every dime possible.

Once you hire a lawyer and are in probate court there is not much anyone can do to help you. You are now in guardianship court hell. In most cases there is just no way to win. Let me repeat that. There is no way to win.

In my father's case it took 5 years, $200,000.00 and three judges to insure my father's golden years were spent with family. In most cases elders end up isolated, medicated and their estates gone. If I had not taken the case public I believe we would have lost him. In many cases the price tag is much higher and the result is death.

The following is an outline on the only way to stay out of court and keep the lawyers from depleting not just the elders estate but family members money as well. Let's be clear. If you end up in court it's an automatic loss for everyone but the lawyers. This is how I now protect my elderly relatives and keep them out of probate court. It's not easy, quick or cheap... but from personal experience I know it works. It worked in my own with family feud and kept a nursing home from filing for guardianship.

1. Call the probate court to get the name of a court approved doctor, and then get a letter of competence from said doctor.
2. Within a period of 60 days go to an estate planning lawyer and got the following documents drawn up. The 60 day time frame is very important.
   a. <u>A Will</u>. Please make sure the lawyer puts in a clause that states that if anyone fights the will OR you letter of future incapacity they will be cut out of will. (They like to forget to tell you this point so that it can be fought in court.)
   b. <u>A Durable Power of Attorney naming the person you trust most</u>. But do not give it to your trusted person. Keep it yourself possession but tell the person named in the document where they can find it something happens to you. You do not want a POA floating around the universe until it is needed.
   c. <u>A letter of future incapacity naming the person you want to take care of you if something happens</u>. In your letter of future incapacity state that if anyone fights your choice, they are cut out of the will.

    d. <u>A trust</u>…if needed. In the trust state that if anyone fights who controls the trust they are out of the trust.

3. Make a video record of you end of life wishes.

    a. Buy or rent a video camera, or hire a videographer.

    b. Gather everyone who could possibly want your assets or could possibly want to be the one caring for you in a room.

    c. Speak to the camera. Write a script of includes the following information.

        (a) Give the date of the recording.

        (b) Your name

        (c) The name of everyone in the room

        (d) State that you are not drunk, on any medication that would cause you to be incompetent and that you have a letter from a court approved doctor stating you are competent that is less than 60 days old.

    d. Point the camera at every person in the room. Make a list of question and ask them the following questions.

        (a) Ask them their name, their relationship to you and the date.

        (b) Ask them if they believe that you are not drunk, on drugs and are competent.

        (c) If anyone won't do it…tell them they are out of the will and to leave the room. They will do it. The only ones that might refuse are the ones you need to worry about. If you value your freedom and dignity you have to stand tough.

4. Read the letter of future incapacity into the video camera.

5. Have plenty of food and drink available while you are reading the document.

6. After everyone leaves read the will and if needed the trust into the camera.

7. Don't leave out a single element. Every detail is important, even the date.

8. Make a DVD copy of the letter incapacity only portion of the recording for everyone in the room.
9. Make 5 extra copies for yourself to put in a safety deposit box and have a trusted friend hold at least one copy for you.
10. Don't give it to a lawyer. It will get "lost". Many lawyers advise against making these video. It's my belief this is because the video makes it difficult for a lawyer defraud his client.
11. The purpose of making this video is to keep your own family members or anyone from forcing you into a guardianship in probate court.

Trust, it all comes down to trust. There is a misplaced trust in the probate courts of the U.S. Families who have issues as to who will control and care for their elder or disabled sibling are unwisely trusting the courts to figure out the truth and make a decision between rival petitioners for guardianship. Why is it unwise? The court will almost never pick one family member over another. Instead they will hire a <u>Paid Professional Guardian</u> to take over the elder or disabled person's life. Why is this the pattern in a majority of the cases where family squabbles in up in probate court?

It started in 2001 when a lawyer who was the president of the *National Association of Guardians* stated traveling around the county to judge's conventions and told judges that they didn't have to make the hard decisions any more. There was now a third alternative that would not only let them sleep at night but would reward their cronies.

By 2005 many states, with the unlawful lobbying of judges, rushed to write new laws based on this "third party" guardianship that was intended to protect our most vulnerable from abuse. Instead, the new laws created a new billion dollar industry called <u>Certified Guardianship</u> and made the judges jobs much easier.

I ask you to trust the following. Judges never believe either side of a family fight. Judges don't want to hear about the he said she said. Judges don't know or care to get to know the details about any elder or disabled person's case. Judges could care less if the law doesn't agree with what they want to do. They feel no obligation to follow the law. If they get over-turned by a higher court for acting "unlawfully" that's okay, the next time their legislators meet they well just get the law changed once again so they can do as they like. Judges will pick the stranger over a family member just to get the fighting to stop.

Your only defense is to stay out of probate court. Probate Pirates will plunder the estate and turn your loved one over to a paid stranger.

Did I mention that you can't win? The reason? All the laws in probate court have been written by lawyers, for lawyers. Not the elder, the lawyers. The minute you file a motion in probate court to ask for guardianship of an elder you just started an income stream for:

1. Your lawyer
2. A guardian Ad litem
3. An Attorney Ad litem
4. At least one doctor (maybe more).
    That's if you are an only child and no one is contesting the guardianship.
    In a contested guardianship add the following:
5. The other side's lawyer
6. Security of costs -- a large cash deposit upfront in case you lose and you have to pay the other sides attorney's fees. (Also known as "pay to play.")
7. A paid professional guardian or fiduciary (If you take the family feud to court chances are that neither of you will win financial guardianship of the elder.)
8. he paid professional guardian's lawyer.

Now you would think that you would only be responsible for your own lawyer's fees. Unfortunately that is not true.

The lawyers have gotten laws passed that insure they get paid one way or another.

Unfortunately, this happens far too often now as more adults are seeing a decrease in their mental ability. Unfortunately, many elders are taken advantage of by people who are closest to them, including their caretakers, children, friends, and other relatives.

LAST BUT NOT LEAST: It is important to always have your estate planning documents in order so you will not be taken advantage of when you are older and your mental capacity becomes limited.

CHAPTER 5

Legislators, Law Enforcement, Medical Personnel, Attorneys, and other Professionals: A New System is Needed

• • •

Brooke Astor is a well-publicized example of betrayal by both family and professional servers. Her son, Anthony Marshall, was an attorney, decorated Marine, and US Ambassador. He was convicted of looting his mother's fortune and sentenced to two years in prison.

ANTHONY MARSHALL, CONVICTED OF LOOTING MOTHER BROOKE ASTOR'S FORTUNE, DEAD AT NINETY: LAWYER

THE ONLY CHILD OF THE legendary philanthropist was convicted of changing her will to steal $185 million. His wife, Charlene, published a farewell for the former US Marine and diplomat—but made no mention of his mother or his two children, who heard about his death through media reports.

By: Shayna Jacobs, Corky Siemaszko NEW YORK DAILY NEWS
Updated: Tuesday, December 2, 2014, 12:15 a.m.

ANTHONY MARSHALL, THE ONLY CHILD OF THE LEGENDARY
PHILANTHROPIST BROOKE ASTOR, SPENT TIME IN PRISON FOR ALLEGEDLY
STEALING MILLIONS OF DOLLARS FROM HIS MOTHER'S FORTUNE.
Anthony Marshall, who plundered his mother Brooke Astor's fortune and forced the beloved philanthropist to spend her final years languishing on a urine-stained couch, is dead at age 90.

Marshall, who suffered from Parkinson's and congestive heart failure, died early Sunday at New York-Presbyterian Hospital, his defense attorney Ken Warner said Monday.

In a paid obituary for the former Marine and diplomat, Marshall's wife, Charlene, called him "a very great man."

It ended with the widow declaring, "Semper Fi my Tonyness, Your beloved Charlene."

Nowhere in the obituary, which appeared in *The New York Times*, was there any mention of Astor; Marshall's twin sons, Alexander and Philip, or the scandal that ruined her husband's reputation.

Instead, Charlene Marshall listed the stepchildren and step-grandchildren "who showered him with love," mentioned that Marshall fought at Iwo Jima in World War II and was awarded a Purple Heart, and traced his diplomatic career.

MARSHALL WAS CONVICTED OF SWINDLING MILLIONS OF DOLLARS FROM HIS PHILANTHROPIST MOTHER BROOKE ASTOR, WHO DIED AFTER SUFFERING FROM ALZHEIMER'S DISEASE.

Marshall, she wrote, "had the tenderest of hearts, a brilliant mind and an outrageous sense of humor."

Philip Marshall, whose elder abuse accusations against his father led to the investigation that resulted in Marshall's conviction last year for defrauding Astor's $185 million estate, said Charlene made no attempt to contact him.

"The fact I first heard the sad news of my father's death from the press speaks volumes about the devastating effect elder abuse can have on families," Philip Marshall said in a statement to the Daily News.

Brooke Astor died in 2007 at 105.

And the six-month trial of Marshall and his lawyer pal Francis Morrissey stripped the veneer off one of New York's most famous blue blood families.

ANTHONY MARSHALL AND HIS WIFE CHARLENE LEAVE THEIR HOME AFTER HIS MOTHER, LEGENDARY PHILANTHROPIST BROOKE ASTOR, DIED IN 2007. They were convicted of swiping $60 million—money that was earmarked for charity—from a then-101-year-old Astor by getting the Alzheimer's-afflicted grande dame to sign will updates.

The allegations were astonishing. Astor was considered the first lady of New York philanthropy, and was known for always being proper, and looking and dressing her best.

She was awarded the nation's highest civilian honor, the Presidential Medal of Freedom, by President Bill Clinton in 1998.

But in the years that followed, her son cut back on her care, convincing her she was going broke, prosecutors said.

While Astor lived in a filthy Park Ave. duplex and slept in a dirty nightgown, Marshall blew his mother's dough on his third wife, Charlene.

FORMER PRESIDENT BILL CLINTON IS SEEN WITH BROOKE ASTOR.
He denied any wrongdoing and was eventually sentenced to one to three years in prison. He was sprung for medical reasons after serving just three months.

He spent his final months with Charlene in their Upper East Side townhouse.

In a statement, Warner said Marshall died "knowing he was deeply loved by his wife, Charlene, who as always was at his side."

"In the end I hope he is remembered for his integrity and decency, not for the injustices he suffered," Warner said.

This article describes professional guardianship kidnapping. August 30, 2016, the court-appointed Emergency Temporary Guardian abducted Lillie from her doctor's office while her niece was in the other room filling out papers.

Is Elder Guardianship A New Form Of Human Trafficking?

By: Dr. Terri Kennedy President, Power Living Enterprises, Inc. 9/13/16

As the 71st session of the General Assembly of the United Nations begins to discuss international issues that affect the lives of millions throughout the world, the United States needs to step up its commitment to safeguard human rights and promote the rule of law in its own backyard- specifically, escalating abuse in the U.S. Elder Guardianship system.

It's legal, but is it right?

Imagine you've worked hard all of your life and suddenly you are deemed incapacitated and are stripped of your dignity and basic individual rights. You have been abducted from your home, isolated from your family, and "placed" somewhere to be medicated while your assets are being pillaged. The authorities that should be protecting you are the ones committing these heinous acts. It sounds like Nazi Germany, but this is happening in the United States today.

The victims are seniors. The partners in crime are financial predators and agents of the Elder Guardianship system — attorneys, professional guardians, medical experts, and others who are paid out of the senior's assets. There are some good judges but many are overworked and some are actively aiding the exploitation. Anyone can file to deem you incapacitated. The entire process from filing an incapacity petition to plenary guardianship where all rights are removed can happen within days. Yet, once you're caught in the web, it's almost impossible to break free... AND you are forced to pay your abusers in the process.

A 2013 AARP report gave a "best guess" estimate of the number of adults under guardianship nationally at 1.5 million. Idaho and Minnesota are the only states that track the amount of money being controlled by guardians or conservators; the combined total for just two states is over $1 billion. *Guardianship is supposed to protect older citizens. However, what happens when the system is broken?* A 2010 federal study by the U.S. Government Accountability Office (GAO) identified hundreds of allegations of physical abuse, neglect and financial exploitation by guardians in 45 states and the District of Columbia between 1990 and 2010. In 20 cases, the GAO found that guardians stole or improperly obtained $5.4 million in assets from 158 incapacitated victims.

THE ABDUCTION OF LILLIE

Tuesday, September 6, 2016 was Lillie's 88th birthday and her family didn't know where she was. A week earlier, on August 30, the court-appointed Emergency Temporary Guardian abducted her from a doctor's office while her niece was in the other room filling out papers. Although Lillie was happy and safe in her Palm Coast home of twenty years, the guardian "placed" her into assisted living and refused to tell her family the location. Lillie was not in danger and there was no emergency situation or other credible justification of such extreme and deceptive action. Video of Lillie from July 30, 2016 — just a month before — shows a vibrant African-American woman enjoying her home and family, and vocal about her financial affairs and this case. In fact, she does not seem incapacitated at all.

Since the case started in 2012, three good doctor's reports that could have given Lillie her rights back went stale through a legal shell game of loopholes, frivolous objections and unethical behavior. Now, while she is sequestered and possibly sedated, they are pushing hard for plenary guardianship, which would take away her last two remaining rights: the right to vote (she is a registered Democrat excited about voting for Hillary Clinton) and the right to choose with whom she socializes. Over a dozen attorneys and others have been invoicing against Lillie's assets, while the temporary guardian has not paid Lillie's basic bills or given her a penny of her *own* money for food or personal living expenses. The temporary guardian has been neglecting her fiduciary responsibilities and violating standards of practice, but Lillie's sister and over 50 nieces and nephews are the ones being shut out.

The sudden manner by which Lillie was involuntarily placed in an anonymous location and isolated from her family and support system was likely traumatizing to her particularly given her past victimization. The initial evaluation for incapacity happened in 2012 when she was held captive for eight months at the home of a family friend. She eventually called 911 and escaped. Now, after five years of systemic abuse, Lillie is being violated again — this time by the temporary guardian who is supposed to be her advocate. *Getting old is not a crime, yet Lillie is being treated like a criminal.* Tonight, she is somewhere alone in assisted living probably wondering why her family has abandoned her.

Captors use social isolation to torture prisoners of war. Social isolation of otherwise healthy, well-functioning individuals eventually results in psychological and physical disintegration, and even death. Nevertheless, the Emergency Motions filed in court to get Lillie returned to her home and family have been ignored.

Florida's "Liquidate, Isolate, Medicate"

In Florida, there are 5 million people age 60 and older and that demographic is expected to account for most of the state's population growth in the next 15 years. Yet, seniors who have come to this retirement haven are actively being deprived of life, liberty and property without due process of law. The guardianship system oversteps constitutional rights and goes against the Equal Protection Clause of the 14th Amendment that forbids states from discriminating invidiously against some of their citizens.

Professional guardianship is considered a "growth business," with the number increasing from 12 registered professional guardians in 2003 to 456 in 2015, according to the Florida Department of Elder Affairs. The abuse is so rampant that the process itself has been called "Liquidate, Isolate, Medicate." With 40 hours of training and a modest background check, a professional guardian can start earning $85 an hour and have control over a ward's property, finances, medical decisions, housing and social relationships. In other words, the guardian has the ability to: *liquidate* your assets by selling your home, car, etc.; *isolate* you from your family as guardian of "your person;" and put you in a nursing home to *medicate* you until you die. All of this is supposed to be in your "best interest." An ABC13 Investigates report dubbed it "The Grey Prison."

For example, 89-year-old Marie, featured in the *Sarasota Herald-Tribune*'s Elder guardianship: A well-oiled machine, had her rights removed at the request of her stepson-in law. The court ordered a trust company to pay out some $635,000 to attorneys, guardians and other involved in her case. She survived wartime Poland and said even Hitler's Germany failed to prepare her for this travesty. Republican member of the Florida House of Representatives Larry Ahern said, "In extreme cases, the wards are sometimes prevented from regaining their competency and remain, in effect, prisoners of guardians." How many seniors, like Lillie and Marie, are being exploited in this cruel and systemic manner?

Due to a string of horror stories and rising complaints, on March 10, 2016 Governor Rick Scott signed into law Senate Bill 232 creating the Office of Public & Professional Guardians to replace the Statewide Public Guardianship Office within the Florida Department of Elder Affairs. In April, they initiated rule making procedures to address the regulation of professional guardians, including standards of practice and disciplinary guidelines. These are expected to be in place October 2016. While these necessary changes are underway, what happens to seniors, like Lillie and Marie, who are being victimized *this moment* in Florida? Will they get a pardon and be set free?

A NEW FORM OF HUMAN TRAFFICKING?

According to the United Nations Office on Drugs and Crime, Article 3, paragraph (a) of the Protocol to Prevent, Suppress and Punish Trafficking in Persons defines Trafficking in Persons as the "recruitment, transportation, transfer, harbouring or receipt of persons, by means of the threat or use of force or other forms of coercion, of abduction, of fraud, of deception, of the abuse of power or of a position of vulnerability or of the giving or receiving of payments or benefits to achieve the consent of a person having control over another person, for the purpose of exploitation. Exploitation shall include, at a minimum, the exploitation of the prostitution of others or other forms of sexual exploitation, forced labour or services, slavery or practices similar to slavery, servitude or the removal of organs."

Trafficking involves psychological coercion to render someone a slave. To do this, perpetrators employ "tactics that can lead to the psychological consequence of learned helplessness for the victims, where they sense that they no longer have any autonomy or control over their lives. Traffickers may hold their victims captive, expose them to large amounts of alcohol or use drugs, keep them in isolation, or withhold food or sleep. During this time the victim often begins to feel the onset of depression, guilt and self-blame, anger and rage, and sleep disturbances, PTSD, numbing, and extreme stress. Under these pressures, the victim can fall into the hopeless mental state of learned helplessness."

An argument can be made that the "Liquidate, Isolate, Medicate" Elder Guardianship process in Florida at its worse is a form of human trafficking. On the basis of the definition, it is evident that trafficking in persons has three constituent elements: a) The Act (What is done) — In this case, the transfer and harbouring of a person, b) The Means (How it is done) — Abduction, deception, abuse of power or vulnerability, and c) The Purpose (Why it is done) - In the case of guardianships, the purpose is financial exploitation — a form of servitude. Seniors are sedated in locked assisted living facilities while their assets are spent down.

THE RIGHT TO BE PROTECTED & RESPECTED

Probably the most famous case of financial elder abuse is that of one-time New York socialite Brooke Astor when she was more than 100 years old. Her grandson Philip C. Marshall testified against his father and helped put him in jail. In his 2015 testimony to the Senate's Special Committee on Aging, Mr. Marshall said, "To be complacent about elder justice is to be complicit in elder abuse."

Given demographic trends, elder financial abuse is expected to grow dramatically unless we do something. The baby boom generation is reaching retirement age at a rate of 10,000 people per day. Those 65+ will make up 20% of the population by 2050. The 2015 White House Conference on Aging has made "elder justice" one of its four tracks. There is now a federal home for Adult Protective Services and a new Elder Justice website called a "one-stop shopping site for victims, families, prosecutors, researchers and practitioners." President Barack Obama declared June 15, 2016 as World Elder Abuse Awareness Day.

Awareness is good, but immediate action is needed. If states are not doing their jobs, the federal government needs to step in. It's time to reform the Elder Guardianship system in the U.S., prosecute predators and hold legal agents — judges, attorneys, evaluators, professional guardians, etc. — to a higher standard. As Vice President Hubert Humphrey said, "The moral test of government is how that government treats those who are in the dawn of life, the children; those who are in the twilight of life, the elderly; those who are in the shadows of life — the sick, the needy and the handicapped."

Just as we continue to make strides with human rights issues around the world, we need to shine a brighter light on elder abuse on our soil — particularly this type of vicious and systemic financial exploitation. To be an elder is a privilege, not a condition causing you to be tossed aside and abused. Our elders need to be protected and respected. If we're lucky, we will all get old. Let's create a society where we can age with grace and dignity.

Teresa Kay-Aba Kennedy is a Harvard Business School-trained strategist and President of Power Living Enterprises, Inc. Her mission is to raise the consciousness of the planet and create a more sustainable world by releasing the potential in individuals. A seasoned life coach/speaker and founder of the first yoga studio in Harlem, she has been featured on the cover of Yoga Journal, in Oprah's book, Live Your Best Life!, and was selected as a World Economic Forum Young Global Leader. An early Internet pioneer and TV executive, she has advised billion-dollar companies on their multi-platform engagement strategies. Her latest award-winning book — co-authored with her mother Columbia University-trained journalist Janie Sykes-Kennedy — is Dancing Light: The Spiritual Side of Being Through the Eyes of a Modern Yoga Master on her teacher/mentor 98-year-old yoga master Tao Porchon-Lynch.

On June 20, 2016, Kennedy moderated a conversation with Tao Porchon-Lynch at the United Nations for International Day of Yoga on "Yoga for the Achievement of the Sustainable Development Goals." On October 3, 2016, for International Day of Non-Violence, she will facilitate a conversation with Ms. Porchon-Lynch on Mahatma Gandhi and Dr. Martin Luther King, Jr. hosted by the Indian Consulate in New York. On November 19, 2016, she will moderate another discussion with Ms. Porchon-Lynch at the United Nations for Women's Entrepreneurship Day.

Note: Kennedy is the niece of Lillie featured in this article. As of September 13, 2016, Lillie's family still does not know where she is and the temporary guardian refuses to tell them. For more, go to www.elderdignity.org. Watch the video and let us know what you think. For specific questions or suggestions, email elderdignity@hotmail.com.

The public is picking up the tab when lawsuits are successful against corrupt public officials. The public also picks up the tab when a wealthy person is stripped of their assets and dumped into a public care facility until they die.

Lyon County to Pay $2.1M for Public Guardian's Theft
By: Carri Geer Thevenot *Las Vegas Review-Journal* December 18, 2015

Lyon County and former Public Administrator Richard Glover must pay $2.1 million to the heirs of a man whose Wellington home was looted after his death in May 2006, a federal jury ruled Tuesday.

"It's been a really long haul," Las Vegas resident Richard Mathis said after hearing the verdict.

The verdict stemmed from a civil rights lawsuit filed by Mathis and his two brothers, Anthony and James, who accused Glover, a public guardian who handles the affairs of people deemed mentally or physically incompetent, of illegally seizing and stealing nearly $1 million of heirlooms and other property from the home of their 85-year-old father, Joe, shortly after his death.

Anthony Mathis, who lives in Vermont, and Richard Mathis came to court Tuesday afternoon to hear the jury's verdict. Glover also came to court, but he and his attorneys declined to comment.

Later, as Richard Mathis left the federal courthouse in Las Vegas, juror Kristine Anderson approached him and said, "I hope you guys are able to move on now."

Anderson told the Review-Journal that jurors wanted to hold Lyon County accountable for failing to have written policies to guide its public administrator in overseeing assets of vulnerable wards, and for failing to protect its citizens.

"The family clearly wasn't notified that the property was going to be removed from the home," she said.

The jury's verdict included about $1.6 million in damages against Lyon County and $180,000 in damages against Glover for emotional distress, as well as about $217,00 in damages against both defendants for stolen property. In addition, the jury ordered Glover to pay $100,000 in punitive damages.

"I hope that this'll teach Lyon county not to do this to somebody again, but I don't think it will," Richard Mathis said.

The Mathis brothers had sought a $4.5 million verdict. Their attorneys argued that the stolen property included $800,000 worth of opals.

"It's hard to value property that's missing," Anthony Mathis said.

U.S. District Judge Andrew Gordon presided over the trial, which began Nov. 2.

"At its core, this case is about a Nevada county that was deliberately indifferent to the constitutional rights of its citizens," attorneys for the Mathis brothers wrote in their trial brief. "The evidence in this case shows that Lyon County has elected numerous public administrators that have overtly violated the constitutional rights of Lyon County citizens for more than a decade."

Glover was investigated but never faced criminal charges related to the missing Mathis property. However, records show he was charged with a crime in connection with the estate of Carl Liberty and pleaded guilty to a misdemeanor in 2010.

Joe Mathis' six children, including three daughters, were raised in Smith Valley, where the western Nevada town of Wellington is located.

Depression is a main cause of pseudodementia, a disorder that resembles dementia. Things as simple as not getting enough water and exercise or an anxiety attack or stroke can also lead to pseudodementia. Statistics show the number of people experiencing pseudodementia vs. dementia can be as high as 32 percent. A person diagnosed with this disorder is subject to guardianship often without a full evaluation.

REVERSIBLE COGNITIVE DISORDERS—PSEUDODEMENTIA
By: Carrie Hill, Ph.D. and Natalie Reiss, Ph.D. Updated: Jul 3rd 2008

A primary reason that accurate diagnosis is so important among people exhibiting cognitive problems is that some causes of cognitive impairment are reversible. Consider the costs—physically, emotionally, and financially—of diagnosing someone with irreversible dementia when, in fact, the problem could have been reversed. Reversible conditions creating cognitive problems include pseudodementia, medical conditions, and delirium.

PSEUDODEMENTIA
Pseudodementia is a situation where a person who has depression also has cognitive impairment that looks like dementia. Depression is a mental disorder that includes a depressed mood that lasts at least two weeks accompanied by the loss of interest or pleasure in nearly all activities, feelings of

guilt or suicidality, social withdrawal, and sleep and appetite disturbances. Depression can also create cognitive symptoms such as difficulty thinking clearly, problems concentrating, and difficulty making decisions. For more detailed information about the symptoms of depression, please click here to visit our associated topic center. Pseudodementia is not permanent; once a person's depression is successfully treated, his or her cognitive symptoms will go away as well.

DIAGNOSIS

Estimates suggest that between 2% and 32% of older individuals who experience cognitive problems actually have pseudodementia. However, this number may not be completely accurate, because it is often tricky to distinguish between depression and dementia in older adults. A thorough clinical interview can reveal important clues about the proper diagnosis. For instance, while people with depression may complain of having memory problems and appear upset about them, they will usually perform well on objective neuropsychological tests of memory administered in a clinician's office. On the other hand, individuals with dementia will often deny having any problems with memory or minimize their importance, and display impairment on neuropsychological tests.

The Geriatric Depression Scale (GDS) (described in an earlier section is often used to help differentiate between pseudodementia and other forms of dementia. Results from the GDS are combined other information about a person's history and current functioning to help with diagnosis. For example, people with pseudodementia typically do not have a history of mood swings (unless they have Bipolar Disorder, an illness characterized by repetitive swings in mood and energy levels) and are likely to score high (high = more depressed) on the GDS. In contrast, people with dementia usually show a range of emotions, sometimes responding to situations with an inappropriate emotion (e.g., laughing while others are sad).

A MENTAL HEALTH EXPERT'S PRIMER ON ASSESSING AND TREATING A LOVED ONE WITH DELIRIUM
By Jo-Ann Marks Special to the Arizona Daily Star

Brief reactive psychosis better describes what hospital patients display when we (family & visitors) and medical staff see a change in behavior. The "simple" test used in this article (CAM — Confusion Assessment Method) is something many of us could not pass on a good day, nor does it address the cause of the confusion.

Psychosis is a change in the way the patient experiences their environment. Psychotic features are seeing, hearing, smelling, feeling or thinking that seems odd and not verifiable to the observer. Just being in the hospital is cause for psychotic symptoms and add the physical reason for hospitalization — they're enough to unbalance anyone's normal functioning.

So please don't become overly concerned by the onset of the psychotic symptoms. It is more important to backtrack to that point where the psychosis began.

Typical causes for psychotic features (changes in the five senses and thinking) are: medicine reactions or interactions, the trauma of the injury no matter how small, and new people (doctors, nurses, techs, housing keeping, social workers, etc.,) who keep bombarding the patient with the same set of questions is enough to make anyone feel a loss of reality as well as moving patient to diagnostic rooms for "more tests" or for hospital convenience. Constant taking of blood and vitals is very intrusive to the patient even if deemed essential, which I sometimes doubt. Waking a patient up to do these tests is nuts. No one likes being awoken by a stranger. Monitors exist that can do all this automatically.

I am in total agreement that if your loved one does not need round-the-clock medical supervision, opt to take them home with visiting nurses if necessary. Coming home will eliminate 50 percent of the symptoms once a patient is in a reliable environment with outsiders kept to a minimum.

Every time my husband was hospitalized, he would call me in the middle of the night to tell me the staff was trying to kill him and I needed to get him out of there. Nurses would follow up with apology calls, but I would advise to always allow him to call whenever he needed reassurance.

My husband believed the Japanese were attacking him, was unable to recognize his daughters at times, believed the hospital was poisoning him, and threw a plate of food across the room to show his unhappiness with his predicament. All disturbances in his five senses and thinking. Believe it or not, medical personnel are not competent to make psychiatric diagnoses. They do not have the training, education or experience. Ask for a psych consult if you are concerned.

I am thankful for hospitals and medical professionals; however, the experience of the patient is rarely the focus of their care. They think nothing of letting an intern examine (question and poke) your loved one so they can gain experience. I say, go experiment on someone else.

It is up to the family to monitor the intrusions during the patients hospital stay to lessen the psychosis. Ask about why the patient is on all these meds. Does he really need a stool softener or sedative? Anti-anxiety meds can often have the reverse effect, causing the patient to be confused or agitated. After ingesting Ativan, my mother started talking in Italian, returning to childhood, asking my dad who I was. By the way, I requested the Ativan.

Other things that can cause psychotic symptoms are a low hematocrit (low red blood cells), low potassium/minerals or adjustment to the medical condition that resulted in hospitalization can cause interruption in the normal brain chemistry functioning.

Ask for a comprehensive blood panel that includes all measures of vital elements.

An experienced psychology professional can do wonders to help you through the maze of hospitalization symptoms. As with this article, psychiatric and mental health professionals are rarely consulted for their expert advice when they are the best prepared to assess and diagnose these psychiatric symptoms.

Jo-Ann Marks is an licensed psychotherapist with 25 years diagnosing and treating serious mental illnesses.

The court commissioner mentioned in the next two articles often teaches Washington State Bar Association CLE classes. Commissioners, judges, and attorneys involved inthis racketeering enterprise often teach continuing education classes to send a clear and chilling message to honest attorneys not to buck the system. It's also a signal that the corruption goes all the way up.

LEGISLATION NEEDED TO FIGHT ELDER ABUSE AND GUARDIANSHIP FRAUD
By: Anthony Domanico, NJ 2014

As we consider all of our blessings living in the United States, one of the greatest is our civil rights. We're witnessing a disenfranchisement of those rights through legal manipulation, overmedication, and isolation that perhaps can be lessened through legislation.

Improved legislation on behalf of alleged vulnerable adults and guardianship reform is needed. Currently, the supervisory boards in many states are for-profit guardianship firms that write the regulations that legislators apply toward sanctions against guardianship firms, courts, and attorneys who all may financially benefit from guardianship fraud.

Guardianship fraud is a multibillion-dollar industry, often carried out by the legal system and affecting the lives of approximately five million seniors a year.

Under court-ordered guardianship in most states, the alleged vulnerable adults lose all civil rights and essentially face civil/legal death. They cannot vote, marry, contract, divorce, decide where they live, what medical care they can get, what drugs they can take or refuse to take, and even if or when they will die. All of these decisions are assigned to a stranger, in most cases, who will run the person's life. The alleged vulnerable adult loses complete control of her or his money and property. Current laws in some states pronounce that a death certificate of a person declared an alleged vulnerable adult can only state the death is by natural cause.

An example as reported in *The Seattle Times* is a matter regarding Guardian Services of Seattle (GSS), the largest for-profit guardianship firm in the state of Washington. They obtained $82 million when a client with severe bipolar disorder was pronounced to have a "sound mind" by the GSS psychiatrist so he could change his will, leaving his entire estate to a GSS foundation. He died unexpectedly at the age of 52. His death announcement was not posted in the newspaper. The family sued, and GSS settled out of court.

The National Association to Stop Guardian Abuse also mentions GSS in the Stamm v. Guardianship Services of Seattle—Reply Brief by attorney Margaret Dore. Ms. Dore stated in her brief: "It is undisputed that GSS submitted a false statement under oath to obtain the discharge of Mr. Stamm's attorney. In Kuvara, the attorney who engaged in similar conduct was disbarred. GSS committed other breaches of duty, many of which are established as a matter of law. GSS's fees should be disallowed in their entirety. Otherwise, the wrong message will be sent." Ms. Dore was able to get Mr. Stamm released from guardianship.

This case is noted because no sanctions were brought against GSS. Commissioner Velategui, who hears most of the cases for GSS, has himself been written up by *The Seattle Times* and in numerous Internet articles. One especially notable article is entitled "A Horrifying Thought, Junk Justice and Judicial Serpents," and it states, "The victims of this judicial sham have done as I've done—reported the judicial malfeasance to the commissions required to monitor the judiciary, asked the Attorney General's office to investigate this court supported crime, reported to the ACLU, to AARP, the Adult Protective Service of DSHS, the police—all with the same result—nothing."

The Seattle Times noted in articles that Commissioner Velategui sealed many of his guardianship cases that were related to apparent misconduct such as noted in the above article by Dr. Woodhull. In one guardianship case, the wife brought a case against her husband's trusted friends. A GAL was called because the attorney told the court in a petition against the friends that her husband had been *diagnosed with dementia several years earlier.* At the hearing, the attorney told Commissioner Velategui that the actual baseline *neuropsychological evaluation had been done the day prior to the hearing and wasn't available.* Instead of dismissing the case, Commissioner Velategui ordered a GAL to intervene. This same alleged vulnerable adult had filed for divorce from his wife and inherited a substantial fortune. It can only be guessed that because the GAL realized the circumstances, she recommended that he retain the right to vote, which she stated on the front of her report. GSS gave the wife full rights to her husband, she kept visitors from seeing him, and GSS withdrew her husband's petition for divorce.

Additionally, the commissioner imposed a gag order on the friends who tried to help him that limited them from going to law enforcement or government agencies.

During the year following this man's guardianship with GSS, both the attorney for GSS and the director of GSS made false statements to the guardianship court to obtain the release of confidential papers sent to Adult Protective Services by a nurse who reviewed his neuropsychological exam and thought it was highly suspicious since there was no input by his physician, and the information about his condition was stated as inconclusive. Commissioner Velategui sealed the file. GSS went after the nurse's license to attempt to get it revoked for giving an opinion regarding the neuropsychological exam and for writing to authorities about her concerns. Because so many friends inquired about this alleged vulnerable adult's well-being, the wife changed the locks on the doors and changed the phone number to an unlisted number.

It is hoped these examples indicate that in order to curtail this multi-billion-dollar fraud against innocent Americans, legislative changes need to be made that better regulate the growing guardianship industry. Some states have already turned to CASA(Court Appointed Special Advocate) volunteers, who do not financially profit from their investigation, as a means of curtailing guardianship abuse. Since the supervisory boards in many states are for-profit guardianship firms that write the regulations, the supervisory boards need to be comprised of other agencies to safe-guard civil rights. Remember, the life you safeguard may be yours or that of a loved one down the road.

In another article from the *National Association to Stop Guardian Abuse* states:

"Once an appointment of a professional guardian has been made, the family can be completely excluded from the ward's life. Worse, if there can be a worse, the ward is completely at the mercy of the guardian for better or for worse.

People who don't understand the harm isolation can do, should spend a couple of months alone in a room with no stimulation and the only human contact (and brief words exchanged) being when someone brings a meal and picks up the tray. That experiment will give you a taste of what many under guardianship go through and what you may on day be looking forward to, if the laws are not changed."

SEQUEL TO *BARBARIANS AT THE GATE*

1. Five million elders lose their life savings, homes, etc. every single year to elder financial abuse.
2. Family members and friends perpetrate 65 percent of all elder financial abuse. Guardians and attorneys or individuals in public positions usually perpetrate the other 35 percent.
3. Law enforcement is reluctant to prosecute elder financial abuse perpetrators due to lack of funding and the fact that elders make poor witnesses.
4. Elder financial abuse is the crime of the twenty-first century.
5. It is easier to find an attorney to defend the abuser than to find one who is willing to litigate on behalf of the victim of elder financial abuse.
6. The crime of elder financial abuse is costing elders more than $2.6 billion every year.
7. Only one of every nine elder financial abuse cases is reported.
8. Of the reported elder financial abuse crimes, very few get prosecuted. The perpetrators who perpetrate this as a daily business are so slick they believe they are infallible. The family or friends

who prey on elders know that the elder will most likely never prosecute.

9. Nursing homes also commit elder financial abuse when they drug the elders and list maladies they do not actually have because there is more money in "memory care" than regular medical care. It becomes convenient for every resident to acquire Alzheimer-like symptoms through unnecessary medications. This also cuts back on the amount of staff needed, causing these homes to work "short" so the profit margin is larger.

National Association to Stop Guardian Abuse: **The Trial Lawyers Association: Holding Our Courts Hostage, State of Washington:** *"They have enough hand-picked lawyers on the Bar Associations, in the legislature, in judicial positions and on various commissions, boards and other influential positions to control the corrupt courts we are forced to endure.*

Should a citizen 'file a complaint' that complaint is heard by the very 'lawyers' that are responsible for the nature of the complaint. In other words, lawyers set the rules, interpret the rules, administer the rules, and impose penalties if they feel the rules have been broken."

This man's experience with a corrupt court sums up the experiences, the emotions, and the terribleness faced by millions of families when dealing with professional guardianship fraud.

A HORRIFYING THOUGHT JUNK JUSTICE AND JUDICIAL SERPENTS
By: Author Unknown, Washington State

The guardians are fairly easy to understand. I once spent the night in an emergency room with a police officer. As we chatted the night away, he told me about highway accidents. He said that there were many kinds of people present at serious car accidents. There were those who had skills and offered them freely to assist the injured. These are the people who pull the injured out of burning cars, who offer first aide, and who rush back with blankets and water. Then there are those who would like to help but at that moment have nothing to offer. So they stand quietly to the side waiting to see if they can help. There are also the gawkers—the somewhat immature who watch what is happening as if they were watching t.v. Lastly, there are the few, the fraction of one percent who hurry to the scene to see if there is an unattended purse or wallet, a nice watch, or anything they might have a use for. These are the guardians—opportunistic vultures. The victim is down, there's money or its equivalent to be had. This is an irresistible opportunity for this minority. They can strip the victim bare in no time and be out without being noticed in the excitement. They have no concern for the pain, fear or suffering of those they are stripping.

That image horrified me and has stayed with me all of my life. I always felt fortunate that I had never known such people—they weren't in my life—not even on the periphery. But they are in my life now. They are in all of our lives. They are the ones standing on the edges waiting for the accident that will put some unfortunate soul in their hands. They are the guardians and their sleazy attorneys, camouflaged to look like average citizens, cloaked in the attire of "professionals," and yet nastier, meaner, greedier than any nose-dripping, dirty, sick coke addict desperately looking to get the next fix. We can recognize the addicts—their appearance and surroundings often give them away—and that affords a bit of protection. But the guardians come securely wrapped in the "justice" system, they dwell in the courts. That makes them much harder to identify and gives them the benefit of the surprise attack. In the end, their crimes are even more lethal than the crimes of the neediest addicts. They represent a far greater danger to all of us.

This unmonitored program has been structured to bring the accidents right to their greedy, dirty hands. They don't have to lurk on the highway and wait. The word has gone out that they can steal with impunity, and like maggots they have come to the carcass to feast. The knowledge that there are no restraints, no laws, no accountability has attracted the least desirable of humanity—those who lower the standard of what it means to be human. A valuable item left unattended will be snatched immediately.

Even the lowest criminals, however, unlike the guardians, have a morality that prevents stripping the helpless of all that they have.

I realize that there are probably some guardians and some guardians' attorneys who are decent, law abiding, empathetic, fair people who live by the standards shared by most of us. But I can truthfully say that in five years of talking to hundreds of people state and nationwide, I have never heard of them. Not once has anyone ever praised a guardian. Not once. Nothing even close to praise.

The judiciary is a different matter. I have given a lot of thought to **Commissioner Carlos Velategui** over the last five years. I've wondered how it could matter so little to him that a court appointed guardianship and its sleazy attorney could use that appointment to exploit a woman who was unable to protect herself from their greed. The guardians are required by law to "guard" her.

The commissioner is required by law to monitor their "guarding." Yet, from our first meeting, this commissioner was determined to not to waste any time on this matter. The fact that they failed to note her mixed up medications, the fact that despite my urging and their promises, she received no physical therapy for the hip she had broken only months earlier mattered not at all to him. She is permanently in a wheelchair, a fact I attribute to their neglect. **The commissioner is free to ignore any facts that might require him to apply the law.**

When I asked him about the double charge (there were five of them) he responded with "I don't believe they double charged." However, the double charge was right in front of him, undeniably so. In the absence of any kind of explanation from the guardians, what he was really saying was that he wasn't going to be bothered with details. But those details were money my mother earned honestly and with hard work. Those details were money the guardians and their attorney did not earn. **By refusing to ask for an explanation which could be believed or not believed, the commissioner was enabling the theft of an eighty-five-year-old woman whose earning days were over and who counted on those savings to provide for the many needs she know old age would bring. If the details are time-consuming, the commissioner doesn't need to** be bothered with them even when those details would prevent some part of the theft of a vulnerable human being.

If neither the guardians nor the attorney had an answer to my complaints, the commissioner supplied one for them. His answers were insulting and unbelievably ludicrous. They are on tape. My mother was charged interest because I delayed payment while I fought the theft in court. The guardians and attorney were five weeks late in violation of a statute and a court order. That court order was issued by Commissioner Velategui himself! Believing that the court would never accept a late bill in the absence of a request for an extension, we moved her money markets accounts to cd's. When the commissioner gave blanket approval to the entire bogus bill, she lost money on the cd's. Needless to say, they were fined nothing. My mother was fined though. According to the commissioner, "they waited long enough." My mother was charged over three hundred dollars because I fought their theft in court. **The commissioner can be as biased and partial as it pleases him to be. He does not even need to try to appear to be fair or impartial.**

I lost my attorney when the guardians, knowing they would be robbing my mother, didn't want me to keep an effective attorney who knew the facts. They withdrew their waiver of his conflict. He withdrew. In retrospect, I realize that he should not have withdrawn, that once the conflict was waived, it should be waived permanently. My attorney did me a disservice. After I read the LA investigative reports, I realized that this was a part of the scam. I suspect there is a <u>Predators for Dummies </u>book out there somewhere. I went to the attorney he recommended. After hearing it was a guardianship of the person of only six weeks duration, that attorney told me "You don't want to pay me $1000 for a $1000 bill." When the bill came in for $18,000, it was so obviously bloated and dishonest that I never dreamed the commissioner would even look at it. **Logic and common sense need not be a part of the commissioner's determination.**

I was right, the commissioner never even looked at it—he just gave it his blanket approval—the whole thing—every cent. He never asked the free-loading attorney why he invited himself to every unnecessary event. He never asked the guardians if they were going to pay the attorney's obviously bogus charges if the court didn't approve them. No business could survive if they were being milked by their own attorney. They knew that his bogus charges would be dumped on my helpless mother. That fact, of course, was kept from me.

When I discovered that the guardians and their loathsome attorney had not even bothered to match their bogus charges, I brought an action for fraud. The boldness of the fraud was evidence to me of their assurance that the bill would be rubberstamped. It was evidence also of their profound contempt for the commissioner, the court, and for the judicial process. And that is to say nothing of the repeated lies, their serial perjury in the courtroom, in front of the commissioner, and in front of me. I brought a motion to vacate for fraud. I'm embarrassed to say it, but I believed the commissioner would be happy to discover his mistake and take those low class thugs off the street and away from the vulnerable.

I was wrong and those shameless guardians and their equally shameless attorney were absolutely right in their assuredness of the commissioner's corruption and his utter disregard for the law, for right and wrong, and for the responsibility of the guardians and the court to the vulnerable. **When I pointed out the theft, since he, as usual, had read nothing, he responded that I should have shown it to him earlier. But that wasn't my job. And to suggest that it is, is pure nonsense—just a way to momentarily get him off the hook. By law, he is required to monitor the guardians, not me. There was nothing to stop that judicial farce from applying the law to the guardian's and their attorney's greedy exploitation of the vulnerable woman in their care. In fact, that is exactly what the law required him to do. Needless to say, that sick man perverted the law, the intention of the law, and a glitch in the law to find that despite having POA, despite having a law degree and a license to practice in WA State which I had changed to inactive because I didn't have time to take the supplementary course work, despite the fact that for the last five years I had been my incapacitated mother's caretaker—and despite the fact that the guardians and their dishonest attorney had used a court appointment to steal from her, that farce of a commissioner used the law to satisfy his** own sick needs. **The commissioner can ignore the criminal behavior (and indeed support and encourage it) if it is committed by the side he prefers.**

He found that I was practicing law without a license, I had no standing, and a few other things that I can't bring to mind. He fined me the thieves' legal fees, about eleven thousand dollars. I paid the attorney who itemized—a mistake I will regret till the day I die. I didn't pay the other one because she pretended that she couldn't itemize due to attorney client privilege—which in this case is the community privilege of thieves. I will take to the streets before I pay a cent to that garbage. It is no different than being required to write a thank you note to a rapist. The commissioner is what many small men become—a bully. He thinks he can pervert the law to force me into silence, to force me to acquiesce to the guardians' and attorney's theft of my helpless mother, to force me to accept his sick, sick rendition of justice. People like Carlos Velategui can never bully people like me. As much as I love my mother and care about the helpless, I love, at least equally, the notions that gave rise to our "justice" system—impartiality, equality in the eyes of the law, and the rule of law. Good people can only despise what this "jurist" represents. **The commissioner ignored the law, ignored the theft, ignored his obligation to be impartial, ignored his legal responsibility to monitor the program and by doing so protect those who come into it. He used what the bar called a "glitch" in the law to serve his own sick perverse needs. He used the law as a club to assault my mother, the judicial system, and me. The commissioners "reasoning" can be a specious as he chooses and need to have no relationship to justice, to the law, to basic notions of right and wrong. It came to me, belatedly perhaps, that these guardians are judicial creations. If the judiciary weren't there ignoring their crimes, rubberstamping their theft, defending them, and punishing those who refuse to just accept that that "is just how things are" then the police would act, the APS would act, the DA's office would act, who knows, maybe even the board would act! The guardians and their attorneys would be where they belong—IN JAIL—along with, I would hope, that judicial impersonator—Carlos Velategui.**

9/11 taught us much about ourselves. Among many other things, we learned that America was not safe from attack; we learned that we and our loved ones could be the victims of outrageous plots and crimes that are incomprehensible. We learned that we are not universally loved, and often not even liked. We learned we can be hated by those we've never met. This experience with a criminal guardian and a protective judiciary is an equally horrifying 9/11.

I assumed that Velategui was a rogue commissioner, a sick little man, or a man with a Napoleon complex, or a man of perverse needs, a man on the take. I've thought and heard it all. But I have heard from many people across the nation repeating stories worse, much worse than mine. I have heard enough horrific stories to know that while he may not be the rule, Velategui is not the exception. There are many Velateguis in the probate courts of America. In New York, they were on the take. I received copies of the front page reports in N.Y. when the judges and commissioners were jailed for their part in the guardianship scam. Recently, a reader of the *Los Angeles Times* was so outraged that he suggested the judges be "lynched" for their handling of the California's conservatorships. A little extreme, perhaps, but at the very least they need to be removed from the bench. They not only harm the most helpless among us, but they make a mockery of this branch of the government.

Most guardianship programs have been given to the judiciary to monitor. Most courts simply don't have the time to really monitor. To be able to flap their wings and crow about their clean desks, these judges and commissioners have sold out justice and instead just bring out the rubber-stamp to clear off the desk. Some judges and commissioners have chosen to rely on those they know and trust—the guardians and their attorneys who come before them frequently. It's called bias, and it has no place in a courtroom. Some judges and commissioners are splitting the spoils with the guardians and their attorneys, for example, New York. No matter what the reason, the result is the same—the citizens who have paid for these courts with their wages, their trust, and in times of war, their lives and health—are getting in return, less than nothing. In Velategui's court and in the courts of others like him justice is not even a distant hope, the only laws that matter are those that serve his agenda, bias is the rule, and the whole thing cannot even rise to low level farce.

The victims of this judicial sham have done as I've done—reported the judicial malfeasance to the commissions required to monitor the judiciary, asked the Attorney General's office to investigate this court supported crime, reported to the ACLU, to AARP, the Adult Protective Service of DSHS, the police—all with the same result—NOTHING. The commissions on judicial conduct are incredibly ineffective—I'm not sure what a commissioner has to do to be rebuked, but apparently bias, ignoring the law, not reading the pleadings, the rubberstamp, the approval of the theft of the vulnerable just don't count—and they don't count in any of the states from which I've heard. The only thing that has made a difference has been media attention. If you can get the stories to the public, you can get something done. The specter of Presiding Judge Eadie hurrying to open improperly closed files is worth a good laugh. He knew those files were closed improperly, but it didn't matter until the media got ahold of it.

I just recently realized—and I do admit to a certain amount of naiveté—that if the commissioner could impose himself on the law in the manner he did—to subvert it to his needs, then what about those situations where the justices apply their judgment and not the law. I am talking about child custody, alimony (not the amount), living arrangements for children, division of property, and the list goes on and on. How many of them are sick, biased, needy individuals? Judges and commissioners have legal training. How many of them are judicial serpents, satisfying their own needs rather than the needs of justice. Their training doesn't include common sense. It doesn't include right and wrong. It doesn't include wisdom. How can such matters be put in their hands? How many of them apply their judgement to find the conclusion that suits their needs, their desires, and not the requirements of justice?

How many Americans are being shortchanged in the "halls of justice?" How many of them are going about their lives foolishly secure in the belief that should a wrong occur, the justice system will do all that the law permits to remedy the wrong, unaware that in too many courts all that can be found are judicial serpents, buffoons, and junk justice? IA small man can convert even a small power into an enormous and sickening wrong. Velategui is living proof of that.

There is no recourse from a rogue justice—none whatsoever. The SPD—Fraud Unit recognized that theft had occurred as did members of APS, and the ACLU, but they wouldn't interfere with a court order. The Commissions on Judicial Conduct throughout the United States are reportedly uniformly ineffective. The court of appeals does not address lousy judgement, nor does it address sick and biased judgment. It addresses only very specific errors of law. The lower courts can subvert justice, pervert justice, and ignore justice without committing one of those very specific errors. The notion of judicial discretion serves an important purpose as does the notion of judicial independence. But those notions are not meant to cover up lawlessness, crime, bias, or the denial of justice. **The truth is, there is no recourse. None.** All over America fine justices are making careful, wise decisions. But also, all over America, rogue justices are making nasty decisions, perverted decisions, twisted decisions and the victims have no recourse. The only people who know are those who use the services of a particular court. That ends up being a small percentage of the population. So you don't have the huge numbers that would prohibit the perversions. We know what our legislators are doing. Their records are easily available. Their activities are in the pages of our papers. But we don't know what the judges we vote for are doing unless we happened to be in his or her courtroom. If you haven't had a divorce in the last four years or adopted a child or had a property dispute, you really don't know anything. Our vote is meaningless if we don't know for whom we are voting.

If **Commissioner Carlos Velategui** can ignore and pervert the law to achieve his own ends in the ex parte department, think what a justice can do in all of the other varieties of courts across America. The judicial system is doomed if there is not a way to get the Veleteguis out of it. I would prefer to take my chances with a jury any time. It would be good to see much greater use of the jury system. The risk of catching a Velategui is simply too high. The jury system isn't perfect but you can at least count on their knowing right from wrong. If that isn't possible, then the commissions on judicial conduct have to take a much more active role in policing the judiciary. The commissions need to be composed primarily of non-legal folks. Perhaps the legal community is simply too dirty to police itself. **Judges and commissioners must be policed.** Commissions, boards, bars, are all composted of members of the legal community. Four hundred years ago, Shakespeare advised that we should "Kill all the lawyers." Every time a comic mentions attorneys, they do so with the equivalent of a finger down the throat. In four hundred years, nothing has changed. I'm not an advocate of the "Where there is smoke, there is fire," bandwagon. But where there is four hundred years of unrelenting smoke, there probably is fire. No other profession, no matter how highly paid, generates anything like the amount of contempt earned by attorneys. We have put our judicial system, our laws, our rights in the hands of the most despised profession in our country. Judges, commissioners, guardianship boards, commissions on judicial conduct, the bar are all composed in large part of attorneys. They have not policed themselves and they need to give up the pretense. It is beyond horrifying to realize that there may be thousands of Velateguis out there. For my part, I would trust a jury of my peers over any commissioner and over most of the judges I've met. In truth, I would trust a jury of ten-year olds over what I experienced in Commissioner Velategui's courtroom.

How can it be that the one place in America where it is all right to steal, to loot, to plunder the assets of another—where, in fact, the perpetrators are encouraged and even supported in the theft—is in that place formerly known as the "temple of justice" but revealed instead to be a sewer or a cesspool. Anywhere else in the world would have quick and severe consequences for theft and additional consequences for the theft of a vulnerable, defenseless human being. But in the probate courts of America, the helplessness of the victims is an added bonus. It makes the theft easier and the rubberstamp both quicker and surer.

My cats' litterboxes are cleaner than Velategui's courtroom and cleaner than most of the probate courts in America. That's outrageous! Absolutely outrageous!

Where are the presiding judges? Where are the Commissions on Judicial Conduct? Where are the state BARS? One can only assume since they, like the attorneys and judges in the probate and ex parte departments are also lawyers—they too are working their own illicit scams and certainly won't rat out peers who have created lucrative cash cows for themselves. These people share a value system almost identical to that of the lowest criminal groups, with one exception—even the most degraded criminals spit on those who chose the most vulnerable to be their victims of choice.

Only shared degeneracy can account for the absolute indifference to crimes that, when the word gets out, will horrify and infuriate decent, hard-working Americans who have EARNED, not stolen, what they have acquired. When the citizens find that there is a predatory subculture created by a lawless, valueless judiciary who are free to harvest the lifelong savings and sacrifices of those too sick to defend themselves, they will demand change. It is my hope that they will also demand accountability.

> *"Allegations of financial exploitation and abuse are rife, despite waves of overhaul efforts." WSJ*

COURT APPOINTED GUARDIAN CERTIFICATION
By: Michael Larsen

The Center for Guardian Certification/CGC is a private, non-profit organization certifying body. Once a guardian is certified, CGC oversees some guardians, and many states have separate bureaus that oversee guardianship. It was not until January 2012, CGC instituted verification of social security numbers, educational background, and felony checks on applicants and certificants. In a CGC recent newsletter under <u>New Web-Based Application and Examination Process Now Available</u>, it states: *"Now, the application process for both taking the guardianship certification examination and renewing your certification (if you are already an NCG or an NMG) is easier than ever! All applications can now be completed online and your credit card will automatically be charged. You are no longer required to seek the services of a notary for your application(s), and you won't have to cut a check or pay for postage.*" **Further down it states:** "*Practice tests will be available to you prior to the exam, so you can test the system and make sure that everything is in good working condition prior to your exam day.*"

The federal government has acknowledged court appointed guardianship abuse at least since its 1987 report by a House subcommittee of the Select Committee on Aging. The system of court appointed guardians is overseen by the family law attorney lobby, and there is a dramatic increase of people signing up to become court appointed guardians. The problems with court appointed guardians appear to be barely studied by government offices, while at the same time the severity of the problems with court appointed guardians are documented as getting much worse.

John Ahern, investigator with the Department of Health and Human Services, Government Accountability Office, has started another study of guardianship abuse (2016). GAO is reaching out to the **National Association to Stop Guardianship Abuse**, and organization that documents thousands of cases of guardianship abuse yearly, for input into his study, almost all of which are court appointed guardian cases. The guardian creates a trust account; however, trust accounts are not audited by the court. While many call for reform, because this system is open to financial abuse, it is believed by numerous families caught in guardianship financial fraud that reform will not work; the system needs to be changed.

This **WSJ** article documents two guardianship cases – one in Washington and one in Florida:

ABUSE PLAGUES SYSTEM OF LEGAL GUARDIANS FOR ADULTS

THE WALL STREET JOURNAL
By: Arian Campo-Flores, Ashby Jones

One day in March 2012, 71-year-old Linda McDowell received a knock at the door of her small Vancouver, Wash., home. Ms. McDowell needed court-appointed help, the visitor told her.

It turned out that Ms. McDowell's former housemate and companion had pushed for a court petition claiming Ms. McDowell was unable to take care of herself. The petition said Ms. McDowell had recently made an unsafe driving maneuver, had been disruptive in a doctor's office and, in a recent phone call, had seemed confused over the whereabouts of some personal papers.

Based on the motion, a judge ordered an attorney to act as a temporary guardian with control over Ms. McDowell's money and medical care. Ms. McDowell was also to pay for these services.

"I was shocked," says Ms. McDowell, who once worked as a conference manager for the National Aeronautics and Space Administration before a second career in real-estate investing. "I had never met this person, and here she was telling me I basically belonged to her."

The visit marked the start of a 30-month stretch in Washington's guardianship system that upended her life and drained much of her $700,000 in assets. People involved in her case still disagree about whether Ms. McDowell ever needed a guardian. But by the time a judge decided that one wasn't necessary, the value of her assets had dropped by about $470,000, much of which was spent on several guardians and related expenses, court and bank records show.

"My savings are gone," says Ms. McDowell, now living in a motor home near Sequim, Wash., with her dog, Sam. "They took everything."

For decades, states have granted courts the power to appoint guardians or conservators for elderly or disabled people unable to tend to their basic needs. Most appointed guardians are family members, but judges can turn to a growing industry of professional, unrelated guardians.

The caretakers' authority varies by case and jurisdiction, but often they are granted broad authority over a ward's finances, medical care and living conditions. Unlike a power of attorney, which one person can grant to another and revoke at any time, guardianship is established by a judge and can only be revoked by the court.

But guardianship systems across the country are plagued by allegations of financial exploitation and abuse, despite waves of reform efforts. As a result, critics say, many elderly people with significant assets become ensnared in a system that seems mainly to succeed at generating billings. "These laws which were designed to protect the vulnerable are being used against them to exploit them," says Dr. Sam Sugar, founder of Americans Against Abusive Probate Guardianship, an advocacy group.

Because guardianship systems vary by state and county and record-keeping systems are inconsistent, precise national data is unavailable. But the roughly 1.5 million adult guardianships in the U.S. involve an estimated $273 billion in assets, according to Anthony Palmieri, auditor for the guardianship fraud program in Palm Beach County, Fla.

According to a survey on guardianship conducted last year by the Administrative Conference of the United States, a federal agency, 64% of the 855 judges and staff who responded said their courts had taken action against at least one guardian for misconduct-related issues in the previous three years.

Guardians across the country have faced prosecution for wrongdoing in the past year. In July, Stephen Grisham, a guardian in Minneapolis, was sentenced to a year in prison and ordered to pay restitution of nearly $160,000 after pleading guilty to stealing from his wards. He is "a very good person who made a horrible mistake," says his attorney, Thomas Plunkett.

The problems are more urgent as aging baby boomers cause the population of seniors nearly to double by 2050, according to Census estimates. In New Jersey, the number of adult guardianships added annually increased 21% from 2009 to 2014, to 2,689 cases.

Guardians properly supervised by courts typically do a good job protecting elderly people from exploitation by acquaintances and others, says Catherine Seal, a guardianship attorney in Colorado Springs, Colo., and president-elect of the National Academy of Elder Law Attorneys. "The worst cases that I see are the ones where there is no guardian," she says.

In one case Ms. Seal handled several years ago, she says an elderly woman was befriended by a neighbor who persuaded her to buy a condo and include the neighbor's name on the title. A year later, the neighbor had the woman transfer full ownership to her and moved in to the unit. After

Ms. Seal was appointed conservator, she sold the condo and recovered the investment for the elderly woman.

Expenses that arise as a result of a guardianship, including lawyers for both the guardians and wards, typically get paid from the ward's assets. (In some jurisdictions, there is a public guardian's office that handles cases for indigent clients.) The financial arrangement, critics say, encourages lawyers and guardians to perpetuate guardianships indefinitely.

Charles and Douglas Franks say that is what happened to them. As their 89-year-old mother grew increasingly frail, the brothers clashed over where she should live—close to Charles in New Orleans, as he wished, or in her own home in Pensacola, Fla., as Douglas wanted. In 2012, Charles says he followed the advice of a financial adviser and petitioned a state court in Pensacola to appoint a guardian to settle the matter.

Their mother, Ernestine Franks, had granted Douglas a power of attorney and signed advance directives designating him as her guardian if she were ever deemed incapacitated. But a probate judge nullified the power of attorney and appointed a professional guardianship company instead. "There seems to be a lot of conflict" involving the Franks brothers, said Judge Jan Shackelford in the initial proceeding, according to a transcript. A judicial assistant says Judge Shackelford couldn't comment on pending cases.

Soon after being appointed, the guardianship company, Gulf Coast Caring Solutions in Pensacola, suspended the brothers' visits to Ms. Franks for three weeks and later permitted them for only a few hours at a time, citing their conflict. The brothers, who have since repaired their rift, say their relationship with the guardians quickly became contentious. As a result, the judge ordered that their visits with their mother be supervised by a monitor, who charges Ms. Franks $100 an hour.

Under guardianship, withdrawals from a $1.3 million trust set up to pay Ms. Franks's expenses jumped to $297,000 in 2014 from $94,000 in 2011, when Ms. Franks mostly made her own financial decisions, according to documentation provided by the Franks brothers. More than $75,000 in 2014 went to lawyers for Gulf Coast, which has been embroiled in litigation with the Franks brothers over issues ranging from expenses to home-care providers. The company said in a court filing this month it was resigning as guardian and recommended the appointment of a successor. A new judge overseeing the case scheduled a hearing for November.

Gulf Coast and its attorneys didn't respond to requests for comment. In court filings, the company accuses the brothers of harassing its care-givers and of unsettling their mother with the squabbling. Gulf Coast says that from the start, the brothers have "engaged in a relentless battle against the guardian" in an attempt to get the company removed and "re-gain control of their mother and her finances."

Charles Franks says initially he thought seeking a guardian would be "a good thing." Now, he says, "I am tortured by that decision."

Ginny Casazza, president of the National Guardianship Association, says some critics of guardians' fees don't realize how time-consuming some duties are, such as accompanying wards to medical appointments. Many charges billed to a ward don't come from guardians, she says, but from other professionals like lawyers—whose hourly rates are usually much higher than those of guardians.

Ms. Casazza says fee disputes can be minimized if guardians at the outset provide an estimate of their annual fees, as the NGA recommends. She also says the current inconsistency in fees—which usually are deter-mined by what a court finds reasonable—could be addressed by establish-ing fee guidelines like those created in Arizona in 2012.

Guardianship expenses are usually filed to courts for a judge's ap-proval annually, though some guardians submit requests for approval of fees more frequently. The accountings vary in detail, but generally they include some breakdown of costs, such as food, prescription medication and travel to medical appointments.

Some legal experts say guardianship laws aren't well-enforced by overworked judges in underfunded courts who too often rubber-stamp expense reports filed by guardians, or don't crack down when the docu-ments aren't filed on time.

Judges acknowledge they struggle to keep up with the rising flood of paperwork. Some, like Jean Stewart, a former probate judge in Denver, point fingers at state lawmakers who haven't increased judicial budgets to address the problem. "It's just plain manpower," said Ms. Stewart, who recalled spending "many Sunday afternoons" reviewing guardianship reports.

In recent years, states have tried to stamp out abuses: From 2004 through 2014, legislatures passed a total of 292 bills addressing adult guardianship, according to the American Bar Association. Many states now screen the financial and criminal backgrounds of potential guardians and require guardians to post bonds at the outset of a guardianship to insure that a ward's assets will stay protected.

Florida lawmakers this year added restrictions on suspending a power of attorney that a potential ward has granted a family member, and enacted a requirement that suspected abuse, neglect or exploitation by a guardian be reported to a state hotline.

And Texas passed a law this year believed to be the first in the U.S. to establish an alternative to guardianship known as "supported decision-making." Under the model, disabled individuals voluntarily sign agreements with people who can help them make decisions on finances and other specific issues.

In 2011, the Washington state legislature added training requirements for prospective guardians and gave courts the authority to sanction a guardian if the guardian fails to file a required report or attend a hearing.

The changes weren't enough to keep Ms. McDowell in Vancouver from a costly trip through guardianship.

In early 2012, Ms. McDowell and her longtime friend and housemate Annette Snyder were going through a difficult period in their relationship. Ms. Snyder had recently moved out of their shared home.

Ms. Snyder says she became concerned that an emotionally distraught Ms. McDowell would do something rash before they could settle their differences over their finances and possessions. She consulted a lawyer who suggested guardianship. Rather than file the petition under her own name and risk further stoking tensions with Ms. McDowell, Ms. Snyder asked a mutual friend to do it.

On March 8, 2012, a guardianship petition filed with the Clark County Superior Court claimed that Ms. McDowell had behaved erratically throughout much of the previous year. She recently had been admitted to a hospital for a small stroke, it alleged, but "became unjustifiably fearful, pulled out her IV, and left the hospital against medical advice."

The court held a hearing that same day, after which Clark County Judge Scott A. Collier appointed Kathleen McCann, an attorney, to become a temporary guardian. Ms. McCann was asked to investigate and offer an opinion on whether the court should appoint a longer-term caregiver.

On May 4, Ms. McCann advised that long-term care was needed. She submitted a report from a psychologist who said that Ms. McDowell displayed paranoia and "cognitive disorganization" and "impaired" reasoning ability. Ms. McCann didn't respond to requests for comment.

At the May hearing, the court-appointed lawyer for Ms. McDowell, James Senescu, appeared but didn't oppose the petition for guardianship. Ms. McDowell says she stood up and tried to object, but to no avail. "My attorney said nothing, and the hearing was over in about three minutes," she says. Mr. Senescu declined to comment.

Stacey Bollinger of Halo Guardianship Service Inc. was appointed her new guardian and remained so for nearly two years.

The bills piled up. Ms. Bollinger billed Ms. McDowell $332.50 to take her to breakfast, $95 for a one-hour birthday visit and $47.50 for a phone call on Thanksgiving, according to Halo Guardianship invoices filed with the court. Ms. McDowell was allotted a $500 monthly allowance. Over her objections, her house was sold, effectively forcing her into an assisted living facility.

In early 2013, Ms. McDowell enlisted lawyer MarCine Miles to help her. Ms. Miles, who says she worked pro bono because her client didn't have the authority to pay the fees, says there are still far too few checks on the system.

Guardians "hand their bills to a court, and the court just says 'OK,'" she says. Judges "never seem to ask why it took a guardian three hours to look over a bank statement."

Calls to the Clark County Superior Court administrator, Jeffrey Amram, weren't returned.

Months later, Ms. Miles arranged for her client to move out of assisted living into her motor home, and in March 2014, she helped Ms. McDowell get a court order appointing a new guardian who might get along with her better.

Dorine Bright of Riverside Guardian Services Inc., who ended up working with Ms. McDowell for seven months, charged her thousands of dollars for a variety of tasks, including personal visits, mail "processing" and "marshaling assets," according to Riverside invoices filed with the court. Calls to Ms. Bright and Ms. Bollinger and their businesses weren't returned.

Of the nearly $300,000 in total cash expenses Ms. McDowell paid during the guardianships, more than half went to professionals, including lawyers and other "caregiver services," according to bank statements and court records. At the end of the guardianship, Ms. McDowell was left with about $25,000 in cash, in addition to her motor home and a car.

In the summer of 2014, a court—at the urging of Ms. Miles—appointed an investigator to assess the situation. In September, he issued a report citing a variety of doctors and others who over the years of guardianship had examined Ms. McDowell and had attested to her relative well-being. The report included input from a social worker who in March 2013 said that while Ms. McDowell had been "labeled with Dementia by her caretakers and the court," he had seen no impairment in "her level of functioning" during 11 one-hour sessions.

Shortly thereafter, Judge Robert A. Lewis ended the guardianship. All told, a total of 11 people—10 judges and one commissioner—on the Clark County Superior Court made rulings in Ms. McDowell's case. Judge Lewis declined to comment.

Ms. Snyder now says she "deeply regrets" her role in putting Ms. McDowell into guardianship. "At the time, I had no idea what guardianship actually meant, and had no idea that Lin would be taken for such a ride," she says.

Ms. McDowell, now 74 and getting by on about $1,000 a month in Social Security and annuity payments, says that despite some health issues, she feels fine. But the time battling guardianship is "gone forever," she says.

The Catherine Falk Bill is designed to allow family members to be able to "visit" their loved ones at a time convenient for the guardians and often at a high financial cost. Since the ethical standard of the American Bar Association is to never say anything bad about another lawyer, even if they lie, cheat, steal and murder, your own attorney won't fight this issue.

CATHERINE FALK BILL
By: Barbara Stone, Florida October, 2015

As to the Catherine Falk organization, passing bills to "see" one's family is anything but legitimate—these bills are void unlawful, unconstitutional legislation. Nothing is legitimate because guardianship is a criminal racketeering organization.

The only thing that will resolve this ruse of "guardianship" that is actually a human trafficking money laundering racketeering enterprise is to <u>abolish it.</u>

The judges, the attorneys involved, the so called "guardians" are sham shysters who are breaking laws with impunity and destroying people's lives. Once you are in their racket, there is no way out. After they feast on the assets of their victim and deprive them of services, remove them from their home, isolate them and throw them into a feeding tube that is now their latest crime so they can lace their victims easier with drugs, they then move onto the family members who object to and expose their crimes and they become targets—they are sued by the predators in order for them to steal the assets of the family members. It is a racket that goes to the deepest level of the government.

These guardians rackets have become a tsunami—a terrorist enterprise because there is no accountability of their crimes to anyone. the Bar associations oversee the disciple of the lawyers and the judicial qualification commission oversees the judges—a complete conflict in both cases and the statistics show only 1% of the complaint result in any "discipline" in fact what happens is that the information in a complaint is used to help the attorneys and judges cover up for their brethren

We need help. We need strong and repeated coverage of individual cases and the enterprise as a whole by the mainstream media and on the Internet and as much exposure as possible. We need law enforcement who will not fail to investigate and arrest judges and attorneys and guardians who are committing crimes. **Law enforcement pretends it is a "civil" matter. There are crimes being committed against our most vulnerable citizens— special victim crimes. They are being falsely imprisoned, kidnapped, their assets are looted—it is a virtual free for all for these predators— free homes, free art, free jewelry and heirlooms, free cars...**

It is human trafficking at it most venal—money laundering, wired judges. One of the best descriptions I have found of this racket was done by Marti Oakely, a radio show host and an expert on the corrupt guardianship enterprise. I was sending the YouTube video out to everyone and it has now been removed from the Internet—this is how corrupt the system is—they hack, remove, and HIDE their crimes. The YouTube hidden on the Internet is entitled Rense and Marti Oakley—*Guardianship* - Theft, *Looting* And...*FRAUD* AGAINST SENIOR CITIZENS

Considering even a well-known personality such as Brooke Astor became a victim of guardianship fraud, think how easily this can happen to your mother, father, or even you, if the laws are not changed.

GUARDIANSHIP GONE BAD
"ISOLATE. MEDICATE. TAKE THE ESTATE."
By: Susan Hindman

When Robin Westmiller's 80-year-old father suffered a stroke in 2002, causing his health to deteriorate, it attracted the attention of a distant cousin in another state. Over her mother's protests, her father traveled to the cousin's home in March 2004, and within three weeks, the cousin had taken control of his life, refusing to let him talk to his family and convincing him to file for divorce and revoke his wife's power of attorney. When Westmiller was finally able to stop the takeover four months later—by going to court and getting him a temporary emergency guardian—she thought she had taken a step toward getting her father back to his own family. But she had actually created a new roadblock, this one cemented in place by the legal system.

The guardian, she said, "changed (her dad's) name, moved him without telling us, denied him access to a telephone, and no one in the facility or the hospital was told that he had a wife, a daughter, or grandchildren. Once they got hold of him, they drained nearly his entire life savings." When he passed away on June 23, 2007, "there was no life insurance, no stock portfolios, or any other assets," leaving her 83-year-old mother nearly destitute.

Westmiller, a recent law school graduate, wrote a book about her experience, and started a website—the National Association to Stop Guardian Abuse (NASGA) in 2004-then left it to form Advocates for National Guardianship Ethics and Reform (ANGER) in 2008. Both sites detail other horror stories through postings of victims and of published newspaper and magazine articles recounting the stories of others.

Guardians have been accused of draining their elderly wards' life savings, charging exorbitant fees for small tasks, selling homes without permission, throwing away personal belongings and mementos, not paying bills, cashing and pocketing Social Security checks, and making unilateral decisions about where their wards can live and whom they can see. They have even placed them in nursing homes against their will, blocked contact with loved ones, and kept them overmedicated. **As their life savings are redirected toward the guardians and lawyers and dwindle to nothing, seniors are forced to go on Medicaid, leading people close to the issue to call it a form of Medicaid fraud**.

Annie McKenna, media liaison with NASGA and embroiled in her own guardianship battle, says that "abusive guardians have a standard operating procedure: Isolate. Medicate. Take the estate."

How pervasive is this problem? "We're saying it's an epidemic," says Terri Abelar, founder of Aging Solutions, a California eldercare management consulting firm.

Read some of the articles for yourself—in the *Boston Globe* (2008), *Key West: The Newspaper* (2008), *New Haven Advocate* (2007), *Palm Beach Post* (2007), and *Los Angeles Times.* AARP wrote about it in 2004, and *Money* magazine way back in 1989. To watch video reports relating guardianship horror stories, visit Stop Guardian Abuse.org or click *The People of the State of California vs. Joseph T. Quattrochi Sr. Fox 5 News*, from New York City, also did a story, and *The Morning Show with Mike and Juliet* (another Fox program broadcast from New York City) did two stories.

Elderly victims have ranged from average citizens who spent a lifetime saving for retirement to those who are wealthy and familiar faces. One case involved a well-known retired New York judge who became a victim when his court-appointed guardians paid themselves large fees, confined him to a nursing home for two years without being allowed to receive visitors, and sold off his properties. Judge John L. Phillips Jr., a multimillionaire who suffered from Alzheimer's disease, was placed under a guardianship program in 2001. By the time the issue was nearing resolution in 2007, he was destitute. He died at age 83 in February 2008.

And if you think the government doesn't know about this, read the 1987 report by a House subcommittee of the Select Committee on Aging or the 2004 Government Accountability Office (GAO) report on guardianship that followed a yearlong investigation by the Senate Special Committee on Aging, which heard witnesses testify about abuses occurring across the country. What they found, however, was that neither the states nor the federal government has data on the number of elderly people with guardians or the incidences of abuse.

What has happened is the result of an unregulated business pairing with a court system that provides no oversight and government agencies that lack basic statistics.

The Story Of Elizabeth Indig: How homes are sold to cronies.

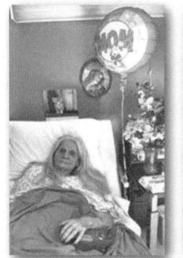

"Ward" Elizabeth Indig and her court appointed for-
hire "guardian," April Parks (*KTNV TV* screen shot)

Elizabeth Indig's house, 43 Pangloss Saint Henderson, market value—$200,000, was allowed to go into foreclosure by April Parks. The house sold at auction for $22,000 to a party in a lawsuit involving Parks' attorney Lee A. Drizin. Parks or Drizin neglected to inform Indig's family or the court of the foreclosure or auction.

Clark County Court records indicate that April Parks' attorney, Lee A. Drizen, was representing a party in a lawsuit against the buyer at auction of Mrs. Indig's house, and should have informed Indig's guardian (Parks) and Indig's family that the house was being auctioned.

According to Clark County Family Court records:

"Parks took control of the Ward's residence at 43 Pangloss Street, Henderson, Nevada 89002 on June 20, 2013, the primary residence of the Ward. The house was in the name of the INDIG FAMILY TRUST. Parks first made a threatening telephone call to Elizabeth (Indig), then came to Elizabeth's home taking her keys to the property and mailbox, and threatening her with trespassing and prison should she (try to re-enter) the property. April Parks was dressed resembling a law enforcement official complete with badge, baton, and wide belt with many keys. Parks also ordered guards at the gate to not let Indig's daughter pass. Parks has already submitted evidence for reimbursement of payment to change the residence locks, and provided an Occupancy Verification to Wells Fargo Bank dated September 24, 2013 signed by her confirming Parks was in control of the residence thus substantiating that Parks controlled the Ward's residence.

Elizabeth's daughter informed Parks verbally on June 20, 2013 that the home and its contents were part of the Indig Family Trust, and that Parks had no jurisdiction or rights to the home and its contents. Parks told the daughter that the court decided that she, April Parks, as an Officer of the Court, was in control of her mother, the home and its contents. Parks again reinforced that she was in charge, and if the daughter interfered with Parks, she would go to prison and never see her mother again. Parks sold the contents of the Indig home between August 10 and August 11, 2013 in violation of NRS 159.113 and 159.1515 which requires notification and permission of the court to sell personal property. Parks did not request permission to sell the Ward's belongings from the court, nor did she inform the court there was a home belonging to the estate.

Parks acted in violation of NRS 159.083 in her negligence to perform her duties to protect and preserve the estate of the Ward. Parks should have been collecting the Ward's mail, and was negligent in NOT PAYING [emphasis added] the HOA fees on the residence. Parks has argued that she had no jurisdiction over the Trust and no responsibility for the home, yet her actions reveal her fraud in taking control of the residence. The past due (HOA fees) were not addressed by Parks which then resulted in the home being foreclosed on by the HOA and sold at auction on November 21, 2013 for $22,000. All of this was unknown to Mrs. Indig's family until August of 2014 when Parks filed the First Annual Accounting almost a year late. Had the First Annual Accounting been filed on time, Mrs. Indig's daughter would have had time to pay the back HOA fees thereby saving the home from foreclosure."

This is the second time April Parks has been reported impersonating a police officer when evicting elderly persons from their home. She was reported wearing such a costume and making similar threats at the time she "kidnapped" Rudy and Rennie North from their home. It was later learned that Parks is not an official "Officer of the Court," and had no right to inform vulnerable people she was acting on an order from the Clark County Family Court.

The Boulder City, Nevada Police Department has launched a criminal investigation into the actions of April Parks in relation to the Indig case (Parks is a Boulder City resident). Judge Steel has been informed of the possible fraud, but has not yet taken court action against Parks, possibly pending the outcome of the Boulder City investigation.

The Story Of Jason Hanson:

"Ward" Jason Hanson (photo by Mike Christ)
and his "guardian" Jared E. Shafer

Jason Hanson's house, 5141 Lindell Rd., # 101, Las Vegas,
market value—$150,000, sold by Shafer for $47,000

The Jason Hanson—Jared E. Shafer Story "Special Administrator"
Jared E. Shafer takes house and inheritance from twenty-four-year-old
man with cerebral palsy

"All I wanted to do was go home, but Shafer takes fervent joy in destroying people's lives." —Jason Hanson:
INSIDE VEGAS by Steve Miller
AmericanMafia.com
March 3, 2014

The Story Of Anna Marie Gaule:

"Ward," the late Anna Marie Gaule, (photo by Thomas
Gaule) and her "guardian" Jared E. Shafer

The fate of the late Anna Marie Gaule was the first published story in my historical record of local guardian abuse.

In 1999, I was visited by Thomas Gaule, Mrs. Gaule's only child and living relative. With him was a retired FBI Special Agent who was a friend of Anna Marie. The gentlemen showed me a photo (above) that had been taken a week earlier of Anna Marie who was then confined to a Las Vegas rest home under the court ordered guardianship of Jared E. Shafer, Clark County's elected Public Guardian at that time.

I had met Mrs. Gaule years earlier while I was a Las Vegas City Councilman, and was aware she owned several valuable commercial properties in my district. I knew she had worked hard all her life to acquire the properties and provide an inheritance for her only child who I later learned was caring for her during her final years as an Alzheimer's victim.

During our visit, Thomas told me that several months earlier, Anna Marie had wandered away from the home they shared, became lost, and was picked up by the police for her safety.

That's when Shafer was informed of Anna Marie's situation, and he immediately petitioned the Family Court for *temporary* legal custody of the woman—and her well heeled estate. In response, Thomas enrolled in Shafer's then offered four week Guardian Course provided to family members for a $1,500 fee at the County Government Center. Thomas passed the course and received a Certificate of Completion. He then petitioned the Family Court for *permanent* custody of his mother. Shafer and his attorney protested, saying Thomas was "unfit" to care for his mother based on the day she wandered away from her house and was picked up by the police. During the course which Shafer taught, Thomas was never informed that his instructor would interfere with his effort to help his mother. However, Thomas reported that Shafer did ask numerous questions about Anna Marrie's real estate holdings. The court sided with Shafer, and granted him *permanent* custody over Anna Marie and her estate. Shafer reportedly didn't take long before beginning to liquidate Mrs. Gaule's assets.

When Thomas and his mother's friend visited me with the shocking photo, I was told that they were trying to rescue her from what was obviously a life threatening situation. I asked if Thomas had informed Jared Shafer of Anna Marie's injuries? Thomas said that Shafer was aware of the extensive injuries, but reported that Anna Marie had "fallen down." Thomas then told me he believed his mother had been beaten at the hands of the Asian caretakers at the Tonopah Drive rest home he visited daily that was used by Shafer to house his wards. Thomas then asked if I wanted to meet his mom.

The three of us immediately drove to the rest home. We were greeted at the door by an Asian man who did not speak English. Thomas informed the man that we were there to visit Anna Marie Gaule. The man said "No No" and tried to shut the door. The retired FBI Agent pushed past the man, and Thomas and I followed him inside the converted house. We went to Mrs. Gaule's room, she was not there. We proceeded to the patio where I took this photo of Anna Marie's facial injuries one week after they occurred. It appeared to me that her nose was broken, and her bruised arms and legs indicated something other than a fall had occurred. It was obvious that she had been beaten, though she could not recall or describe what had happened to her.

Anna Marie Gaule one week after beating (photo by Steve Miller)

Thomas immediately filed a motion in the Clark County Family Court of Judge William Voy. A hearing was scheduled to review Thomas' evidence.

(L to R) Family Court Judge William Voy, then criminal defense attorney Oscar Goodman with law partners Gardner Jolly and David Chesnoff (INSIDE VEGAS photo by Mike Christ)

Thomas, who was acting as his own attorney, asked the retired Agent and I to testify. We arrived at the Family Court at 9:00 a.m. to be informed by the bailiff that we would have to wait outside the court room until we were called. The hearing began and lasted for several hours. We were never called into the court. At noon, a group of smiling men exited the court accompanied by Jared Shafer. Included was local attorney Gardner Jolly who represented Shafer at the time. Thomas followed them out of the court, and informed us that Judge Voy ruled in favor of Shafer, and did not want to hear our testimony. We were disgusted and angry at what had just occurred.

The week following the hearing, Anna Marie was transferred to another Shafer controlled rest home in Pahrump, sixty miles from Las Vegas. Thomas does not drive, so it was very difficult for him to make daily visits to his mother. He was also limited to thirty minutes per visit, and ordered by Shafer to not bring guests, or a camera into the facility.

Anna Marie died shortly after being moved away from her son. An accounting of the disposition of Mrs. Gaule's assets was never provided to Thomas after her passing.

Three Secrets Behind The Ongoing Stories Of Guardianship Fraud In Nevada And The Political Corruption That Enables The Scams To Continue Unabated

Steve Miller is a former Las Vegas City Councilman. In 1991, the readers of the Las Vegas Review Journal voted him the "Most Effective Public Official" in Southern Nevada. Visit his website at: http://www.SteveMiller4LasVegas.com

• • •

"We have one really rich ward whose been dead for over five years." - Patience Bristol, PFSN, Inc. [Leann Marie Peccole Goorjian who died in 2008]

LAS VEGAS - When INSIDE VEGAS stories get stuck in Nevada's judicial or political mud and progress seems at a stand still, I sometimes reveal a few behind the scenes secrets to try to jump start long needed action. This is one of those times.

In the ad nauseam story of local private guardian Jared E. Shafer, and the Clark County Family Court judges who enable him, many readers keep asking the same questions; "Why haven't these guys been prosecuted by the Clark County DA, Nevada AG, or US DOJ for (allegedly) exploiting wealthy court appointed elderly and disabled wards? And where's the Nevada Judicial Discipline Commission when we need them to go after the judges?" The following information may help answer these questions, but don't expect to be satisfied.

SECRET #1, Shafer's private files:

In October 2013, sixty pounds of original documents reportedly disappeared from the office of Professional Fiduciary Services of Nevada, Inc.

(PFSN) on Pecos Road in Henderson. Without my prior knowledge, the documents packed in large cardboard banker's boxes mysteriously appeared on the public sidewalk in front of my house. When I first saw the unsealed boxes sitting there, I looked inside. They contained what I as an investigative commentator considered to be a treasure trove of potentially incriminating evidence about Jared Shafer whom I had been writing about since 1999. Included was an extensive file about what appeared to be an exploitative guardianship of multi-millionaire heiress Leann Peccole Goorjian. I never met Ms. Goorjian though I knew her late father Bill, and several of her closest friends, so I was very intrigued.

The documents and their source (whom I later confirmed) are protected under NRS 49.275, the Nevada Reporter's Shield Law.

I have waited until now to reveal the document's existence based on whether my having shared portions of them with the Las Vegas Metropolitan Police Abuse and Neglect Detail, Clark County District Attorney Steve Wolfson, Nevada Attorney General Adam Laxalt, and federal law enforcement authorities would hopefully inspire comprehensive investigations into what I believe is wide spread criminal guardianship fraud perpetrated against wealthy Southern Nevada retirees and disabled people. So far, the criminal investigations that have occurred were only local and yielded prosecutions of lower level operatives (low hanging fruit), while those who many believe are the masterminds - including several judges - have been allowed to remain unscathed.

The boxes placed on the public sidewalk contained hundreds of what appeared to me to be highly incriminating documents from Shafer's office including canceled checks, handwritten notes, and bank statements pertaining to the court ordered guardianships of a number of hapless, but wealthy, Las Vegas residents including the files of Leanne Peccole Goorjain who died in 2008 at age 51 while under the guardianship of Jared Shafer. After her death, his private records reflect a total of $432,043.00 Shafer paid to himself in "fees" starting with his first self-payment of $294,543.00 on August 4, 2009, eighteen months after Leann passed away, along with two payments of $12,500.00 each, one on March 28, 2013, and another on April 19, 2013, again for "fees." This does not include tens of thousands of dollars Shafer paid over a five year period to his personal attorneys including $4,230 to Elyse Tyrell, accountants, business partners, and other cronies for their "services" to the deceased woman.

Based on my knowledge of the Peccole family's good name and Leann's esteemed relatives who included a Clark County Commissioner and Sheriff, Nevada State Senator, and a billion dollar family owned land development company, and after the documents revealed that the majority of her personal holdings including a two million dollar hillside home somehow became the property of Jared Shafer, with full documentation in hand, I confidently authored the November 18, 2013, INSIDE VEGAS column "Grave Robbery Under Color Of Law."

SECRET #2, It's all legal if a judge approves:

Several months after my column appeared on AmericanMafia.com, I received an unsolicited email from CBS Sixty Minutes Senior Producer Bob Anderson. He said he wanted to speak with me in confidence regarding my Leann Peccole Goorjian column.

The day following our brief phone conversation, Anderson flew to Las Vegas where we met for lunch. He asked me to promise not to talk about our meeting until after an initial Sixty Minutes segment on guardianship fraud had aired.

At the Macaroni Grill on West Sahara, Anderson grilled me about the Peccole case and specifically about her guardian Jared Shafer. Off the record I revealed that I had copies of confidential files from Shafer's office regarding the Peccole case and a number of others, and agreed to share copies of any pertinent documents with him and associate producer Aaron Weisz. Several weeks later, a CBS crew arrived in Las Vegas from New York. Their arrival did not escape local notice. I received a call from George Knapp, a reporter at the CBS affiliate in Las Vegas asking if I knew why Sixty Minutes was snooping around town asking about Jared Shafer. I said I had no comment.

Anderson and I secretly met several more times during the spring and summer of 2014 where he told me of his progress. He said he had obtained an in-prison interview with Patience Bristol, Shafer's assistant who had been convicted of elder exploitation, and was planning a possible "ambush" interview with Shafer at his Pecos Rd. office, a tactic Sixty Minutes is famous for. I was very excited to be a part of exposing what I considered immoral and illegal behavior, and eagerly awaited the planned October 2014 airing of Anderson's first-in-a-series Sixty Minutes story.

In September 2014, I received a call from Anderson. He sounded very despondent. I was told that the CBS News attorneys in New York thoroughly vetted his story and advised that no Nevada laws had been broken in any of the examples he planned to cite on Sixty Minutes. That in each case Anderson investigated, a Clark County Family Court Judge had signed off on Shafer's actions.

I responded that that was the real story! That Family Court Judge Charles Hoskin and his appointed "Hearing Master" Jon Norheim, along with Family Court Judge William Voy had always approved of almost everything Shafer did to his "wards" and their estates, that most of the Nevada Revised Guardianship Statutes they were bound to uphold had been written by Jared Shafer over a thirty-four year span since he was appointed in 1979 by then Clark County Commissioner Manny Cortez (father of United States Senator for Nevada Catherine Cortez Masto, Shafer's god daughter), and some additional "Shafer Laws" were enacted after Shafer's 2003 retirement from the county to go into private practice. Nonetheless, the Sixty Minutes story never aired, but Anderson and Weisz requested I keep them updated, and I have.

In the meantime, I contacted the Goorgian family's attorney Gus Flangas whom I had known for years. Gus was provided Leann's complete file to share with her ex-husband Greg and two sons. Shortly thereafter, I received a call from Greg Goorgian's wife. She said that Leann and Greg's adult sons were told that Shafer is an attorney and that he has their best interests at heart. I explained that Shafer was never an attorney, and that her family needed to put a stop to his obvious exploitation. She said her husband would get back to me soon.

I never heard from Greg Goorgian, but I did have an off the record conversation with attorney Flangus. Because of my respect for Leann's family, and my friendship with her late father Bill, I will not go further other than to say the family did not take action to stop Shafer, and as far as I know, in the eyes of Hearing Master Jon Norheim (left), Leann is still alive - at least on court documents - because Norheim allowed Shafer to receive funds and fees from Leann's trusts and accounts for years after her death in pseudo accord with what's called a "Shafer Law:"

NRS 159.193, "Winding up affairs: 1. The guardian of the estate is entitled to retain possession of the ward's property already in the control of the guardian and is authorized to perform the duties of the guardian to wind up the affairs of the guardianship: (a) Except as otherwise provided in paragraph (b), (c) or (d), for not more than 180 days or a period that is reasonable and necessary as determined by the court after the termination of the guardianship."

SECRET #3, "Shafer Laws," and those who passed or enforce them:

At this point you must be asking how this can take place in a civilized society?

Nevada is a sparsely populated and rural state with an abundance of vacant lots where political signs regularly appear during elections. Our city, county, and state lawmakers and judges learned long ago that the cheapest and most effective way to win a Nevada election is to plaster the desert with signs. Thousands of signs appear on every vacant lot during election season mainly advertising the candidacy of Clark County Family Court Judges, District Attorneys, Sheriffs, Nevada Attorney Generals, Nevada Assembly and State Senate candidates, i.e., "lawmakers."

The majority of these 8' by 12' a-frame portable political signs are provided to politicians by Signs of Nevada, LLC, a business owned by none other than Jared E. Shafer who also owns PFSN, Inc. guardianship service, PO Box 50790, Henderson, NV 89016.

Most of the payers are lawmakers or judges who Shafer supports. In fact, it's almost impossible to win a lower level political post without the use of Shafer's signs, I know because I've run several successful political campaigns. His signs are an absolute must-have item if you intend to win.

The quid pro quo is that many politicians including family court judges who benefited from Shafer's cheap or donated signs have sponsored or judicially enforced horrible legislation that gave Shafer and other Nevada private guardians total control over the persons and fortunes of their wealthy wards of the court (poor people are not assigned guardians). One public official recently expressed a vastly different opinion. On a local TV program hosted by LV Mayor Carolyn Goodman that aired on May 13, Nevada Attorney General Adam Laxalt was asked about guardianship fraud. He replied "We are going to stop private guardians from taking their wards for everything they're worth." I hope he was referring to Shafer, otherwise prosecuting only the low hanging fruit will have little effect on stopping such a multi-billion dollar scam. A much more powerful example must be set, or the AG, DA, and LVMPD will just be wasting taxpayer's money, and there will be many more victims in the future. Retirement, Las Vegas' second largest industry, doesn't need the bad press..

Shafer still owns the political sign company, but sources report that PFSN is no longer in business after recent articles questioning his activities by Colton Lockhead in the *Las Vegas Review Journal*, Dan Roberts and Rana Goodman in *The Vegas Voice*, and Darcy Spears on *KTNV TV Channel 13 News*, not to mention my constant harping in these columns and my frequent E-Briefs. Also, Shafer, his convicted assistant Patience Bristol, and Shafer's bank trust officers at Wells Fargo are defendants in a nasty <u>federal civil racketeering lawsuit</u> brought by the family of one of their purported victims, so it was an opportune time for Shafer to retire.

I have been told that <u>private guardian Denise Comastro,</u> one of Shafer's protégés, has been assigned as successor guardian to his remaining wealthy PFSN "wards."

With "Isolate, Medicate, and Steal the Estate" as the mantra for so many private guardians, I can only wish Comastro's new found "wards" (and their court disempowered heirs) the best of luck during their twilight years, and caution Denise that she will be watched very, very closely. I also hope that law enforcement authorities have not dropped the ball and realize their work has just begun.

Meanwhile, Jared Shafer is said to be enjoying his retirement - while he can. At the same time, *his* judges remain on the bench, and reportedly take lavish European vacations during their time off.

"What happens in Vegas, stays in Vegas?" Not on my watch!

If the reader has been wondering what happens to all the dead bodies of these wards, here is the system one court appointed guardian used:

Man Finds 27 Urns Filled With Human Ashes In Henderson Storage Unit

Posted: May 16, 2017 8:39 PM Updated: May 16, 2017 10:05 PM
Written by Eric Hilt

A man found 27 urns in a storage unit he won at auction.

When Billy Smith bought a Henderson storage unit at auction for a couple hundred dollars, he said he had no idea what he was getting into.

"I've been doing this business off and on as a hobby for the last 20 years," Smith said. "This is the most bizarre thing I've ever found in a unit. I've found lots of crazy things over the years, but nothing like this."

The find: 27 urns, all filled with human ashes.

"I discovered an urn, I thought 'Oh my God, this is somebody's loved one,'" Smith said after going through the small unit at Life Storage near Wagon Wheel and Interstate 515. "Then I found a tub full of remains, and then a second tub full of remains. I was just shocked to see almost 30 sets of remains."

Some of those remains were a few years old, others from the early 2000s. Many of them contained the corresponding paperwork.

"Somebody had the gall to store a family member in a storage unit like that," Smith said.

That somebody, according to Valley funeral home directors, was April Parks, who rented the storage unit before it went up for auction. For decades, she worked as a court-appointed guardian, making legal and financial decisions for senior citizens. But as of May 16, she was behind bars at the Clark County Detention Center, facing hundreds of charges of theft, perjury, and exploitation of her elderly clients.

The charges came after a years-long investigation by the Nevada Attorney General's Office, Metro Police and the Clark County District Attorney's office.

Court documents explained the 270 charges against her and her company. The indictment mentions dozens of victims, including names that were on urns found inside the storage unit.

"Horrendous things, just horrendous things were done to her wards," Elizabeth Indig said. Indig's mother was one of Parks' wards.

Indig's mother is still alive, but Indig said she was still outraged about the ashes being stowed away and then abandoned in the storage unit.

"I shouldn't be shocked because I know all the horrible things that Parks did, but I am shocked, and I am appalled. Words cannot even describe how appalled I am," Indig said.

As appalling as the find may be to people, it likely won't add any charges to the long list Parks is already facing.

Nevada law states: "Cremated remains may be disposed of in any manner upon private property if the agent who ordered the cremation so directs and the owner of the property consents in writing."

By law, Parks was the legal recipient of the ashes, meaning she could store them how she wanted. Her name is on several receipts and burial permits found in the storage unit.

Now, many of those ashes are being stored at a local funeral home as directors work with the Attorney General's office to find relatives to take the urns.

The Attorney General's office would not comment about the recent developments or efforts to find family members. The Clark County District Attorney's office would not comment either.

Below is an incomplete list of urns found inside of the storage unit:

* Gwen D. Belgzin, 10/13/1938 - 7/4/2013
* Bruce Basden, 5/15/1946 - 1/1/2015
* Robert Jones, 5/14/1940 - 12/22/2013
* Fumi Matheson, 6/29/1927 - 7/14/2012
* Thomas Vannote, 7/1/1932 - 11/4/2012
* Sung Ock Kang, 1/10/1934 - 6/2/2014
* Martha Ornelas, 1/30/1948 - 5/25/2015
* Charles Holmquist, 9/30/1931 - 12/13/2013
* Cynthia Hawkes, 5/2/1948 - 10/29/2006

Bribing judges has long been known as a given. This next article explains in detail how this is accomplished.

LAS VEGAS: SIN CITY HARBORS A NEW KIND OF CRIME RING
By: Janet Phelan, May 17, 2017

Las Vegas. These words conjure up visions of glitz, glam, glitter and fabulous wealth. And behind Vegas's casino culture have always lurked rumors of laundered money and organized crime.

The Mob's influence in Vegas is legendary, going back to its inception. Recent concerns have involved the Sands Hotel and Casino, whose owner, Sheldon Adelson, paid $47 million to avoid federal money laundering charges in 2013.

But now, another form of organized money laundering appears to have taken up residence in the centers of power in Sin City. This form of money laundering does not involve casino bosses and mob figures, however. It involves prestigious and reputedly honorable members of government in Nevada.

For not only does money flow freely through the over one hundred casinos in the desert city of Las Vegas. Millions — possibly billions — flow through the probate courts, as well. According to calculations by the Bank of America, in the next 30-40 years 1 trillion dollars may be transferred through inheritances, from one generation to the next. What is happening now in probate courts across the US is an interception of wealth transfer. These interceptions are largely taking place through guardianship proceedings.

How Assets are Plundered in Guardianship Court

Guardianships are generally initiated through court proceedings when there are allegations that an individual may be lacking capacity, possibly suffering from old age afflictions such as dementia or Alzheimer's. Upon the appointment of a guardian by a judge to an alleged incapacitated person (AIP), the guardian assumes the financial and personal responsibility for his ward. This may involve decisions such as selling the AIP's property, reallocation of investments as well as personal decisions such as where the ward lives and who, if anyone, may be allowed to visit him. The opportunity for fraud and abuse when one person has total control over another cannot be overstated.

A recent scandal involving allegations that a Las Vegas guardian for profit, April Parks, misappropriated hundreds of thousands of dollars from her clients recently hit the national news. Parks, owner of the business A Private Professional Guardian, LLC, was charged along with her office manager, Mark Simmons, her husband, Gary Neil Taylor and her attorney, Noel Palmer Simpson.

Parks and her cohorts are being referred to as a "crime ring." Parks, who was arrested in Pennsylvania earlier this year after fleeing the jurisdiction, is claiming indigence and has been appointed a public defender.

The charges state that Parks systematically overbilled and exploited her wards, isolating them from family and friends. She has been charged with over 200 felony counts, including racketeering, theft and exploitation.

Some of the reporters on the Parks story have wondered out loud how she could ever have gotten away with her stealing. In a local television report, tellingly titled Guardianship Crimes Occurred in Courtroom,

Channel 13 wanted to know ... "why all those phony and altered documents were accepted and whether any judges, commissioners or doctors would be held accountable."

"Where was the oversight?" asked 13 reporter Darcy Spears.

The worst-offender guardians seem to have been passed over in the recent rash of arrests. The names of Jared Shafer and Patience Bristol, allegedly conspiring with Guardianship Commissioner Jon Norheim, pop up consistently in the abuse reports. Yet Shafer and Bristol have remained unscathed in the scandal and calls for Norheim to be fired have gone unattended to.

The human cost in these guardianships cannot be quantified. The heartache and loss of a beloved parent to a system which only sees individuals as "cash cows" is a plight that many in Las Vegas have now endured. Leslie Newman, a social worker, recounts how Commissioner Norheim and guardian Shafer "worked" the weak link in her family, her mother's second husband, in order to gain complete control over her mother Enid's assets. She recalls the day in guardianship court when Commissioner Norheim announced that he was going to give temporary guardianship for two weeks only to the husband, Norman. Norman then proceeded to remove Leslie from all the previously prepared documents and formalized a "Family Trust" leaving everything to him and his son from his first marriage. After Norman accomplished this, he was removed as guardian and Shafer and Bristol stepped in.

Leslie maintains that her mother was murdered by the husband, in full sight of police and other so-called protective agencies. And true to form, Shafer ended up with the money.

Leslie's voice quavers as she recalls how a Dr. Rosenstien at Desert Springs Hospital called the police and stated that Enid was being poisoned at home. The police referred the matter to Protective Services, which failed to take action.

To date, arrests have targeted guardians and those in their employ. No judges or other judicial officers have been charged or fired over what is being called the biggest guardianship scandal in Las Vegas history.

ARE THE JUDGES INVOLVED?

However, at least two of the judges involved in Clark County guardianships may have also had their mitts in the cookie jar. A review of the mortgage histories of Family Court Presiding Judge Charles J. Hoskin, who ascended to the bench in 2009 (first having served as a temporary judge since 2002) and Judge William Voy, who has sat on the bench in Clark County since 1998, raises questions about the possibility that they are laundering "extra benefits" through their mortgages.

A money laundering scam using home loans as the vehicle for bribery is exquisitely simple and nearly undetectable: Judge X takes out a loan and Mr. Y pays it back.

Consider this: Since ascending to the bench in 2002, Judge Charles Hoskin has taken out or reconveyed over 2 million dollars in home loans, including an $800,000 loan in 2006 (Mort 20060124-0004304) paid back in 2016. It is of concern that the value of the property, bought by Hoskin in 2003, was declared at $540,000 at that time. One might wonder how Hoskin could have taken out a loan for considerably more than the property is worth.

Hoskin has made some effort to obscure his ownership of the property. The Clark County Assessor's site records his ownership only as "Taxpayer" and records the property location as that of the Assessor's office. The document link to the sale record is also obscured and given the bogus document number of * 99999999:99999

Hoskin's tenure as a permanent judge began in 2009 with a salary of approximately $160,000 per year. Spread equally over 15 years and excluding interest rates, that would amount to over $133,000 per year to pay off the loans, leaving Hoskin with a remainder of $27,000. That would be before taxes.

Something ain't right here.

Hoskin has been central to concerns about guardianship misconduct. He was the formal supervisor for Guardianship Commissioner Jon Norheim and following the uproar in Vegas, which culminated in the formation of a Commission to study and recommend changes in guardianship law, Hoskin and Norheim were both removed from the assignment in adult guardianship court. They were subsequently reassigned to juvenile court.

Judge William "Bill" Voy's name has also popped up in problematic guardianship cases. Voy, who has sat on the bench since 1998, has run up a total of $1,556,988 in loans and/or reconveyances since '98. Voy was appointed by Justice James Hardesty of the Nevada Supreme Court to sit on the Commission to mend the broken guardianship system.

Hardesty's Guardianship Commission was formed in 2015 and issued its final report in September of 2016. Among the Commission's recommendations were to form a permanent body to which complaints about guardianship proceedings could be referred. Such an agency has already been set up in California and in Florida, following news reports of guardianship fraud in those states. These agencies are considered to be dismal failures and are reported to be providing a further level of protection for highly profitable guardianships, replete with fraud and abuse of the ward.

IS THE NEVADA SUPREME COURT INVOLVED?

Justice Hardesty himself may be dipping into the loan trough. According to Washoe County, official records, Hardesty has taken out and/or reconveyed over $1.2 million in loans on his property, located in Sparks, Nevada in the last fifteen years. Records show that Hardesty purchased an acre of land for $22,000 in 1976 and subsequently built a two story home on the land in 1981.

Justice Hardesty was contacted and asked for the proof, via canceled checks, that he personally paid back these loans. He declined to furnish the checks and when queried as to the purpose of the loans, which did not appear to be used for home improvement, he issued a statement through the Supreme Court's press secretary stating only that "I have no further comment."

Through Clark County press officer Mary Ann Price, Judge William Voy issued this reply: "The transactions listed show home sales, refinances and home improvement loans paid through earnings and home sales proceeds. Should an official inquiry be conducted, documentation will be provided to the requesting agency."

Price provided this response from Judge Charles Hoskin: "Judge Hoskin, both before becoming a judge in 2009 and since, has repaid personal home loans through monthly payments from income and refinancing through commercial lenders."

Before this article gets consigned to the pile of "Oh my, more public corruption," it might be useful to consider the implications of the concerns cited herein. If approximately 2/3 of judges (this is the ballpark figure that appears likely) are accepting under the table monies and are fixing cases as a result of being paid off to do so, one must ask the following question:

"Do we even have a functioning justice system in the United States?"

As the promise of justice for all is central to the American vision, the possibility that justice has been waylaid and slain by the powerful and monied is of concern for all of us.

ARE THE FEDS INVOLVED?

Recently, the US Attorney's office in Los Angeles was approached with evidence of the prevalence of bought-off judges. An official with the Public Corruption Unit, Marve Williams, took the call. This is an accurate rendition of what then transpired:

Following accumulating evidence that judges are laundering bribes through their home loans, I called the US Attorney's office in Los Angeles, asking to speak with someone in the public corruption unit.

I shortly received a call back from a Marve Williams, who identified herself as working in the citizens complaint division of that office.

I explained to her that I had amassed evidence pointing to criminal money laundering by California judges.

Ms. Williams informed me (hang onto yer hats....) that the Department of Justice has no jurisdiction over judges. "You will need to contact the Commission on Judicial Performance," she intoned. "Judges police themselves."

"Ma'am!!" I replied. "If judges break the law they are held to the same measure as anyone else. These may be federal crimes and your office indeed has jurisdiction!"

Marve tried to argue this point with me but was clearly losing the battle of words. She then took another tack.

"You are not allowed to report on this conversation or to quote me," she informed me.

"Ma'am!" I yelped. "I identified myself as a journalist in the first minute of our phone call. You cannot inhibit me or instruct me from reporting what transpired here."

"You are not permitted to report this," she retorted.

"Bull puckey!" I replied.

And then Marve disconnected the call.

The Whistleblower Unit of the Senate Judiciary Committee was also contacted in March of this year, as was the Minority leader of the Judiciary Committee, Dianne Feinstein. To date neither office has replied to written and verbal messages citing concern about state judges being bribed to fix cases and also about the attempts by the DOJ to cover up what appears to be widespread money laundering by judges.

And April Parks — low hanging fruit and easy pickins' — may be paying the price for everyone who facilitated her crimes.

It is hoped this book illustrates that a "New System" is needed: Reform will Not Work. These next two articles express how laws need to be changed.

IDEAS TO REDUCE ELDER ABUSE AND FRAUD
By: M Larsen

1   Board of Supervisors over guardianship matters to be a combination of personnel from organizations such as Adult Protective Services, County Sheriff, County Prosecutor, and ACLU, since the civil rights of a person are being relinquished.

2   CASA (Court Appointed Special Advocate) volunteers who are not connected to any of the law firms that represent guardianship organizations to make a thorough evaluation and investigation of the alleged vulnerable adult that includes interviews with all family members, close friends, and family physician.

3   Bank financial statements, stock, bonds, treasury notes, real property holdings, and tax records showing the alleged vulnerable adult's assets at time of guardianship and quarterly thereafter to be available for an outside audit.

4   Liabilities of alleged vulnerable adult to be paid regularly, such as utility bills, mortgage payments, taxes, etc., or missed payments to automatically trigger an outside investigation.

5   Provable record of on-going daily physical and mental stimulation of alleged vulnerable adult.

6   Visitors must be allowed to see and/or talk to the alleged vulnerable adult unless the person personally tells the family member or friend he or she does not wish to see them. Guardians' refusal to let family and friends visit will trigger a formal investigation if a family member or friend states his or her belief that misconduct that is suspicious to the board of supervisors is occurring.

7   Disputes in guardianship matters *mandated* to go into mediation and/or arbitration rather than through the courts, including any initial attempts to take a person into guardianship through the courts prior to CASA involvement.

8   Attending physician to remain the one used by the alleged vulnerable adult, or in the absence of a physician, a physician named jointly by guardian and family members.

9   Medical personnel are allowed to explain the words used in documents such as psych reports to friends and family of alleged vulnerable adults without being sanctioned.

10 All efforts must be made to accommodate the alleged vulnerable adult to stay in her or his own home with family members or caretakers rather than through guardianship unless there is serious proof through a formal investigation by CASA volunteers

that it is in the best interest of the alleged vulnerable adult to be moved.

11 All efforts must be made to free the alleged vulnerable adult from guardianship should her or his condition appear to improve.

12 Courts may not seal files on guardianship cases.

13 Blood tests should be required at the time of death for anyone who died while under the care of others, whether on the basis of formal guardianship or by another type of caregiver. Actual cause of death to be noted on Certificate of Death.

14 Mandatory requirement for attorneys who have knowledge of possible criminal activities carried out by attorneys in alleged vulnerable adult fraud cases to report it to the Office of Prosecutor or Attorney General without fear of ethic charges.

FRAUDULENT GUARDIANSHIPS UNCOVERED MASSIVE FINANCIAL FRAUD SCHEME DETAILED

By: National Alliance to Dissolve Guardianship Miami, Florida, December 1, 2014

A group of Florida victims is going public with their horror stories of their experiences in Probate Court.

Dr. Sam Sugar who founded an organization against abusive probate guardianship stated "Each member of our rapidly growing group has watched in horror as a loved one is taken from them and literally given as a possession to a total stranger who controls every aspect of their loved one's life and all of their life savings and assets with no oversight," Sugar says. He adds "Possession of a vulnerable human being strips away all their civil rights and all their assets.

Immediately upon being placed in "guardianship" all assets and possessions of an elderly disabled person is diverted to a total stranger with no license, no credentials and no supervision. The elderly disabled person themselves becomes the possession of a total stranger who removes all of their rights.

Without rights and absent any meaningful oversight, For Profit Guardians and their Lawyers regularly abuse and isolate their victims often perpetrating massive financial fraud on their innocent victims who have done nothing wrong but to age in Florida. It is a massive industry that rakes in billions a year and it is a threat to every senior. Every single one of us with any assets at all will someday be in probate court."

There are as many as 100,000 guardianships in Florida and could be 5,000,000 or more across the country. Guardians are not State licensed, not trained and have no required medical or financial skills or licenses. They need only pass a 40 hour internet course to be allowed to handle complex medical cases and multimillion dollar estates. In Florida alone the For Profit Guardianship Industry is valued at over 1 billion dollars annually.

Kevin Pizzarello, a family member of a victim has summarized observations:

"A guardian who is put in charge of a vulnerable person remains in charge REGARDLESS of the behavior which takes place while they are in control. <u>Any 'Advanced Directives' are completely ignored.</u> This is a case where not only the "house wins', but it victimizes the elderly, their families and depletes their estate for self-serving benefits. The probability that the abusive and financially exploitive outcomes for the families and victims end up the same 100% of the time is not a random event and one that is impossible to ignore."

Our concerns are for the safety of our loved ones who are trapped in guardianship. We cannot countenance their exploitation, abuse, fraudulent and malicious desecration and the violation of their declared wishes by predatory guardians and lawyers" says Barbara Stone, who has been wrongfully arrested twice just for trying to see and protect her mother who has been unlawfully isolated from her, when her actions, in fact, have saved her mother's life.

The group reports that the For Profit Guardianship Industry uses the exact same tactics in each of their cases: fraudulent claims to initiate and perpetuate guardianships on vulnerable victims and extort massive fees for their services that are rubber stamped by a complicit Judge. In the process their loved ones, the victims of abuse and exploitation, are forced to pay out of their own funds for the perpetration of their own abuse by the guardians and their attorneys who fight the very family members who are trying to rescue their loved ones with the assets of the elderly person they control.

Fabricated "staged" litigation, cooked books, cruel isolation of a senior person to hide rampant abuse and absolutely no oversight agency to provide accountability has erupted into a crisis.

"We are going public with our stories and demand reform. We must not let the millions of baby boomers a percentage of whom predictably may become disabled over time fall prey to this financial fraud scheme" adds Sugar. We are making this horrific scheme into a movement. We are producing a song, a video and a documentary.

We seek your reporting on and exposing of this scheme to the public.

Florida has been reported the most corrupt State by Huffington Post. The proclaimed "probate judges" are engaged in heinous crimes that shame the judiciary and are protected by other judges and law enforcement who close ranks in an immoral cloak of secrecy and breach of fiduciary duty.

We seek indictments and arrests of these judges who are running fully fledged racketeering operations.

THE NEXT HUGE PONZI SCHEME THAT MUST BE EXPOSED

We are family members from all over the country whose parents and loved ones who have been taken from us by a court system gone terribly awry and a gulag of predators known as "Adult For Profit Guardians." Their lives have been snatched and controlled by predator strangers and their lawyers who abuse, isolate, drug and restrain our vulnerable defenseless family members in order to steal their assets. Greed, corruption and abuse of power by judges and a predatory For Profit Guardianship industry has erupted in a society that has become lawless and tramples the lives of defenseless adults and their families.

The For Profit Guardianship Industry intrudes into the lives of families who find themselves in a court arena known as "probate court," a scandalous, merciless breeding ground of corruption often orchestrated by miscreant judges. These courts are supposed to carry out laws designed to protect persons placed in guardianship. Thus family members of a person in a guardianship enter this court under the wrongful impression that they will receive justice in this court. **However, "guardianship" laws are universally ignored in probate court and are likely unconstitutional.**

The For Profit Guardians are total strangers to the "ward" and their family. They prey on persons with significant assets or are parties to settlements that will result in a monetary award such as a malpractice suit or other action that will result in settlement funds. The guardians themselves can then petition in probate court for guardianship after ferreting out an unsuspecting victim.

Guardians can also surface by way of an appointment by a "probate judge" when an unsuspecting family member brings a guardianship action to try to find resolution to family dissension over the care or assets of a parent or other loved one. In these instances, a For Profit Guardian, an un-vetted stranger to the family who is waiting to pounce on their next victim is appointed without their consent by a miscreant judge masquerading as an officer of the law.

A professional guardian then gets control of their victim's money, their assets, their possession, their home, their care and their personal property by alleging they can no longer manage their affairs or are in some kind of imminent danger or unduly influenced and therefore in need of the court's "protection."

Once a "guardian" is appointed, the care and assets of the person placed under their control is transferred pre-death to this complete stranger, a person who has no state license, no regulation, no oversight and no accountability. Guardians actually own the "ward" as their property by law and are free to do with them as they please with little or no oversight. Absent safeguards and oversight it is no wonder the guardianship industry is rife with corruption, greed and abuses.

Even more incredibly, in the ultimate injustice, the victim pays the court cost and fees of the predator guardian and their attorney for this charade of justice.

The heinous crimes of the for-profit guardianship industry are brazen and carried out in open sight as they have no fear of repercussions. With trivial meaningless oversight by a judge who often apparently acts in concert with them to condone their misappropriations, it is easy to predict the unlawful fraud and greed that abet one another and are blessed by the court sworn to protect their innocent vulnerable victims, The guardianship statutes, as originally enacted were intended to protect the indigent among us. They were not intended nor could they constitutionally be applied to circumvent the distribution of assets by testators to their heirs by a pre-death transfer of assets to unlicensed, unregulated persons who operate under color of law abuse, a crime as defined by the F.B.I. With the passage of time and the increasingly evident moral decay of the courts, the outdated, archaic, draconian statutes governing guardianship has morphed into a convenient and impenetrable and extremely lucrative scheme for deceitful lawyers, fraudulent guardians with fabricated credentials and colluding tactics against defenseless adults and seniors who themselves are afforded no presentation under this shameful and immoral statute.

Guardianship is a clearly immoral, illegal, penal system masquerading as law that is cleverly contorted into a brazen opportunity to embezzle the life savings of a citizen of the United States and disinherit their heirs orchestrated by a predator profit and fee driven lawyers and predatory guardians who operate with no real credentials, have no license, no specialized or continuing training, no supervision and no accountability.

The guardianship system is nothing more than a monstrous, MASSIVE criminal racketeering scheme **engaged in human trafficking**

as defined by the F.B.I. and money laundering. It is a preposterous fraud perpetrated by fraudulent guardians, colluding attorney accomplices and miscreant judges in a charade court on the order of Bernie Madoff's Ponzi scheme but vastly larger. It is more brazen and subversive as it has cunningly attached itself to the courts to appear to operate under color of law.

There is a pretense that a lawful proceeding is taking place but the only thing that is occurring is the criminal deprivation of the assets of a disabled, elderly adult by a wired and scamming judge who is working hand in hand with predator attorneys and guardians. These are adult predators committing criminal acts on elderly disabled adults. Just like child molesters, they must be arrested and indicted and their names registered on a predator adult list that must be enacted into legislation.

This deviant scenario is played out all over the country.

The guardianship industry assume free reign to engage in these atrocities because the guardianship statutes strips adults, seniors and the disabled of nearly all of their rights. Once under guardianship, a person has fewer rights than a criminal:

The right to marry, vote, apply for government benefits, have a driver's license or identification, travel, contract, seek or retain employment, sue and defend lawsuits, manage property, make any gift or disposition of property, determine their residence, consent to medical and mental health treatment and make decisional about social environment or other social aspect of their life are all **stripped.**

Any health care surrogate, durable power of attorney or pre-need guardianship **is nullified and the laws protecting those advance directives are trampled in violation of state and Federal statutes.**

Guardianship is all about money. If a person has no assets and little income, they are safe from the pain of adult guardianship. But, imagine the effect of giving someone unlimited and unsupervised access to your money with little or no oversight. Imagine having someone determine every aspect of your life. A person does not necessarily have to be old to be a target.

If family members try to fight this system, the court allows the guardian to use our loved one's money to fight us.

In essence our loved one is being forced by the court to pay for their own abuse of out the rightful inheritance of their heirs—all in order to "protect the ward" —when in fact the ward and the entire family are being legally robbed and attacked with nowhere to turn for help.

Our loved ones suffer heinous crimes. They are routinely isolated from us. If we are permitted to see them, many of us are denied our familial right to hug and embrace our loved ones. Our loved ones are routinely drugged and overmedicated to render them incoherent and compliant. Our loved ones are routinely denied food and services as it is becoming a frequent practice for guardians to force them to have a feeding tube implanted so their care needs are minimized and their assets can be stockpiled and distributed to the "guardian" enterprise who is perpetrating these atrocities.

We, their family members are victims ourselves. As we have banded together to combat this corruption, we have found that a pattern or playbook drives this criminal enterprise. Each of our stories of abuse contain essentially the same elements:

* When we walk into any courtroom, our due process rights and ability to protect our abused and exploited family member goes out the window. Judges are biased in favor of the cronies who inhabit their chambers and are all too eager to pad the wallets of the very people who contribute to and run their re-election campaigns.
* We are isolated from our loved ones by illegal "stay away orders" issued by judges who collude with slanderous, perjured statements of guardians and their attorneys to keep us away from our loved one so they can abuse and exploit our loved ones with troublesome witnesses and in total secrecy.

- Judges are engaged in abetting guardians in a colossal crime spree with the single minded vicious purpose to steal the assets of the person they are supposed to protect.
- We are threatened, maligned, slandered, perjured and subjected to retaliatory diversionary tactics to maliciously interfere with and impede our efforts to protect our loved ones from abuse and exploitation.
- The assets of our loved ones are used by the guardians to fight us in our sadly predictable expensive but futile efforts in court to protect our loved ones. Because "probate courts" perpetrate and abet the abuse and exploitation of our loved ones rather than protect them, we, as family members have taken extreme and desperate measures to protect our loved ones.
- We have been falsely arrested in droves for taking our loved ones out of an abusive guardianship.
- We have fled the country to remove our loved ones to a safe haven.
- We have risked our life savings on futile litigation.
- We have staged pickets and protests.
- We have flown throughout the country to meet with law enforcement.

All to no avail—and as the Baby Boomers age and develop dementias, the problem grows rampant and the abuses proliferate. There are already hundreds of thousands of victims who are isolated from their families, lost their life savings, their constitutional rights and prematurely lost their lives as a result of being victims of abuse in this grotesque scam. Exactly how many is hard to say as all records in Guardianship are illegally sealed and secret. But we know there are at least 7,000 active guardianships in Miami Dade and between 75-100,000 in Florida.

Across America, and particularly in Florida, with its many retirees, The For Profit Guardianship Industry is infested with abuse and fraud. Florida is no longer the sunshine state. It is a dark and dangerous place for unsuspecting adults, seniors and retirees with assets.

A MetLife study calls elder abuse the crime of the 21st century. As early as 1985, elder abuse was called a "national disgrace" by the *US House of Representatives, Subcommittee on Health and Long-Term Care of the Select Committee on Aging*. In December of 1987, Congressman Claude Pepper and the 100th Congress wrote Guardianships in America: a National Disgrace. In 1997, Mark D. Andrews wrote: The Elderly in Guardianships: a Crisis of Constitutional Proportion. More than a quarter-century after the subcommittee report, it continues to be a national disgrace and a breeding ground for subversive activity.

Money **magazine** refers to the "gulag of guardianship" and calls it "a national disgrace." It is a system riddled with abuses. It will, if possible, get even worse as baby boomers provide a stream of new victims.

Once judged incompetent and placed under a conservatorship [or guardianship], a citizen becomes a nonperson, with fewer rights than a convicted felon in a penitentiary. — **Robert Casey, Editor, Bloomberg Wealth Manager**

<u>**We are in a crisis.**</u>

Our stories tell of looting, scams, concealment, high crimes, judicial deceit, wrongful arrest and house arrest, expatriation, witness tampering, retaliation, isolation of our loved ones, orchestrated litigation and other state abated crimes. We wonder- How can this be happening in the USA? The unsuspecting public must be warned of this growing powerful menace. The dangerous, inhumane racketeering Guardianship Industry must be exposed.

The public must be made aware of this scandal. We are victims and advocates locally and nationally who would like to make this story public.

CONTACT INFORMATION:

Doug Franks
678-570.3010
mactechworks@mac.com

Robert Sarhan, MD
305-338.6160
drrob2007@yahoo.com

Teresa Lyles
352-219.5166
tozzolyles@gmail.com

Patty Reid
954-253.5416
pea.reid26@gmail.com

Kevin Pizzarello
841-635.1764
rightsforelderly@gmail.com

Angela Woodhull, PhD
352-219.6994
Chachaangelina@yahoo.com

Barbara Stone
305-397.9369
barbara15151@hotmail.com

Skender Hoti
561-385.6390
skendertravel@hotmail.com

CHAPTER 6

List of Crimes

• • •

This list was developed by Barbara Stone who has been jailed several times trying to see her mother who is a victim of professional guardianship fraud. The judges, lawyers, and guardians have taken well over $1.5 million from Ms. Stone and her mother.

* First degree felonies committing financial fraud and exploitation in a sum of $100,000 or more from an elder person
* Perjury
* Tampering with evidence
* Obstructing justice
* Dereliction of duty
* Violation of Bill of Rights, 1st and 6th Amendments
* United States Constitution Art 3 Sec 3
* Conspiracy under USC 371
* Theft and fraud, fraud on the court, intrinsic and extrinsic fraud, and fraud in the inducement
* Tampering with court records, transcripts, and other records
* Forgery
* Securing writings by deception
* Fabricated evidence that victim lacked capacity to give consent
* Kidnapping
* Abduction
* Unlawful restraint

- Elder abuse and aggravated abuse
- Elder exploitation
- Discrimination
- Retaliation
- Coercion
- Attempted murder
- Premeditated murder
- Official misconduct
- Abuse of power
- Color of law abuse
- Criminal racketeering
- Human trafficking
- Money laundering
- False arrest
- Entrapment
- Battery
- Wire fraud, mail fraud, and bank fraud
- Conversion
- Breach of fiduciary duty
- Lying to the federal government and court system 18 USC 1001
- False imprisonment
- Retaliation under the ADA and 42 USC 12203 Attempted Murder (use of contraindicated drugs, isolation from family members and friends, suspicious falls leading to confinement to bed, etc.)
- 18 US Code § 3-Accessory after the fact
- 18 USC 4 Misprison of felony
- Color of Law/Due Process violations Abuse-42 USC 1983
- Wrongful implantation of a feeding tube without consent, and deprivation of the sensation of food and chewing against her will
- Torture under the international treaties against torture

Conclusion

• • •

By: Captain Elizabeth Griffin, USMC (Retired)

WHEN I HAD THE HONOR of joining the military, I swore an oath to protect the Constitution of the United States. And that means fighting for our sacred constitutional rights, especially our right to freedom. Guardianship takes away every freedom an individual has. I have great respect for those who care for others. However, professional guardianship fraud is about theft and even premeditated murder, and it is often our courts, attorneys, and the guardians that carry it out. I know these are strong words. Yet as I read more and more about this topic, I realized that veterans had to start "stepping up" to help men and women who had served their country and now have lost their right to freedom. I've spent the last year writing to government officials regarding this crime.

There is a large transfer of wealth occurring. This is happening to approximately five million seniors a year, and their wealth is disappearing from the general population into the hands of a few professional guardians, attorneys, and court personnel acting in conspiracy to obtain the victim's wealth with little public knowledge. The victims are chemically restrained, families are torn apart, and life savings are being stolen from families.

The conspirators have the legal resources to sue, fine, and even jail anyone who complains. This is currently the status of many of the families who try to help their loved ones. They are silenced immediately while their loved ones are tortured, raped, drugged, and the family robbed of all assets.

New families continue to come forth to tell their stories and demand reforms that would have mitigated their exploitive experiences. We are seeing those in power and those who benefit financially from this criminal betrayal of the perversion of the courts trample the arguments of victims' families. Evidence and due process are ignored as the civil rights and estates of the vulnerable are trampled by the arguments of the guardians and predatory lawyers that ensure the estate funds line their personal pockets.

We must collectively be voices for the victims who can no longer protect themselves.

In my thirty-three years as a senior revenue officer with the IRS, there is nothing the IRS has ever done that even comes close to the harm that corrupt courts have allowed in guardianship matters.
—Richard M. Schickel, RMS Consulting LLC, Author of *IRS Whistleblower*

M Larsen is a businessman whose family members were embroiled in civil litigation that was in truth a criminal matter. His book relates stories similar to what his family experienced. Larsen provides articles and his own research that spell out an evil crime that knows no bounds. Professional guardianship fraud is greed at its worst carried out by those in power, making this what Lt. James Welskoph calls the perfect crime. Larsen experienced the grief and rage of his family members as he stood by helpless, and he realized that tens of thousands of other families were experiencing the same heartache and murderous rage at the corrupt judicial system. When Larsen searched for answers on the Internet, he found stories and started collecting them to share with his family. Larsen greatly appreciates the help he's received assembling the material for this book and those who have actively participated in sending him articles.

Because the crime is so pervasive in the legal system, and the profits of billions of dollars a year from this criminal activity are so enticing to unscrupulous perpetrators, Larsen hopes this book will reach a larger audience to expose this crime to the general public.

Made in the USA
Middletown, DE
02 January 2021

30614986R00139